Practical Big Data Analytics

Hands-on techniques to implement enterprise analytics and machine learning using Hadoop, Spark, NoSQL and R

Nataraj Dasgupta

BIRMINGHAM - MUMBAI

Practical Big Data Analytics

Commissioning Editor: Veena Pagare
Acquisition Editor: Vinay Argekar
Content Development Editor: Tejas Limkar
Technical Editor: Dinesh Chaudhary
Copy Editor: Safis Editing
Project Coordinator: Manthan Patel
Proofreader: Safis Editing
Indexer: Pratik Shirodkar
Graphics: Tania Dutta
Production Coordinator: Aparna Bhagat

First published: January 2018

Production reference: 1120118

Published by Packt Publishing Ltd.
Livery Place
35 Livery Street
Birmingham
B3 2PB, UK.

ISBN 978-1-78355-439-3

www.packtpub.com

`mapt.io`

Mapt is an online digital library that gives you full access to over 5,000 books and videos, as well as industry leading tools to help you plan your personal development and advance your career. For more information, please visit our website.

Why subscribe?

- Spend less time learning and more time coding with practical eBooks and Videos from over 4,000 industry professionals

- Improve your learning with Skill Plans built especially for you

- Get a free eBook or video every month

- Mapt is fully searchable

- Copy and paste, print, and bookmark content

PacktPub.com

Did you know that Packt offers eBook versions of every book published, with PDF and ePub files available? You can upgrade to the eBook version at `www.PacktPub.com` and as a print book customer, you are entitled to a discount on the eBook copy. Get in touch with us at `service@packtpub.com` for more details.

At `www.PacktPub.com`, you can also read a collection of free technical articles, sign up for a range of free newsletters, and receive exclusive discounts and offers on Packt books and eBooks.

Contributors

About the author

Nataraj Dasgupta is the vice president of Advanced Analytics at RxDataScience Inc. Nataraj has been in the IT industry for more than 19 years and has worked in the technical and analytics divisions of Philip Morris, IBM, UBS Investment Bank and Purdue Pharma. He led the data science division at Purdue Pharma L.P. where he developed the company's award-winning big data and machine learning platform. Prior to Purdue, at UBS, he held the role of associate director working with high frequency and algorithmic trading technologies in the Foreign Exchange trading division of the bank.

I'd like to thank my wife, Suraiya, for her caring, support, and understanding as I worked during long weekends and evening hours and to my parents, in-laws, sister and grandmother for all the support, guidance, tutelage and encouragement over the years.

I'd also like to thank Packt, especially the editors, Tejas, Dinesh, Vinay, and the team whose persistence and attention to detail has been exemplary.

About the reviewer

Giancarlo Zaccone has more than 10 years experience in managing research projects both in scientific and industrial areas. He worked as a researcher at the C.N.R, the National Research Council, where he was involved in projects on parallel numerical computing and scientific visualization.

He is a senior software engineer at a consulting company, developing and testing software systems for space and defense applications.

He holds a master's degree in physics from the Federico II of Naples and a second level postgraduate master course in scientific computing from La Sapienza of Rome.

Packt is searching for authors like you

If you're interested in becoming an author for Packt, please visit `authors.packtpub.com` and apply today. We have worked with thousands of developers and tech professionals, just like you, to help them share their insight with the global tech community. You can make a general application, apply for a specific hot topic that we are recruiting an author for, or submit your own idea.

Table of Contents

Preface

This book introduces the reader to a broad spectrum of topics related to big data as used in the enterprise. Big data is a vast area that encompasses elements of technology, statistics, visualization, business intelligence, and many other related disciplines. To get true value from data that oftentimes remains inaccessible, either due to volume or technical limitations, companies must leverage proper tools both at the software as well as the hardware level.

To that end, the book not only covers the theoretical and practical aspects of big data, but also supplements the information with high-level topics such as the use of big data in the enterprise, big data and data science initiatives and key considerations such as resources, hardware/software stack and other related topics. Such discussions would be useful for IT departments in organizations that are planning to implement or upgrade the organizational big data and/or data science platform.

The book focuses on three primary areas:

1. Data mining on large-scale datasets

Big data is ubiquitous today, just as the term *data warehouse* was omnipresent not too long ago. There are a myriad of solutions in the industry. In particular, Hadoop and products in the Hadoop ecosystem have become both popular and increasingly common in the enterprise. Further, more recent innovations such as Apache Spark have also found a permanent presence in the enterprise - Hadoop clients, realizing that they may not need the complexity of the Hadoop framework have shifted to Spark in large numbers. Finally, NoSQL solutions, such as MongoDB, Redis, Cassandra and commercial solutions such as Teradata, Vertica and kdb+ have provided have taken the place of more conventional database systems.

This book will cover these areas with a fair degree of depth. Hadoop and related products such as Hive, HBase, Pig Latin and others have been covered. We have also covered Spark and explained key concepts in Spark such as Actions and Transformations. NoSQL solutions such as MongoDB and KDB+ have also been covered to a fair extent and hands-on tutorials have also been provided.

2. Machine learning and predictive analytics

The second topic that has been covered is machine learning, also known by various other names, such as Predictive Analytics, Statistical Learning and others. Detailed explanations with corresponding machine learning code written using R and machine learning packages in R have been provided. Algorithms, such as random forest, support vector machines, neural networks, stochastic gradient boosting, decision trees have been discussed. Further, key concepts in machine learning such as bias and variance, regularization, feature section, data pre-processing have also been covered.

3. Data mining in the enterprise

In general, books that cover theoretical topics seldom discuss the more high-level aspects of big data - such as the key requirements for a successful big data initiative. The book includes survey results from IT executives and highlights the shared needs that are common across the industry. The book also includes a step-by-step guide on how to select the right use cases, whether it is for big data or for machine learning based on lessons learned from deploying production solutions in large IT departments.

We believe that with a strong foundational knowledge of these three areas, any practitioner can deliver successful big data and/or data science projects. That is the primary intention behind the overall structure and content of the book.

Who this book is for

The book is intended for a diverse range of audience. In particular, readers who are keen on understanding the concepts of big data, data science and/or machine learning at a holistic level, namely, how they are all inter-related will gain the most benefit from the book.

Technical audience: For technically minded readers, the book contains detailed explanations of the key industry tools for big data and machine learning. Hands-on exercises using Hadoop, developing machine learning use cases using the R programming language, building comprehensive production-grade dashboards with R Shiny have been covered. Other tutorials in Spark and NoSQL have also been included. Besides the practical aspects, the theoretical underpinnings of these key technologies have also been explained.

Business audience: The extensive theoretical and practical treatment of big data has been supplemented with high level topics around the nuances of deploying and implementing robust big data solutions in the workplace. IT management, CIO organizations, business analytics and other groups who are tasked with defining the corporate strategy around data will find such information very useful and directly applicable.

What this book covers

Chapter 1, *A Gentle Primer on Big Data*, covers the basic concepts of big data and machine learning and the tools used, and gives a general understanding of what big data analytics pertains to.

Chapter 2, *Getting started with Big Data Mining*, introduces concepts of big data mining in an enterprise and provides an introduction to the software and hardware architecture stack for enterprise big data.

Chapter 3, *The Analytics Toolkit*, discusses the various tools used for big data and machine Learning and provides step-by-step instructions on where users can download and install tools such as R, Python, and Hadoop.

Chapter 4, *Big Data with Hadoop*, looks at the fundamental concepts of Hadoop and delves into the detailed technical aspects of the Hadoop ecosystem. Core components of Hadoop such as Hadoop Distributed File System (HDFS), Hadoop Yarn, Hadoop MapReduce and concepts in Hadoop 2 such as ResourceManager, NodeManger, Application Master have been explained in this chapter. A step-by-step tutorial on using Hive via the Cloudera Distribution of Hadoop (CDH) has also been included in the chapter.

Chapter 5, *Big Data Analytics with NoSQL*, looks at the various emerging and unique database solutions popularly known as NoSQL, which has upended the traditional model of relational databases. We will discuss the core concepts and technical aspects of NoSQL. The various types of NoSQL systems such as In-Memory, Columnar, Document-based, Key-Value, Graph and others have been covered in this section. A tutorial related to MongoDB and the MongoDB Compass interface as well as an extremely comprehensive tutorial on creating a production-grade R Shiny Dashboard with kdb+ have been included.

Chapter 6, *Spark for Big Data Analytics*, looks at how to use Spark for big data analytics. Both high-level concepts as well as technical topics have been covered. Key concepts such as SparkContext, Directed Acyclic Graphs, Actions & Transformations have been covered. There is also a complete tutorial on using Spark on Databricks, a platform via which users can leverage Spark

Chapter 7, *A Gentle Introduction to Machine Learning Concepts*, speaks about the fundamental concepts in machine learning. Further, core concepts such as supervised vs unsupervised learning, classification, regression, feature engineering, data preprocessing and cross-validation have been discussed. The chapter ends with a brief tutorial on using an R library for Neural Networks.

Chapter 8, *Machine Learning Deep Dive*, delves into some of the more involved aspects of machine learning. Algorithms, bias, variance, regularization, and various other concepts in Machine Learning have been discussed in depth. The chapter also includes explanations of algorithms such as random forest, support vector machines, decision trees. The chapter ends with a comprehensive tutorial on creating a web-based machine learning application.

Chapter 9, *Enterprise Data Science*, discusses the technical considerations for deploying enterprise-scale data science and big data solutions. We will also discuss the various ways enterprises across the world are implementing their big data strategies, including cloud-based solutions. A step-by-step tutorial on using AWS - Amazon Web Services has also been provided in the chapter.

Chapter 10, *Closing Thoughts on Big Data*, discusses corporate big data and Data Science strategies and concludes with some pointers on how to make big data related projects successful.

Appendix A, *Further Reading on Big Data*, contains links for a wider understanding of big data.

To get the most out of this book

1. A general knowledge of Unix would be very helpful, although isn't mandatory
2. Access to a computer with an internet connection will be needed in order to download the necessary tools and software used in the exercises
3. No prior knowledge of the subject area has been assumed as such
4. Installation instructions for all the software and tools have been provided in Chapter 3, *The Analytics Toolkit*.

Download the example code files

You can download the example code files for this book from your account at www.packtpub.com. If you purchased this book elsewhere, you can visit www.packtpub.com/support and register to have the files emailed directly to you.

You can download the code files by following these steps:

1. Log in or register at `www.packtpub.com`.
2. Select the **SUPPORT** tab.
3. Click on **Code Downloads & Errata**.
4. Enter the name of the book in the **Search** box and follow the onscreen instructions.

Once the file is downloaded, please make sure that you unzip or extract the folder using the latest version of:

- WinRAR/7-Zip for Windows
- Zipeg/iZip/UnRarX for Mac
- 7-Zip/PeaZip for Linux

The code bundle for the book is also hosted on GitHub at `https://github.com/PacktPublishing/Practical-Big-Data-Analytics`. We also have other code bundles from our rich catalog of books and videos available at `https://github.com/PacktPublishing/`. Check them out!

Download the color images

We also provide a PDF file that has color images of the screenshots/diagrams used in this book. You can download it here: `http://www.packtpub.com/sites/default/files/downloads/PracticalBigDataAnalytics_ColorImages.pdf`.

Conventions used

There are a number of text conventions used throughout this book.

`CodeInText`: Indicates code words in text, database table names, folder names, filenames, file extensions, pathnames, dummy URLs, user input, and Twitter handles. Here is an example: "The results are stored in HDFS under the `/user/cloudera/output`."

A block of code is set as follows:

```
"_id" : ObjectId("597cdbb193acc5c362e7ae97"),
"firstName" : "Nina",
"age" : 53,
"frequentFlyer" : [
        "Delta",
        "JetBlue",
        "Delta"
```

Any command-line input or output is written as follows:

```
$ cd Downloads/ # cd to the folder where you have downloaded the zip file
```

Bold: Indicates a new term, an important word, or words that you see onscreen. For example, words in menus or dialog boxes appear in the text like this. Here is an example: "This sort of additional overhead can easily be alleviated by using **virtual machines** (**VMs**)"

Warnings or important notes appear like this.

Tips and tricks appear like this.

Get in touch

Feedback from our readers is always welcome.

General feedback: Email feedback@packtpub.com and mention the book title in the subject of your message. If you have questions about any aspect of this book, please email us at questions@packtpub.com.

Errata: Although we have taken every care to ensure the accuracy of our content, mistakes do happen. If you have found a mistake in this book, we would be grateful if you would report this to us. Please visit www.packtpub.com/submit-errata, selecting your book, clicking on the Errata Submission Form link, and entering the details.

Piracy: If you come across any illegal copies of our works in any form on the Internet, we would be grateful if you would provide us with the location address or website name. Please contact us at copyright@packtpub.com with a link to the material.

If you are interested in becoming an author: If there is a topic that you have expertise in and you are interested in either writing or contributing to a book, please visit authors.packtpub.com.

Reviews

Please leave a review. Once you have read and used this book, why not leave a review on the site that you purchased it from? Potential readers can then see and use your unbiased opinion to make purchase decisions, we at Packt can understand what you think about our products, and our authors can see your feedback on their book. Thank you!

For more information about Packt, please visit packtpub.com.

1
Too Big or Not Too Big

Big data analytics constitutes a wide range of functions related to mining, analysis, and predictive modeling on large-scale datasets. The rapid growth of information and technological developments has provided a unique opportunity for individuals and enterprises across the world to derive profits and develop new capabilities redefining traditional business models using large-scale analytics. This chapter aims at providing a gentle overview of the salient characteristics of big data to form a foundation for subsequent chapters that will delve deeper into the various aspects of big data analytics.

In general, this book will provide both theoretical as well as practical hands-on experience with big data analytics systems used across the industry. The book begins with a discussion Big Data and Big Data related platforms such as Hadoop, Spark and NoSQL Systems, followed by Machine Learning where both practical and theoretical topics will be covered and conclude with a thorough analysis of the use of Big Data and more generally, Data Science in the industry. The book will be inclusive of the following topics:

- Big data platforms: Hadoop ecosystem and Spark NoSQL databases such as Cassandra Advanced platforms such as KDB+
- Machine learning: Basic algorithms and concepts Using R and scikit-learn in Python Advanced tools in C/C++ and Unix Real-world machine learning with neural networks Big data infrastructure
- Enterprise cloud architecture with AWS (Amazon Web Services) On-premises enterprise architectures High-performance computing for advanced analytics Business and enterprise use cases for big data analytics and machine learning Building a world-class big data analytics solution

To take the discussion forward, we will have the following concepts cleared in this chapter:

- Definition of Big Data
- Why are we talking about Big Data now if data has always existed?
- A brief history of Big Data
- Types of Big Data
- Where should you start your search for the Big Data solution?

What is big data?

The term *big* is relative and can often take on different meanings, both in terms of magnitude and applications for different situations. A simple, although naïve, definition of big data is a large collection of information, whether it is data stored in your personal laptop or a large corporate server that is non-trivial to analyze using existing or traditional tools.

Today, the industry generally treats data in the order of terabytes or petabytes and beyond as big data. In this chapter, we will discuss what led to the emergence of the big data paradigm and its broad characteristics. Later on, we will delve into the distinct areas in detail.

A brief history of data

The history of computing is a fascinating tale of how, starting with Charles Babbage's Analytical Engine in the mid 1830s to the present-day supercomputers, computing technologies have led global transformations. Due to space limitations, it would be infeasible to cover all the areas, but a high-level introduction to data and storage of data is provided for historical background.

Dawn of the information age

Big data has always existed. The US Library of Congress, the largest library in the world, houses 164 million items in its collection, including 24 million books and 125 million items in its non-classified collection. [Source: https://www.loc.gov/about/general-information/].

Mechanical data storage arguably first started with punch cards, invented by Herman Hollerith in 1880. Based loosely on prior work by Basile Bouchon, who, in 1725 invented punch bands to control looms, Hollerith's punch cards provided an interface to perform tabulations and even printing of aggregates.

IBM pioneered the industrialization of punch cards and it soon became the *de facto* choice for storing information.

Dr. Alan Turing and modern computing

Punch cards established a formidable presence but there was still a missing element--these machines, although complex in design, could not be considered **computational devices**. A formal general-purpose machine that could be versatile enough to solve a diverse set of problems was yet to be invented.

In 1936, after graduating from King's College, Cambridge, Turing published a seminal paper titled *On Computable Numbers, with an Application to the Entscheidungsproblem*, where he built on Kurt Gödel's Incompleteness Theorem to formalize the notion of our present-day digital computing.

The advent of the stored-program computer

The first implementation of a stored-program computer, a device that can hold programs in memory, was the Manchester **Small-Scale Experimental Machine** (SSEM), developed at the Victoria University of Manchester in 1948 [Source: `https://en.wikipedia.org/wiki/Manchester_Small-Scale_Experimental_Machine`]. This introduced the concept of RAM, Random Access Memory (or more generally, **memory**) in computers today. Prior to the SSEM, computers had fixed-storage; namely, all functions had to be prewired into the system. The ability to store data dynamically in a temporary storage device such as RAM meant that machines were no longer bound by the capacity of the storage device, but could hold an arbitrary volume of information.

From magnetic devices to SSDs

In the early 1950's, IBM introduced magnetic tape that essentially used magnetization on a metallic tape to store data. This was followed in quick succession by hard-disk drives in 1956, which, instead of tapes, used magnetic disk platters to store data.

The first models of hard drives had a capacity of less than 4 MB, which occupied the space of approximately two medium-sized refrigerators and cost in excess of $36,000--a factor of 300 million times more expensive related to today's hard drives. Magnetized surfaces soon became the standard in secondary storage and to date, variations of them have been implemented across various removable devices such as floppy disks in the late 90s, CDs, and DVDs.

Solid-state drives (**SSD**), the successor to hard drives, were first invented in the mid-1950's by IBM. In contrast to hard drives, SSD disks stored data using non-volatile memory, which stores data using a charged silicon substrate. As there are no mechanical moving parts, the time to retrieve data stored in an SSD (seek time) is an order of magnitude faster relative to devices such as hard drives.

Why we are talking about big data now if data has always existed

By the early 2000's, rapid advances in computing and technologies, such as storage, allowed users to collect and store data with unprecedented levels of efficiency. The internet further added impetus to this drive by providing a platform that had an unlimited capacity to exchange information at a global scale. Technology advanced at a breathtaking pace and led to major paradigm shifts powered by tools such as social media, connected devices such as smart phones, and the availability of broadband connections, and by extension, user participation, even in remote parts of the world.

By and large, the majority of this data consists of information generated by web-based sources, such as social networks like Facebook and video sharing sites like YouTube. In big data parlance, this is also known as **unstructured** data; namely, data that is not in a fixed format such as a spreadsheet or the kind that can be easily stored in a traditional database system.

 The simultaneous advances in computing capabilities meant that although the rate of data being generated was very high, it was still computationally feasible to analyze it. Algorithms in machine learning, which were once considered intractable due to both the volume as well as algorithmic complexity, could now be analyzed using various new paradigms such as cluster or multinode processing in a much simpler manner that would have earlier necessitated special-purpose machines.

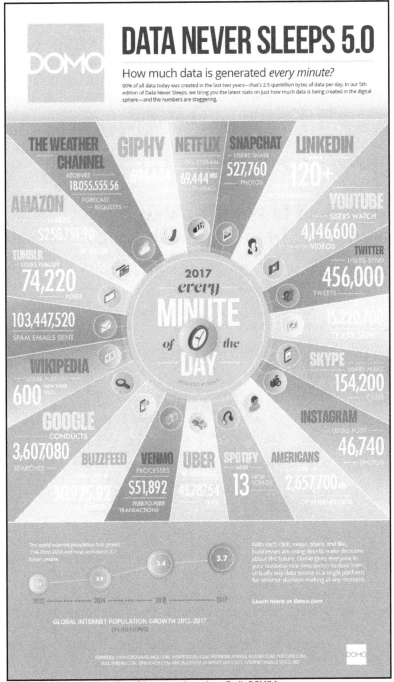

Chart of data generated per minute. Credit: DOMO Inc.

Definition of big data

Collectively, the volume of data being generated has come to be termed big data and analytics that include a wide range of faculties from basic data mining to advanced machine learning is known as **big data analytics**. There isn't, as such, an exact definition due to the relative nature of quantifying what can be large enough to meet the criterion to classify any specific use case as big data analytics. Rather, in a generic sense, performing analysis on large-scale datasets, in the order of tens or hundreds of gigabytes to petabytes, can be termed big data analytics. This can be as simple as finding the number of rows in a large dataset to applying a machine learning algorithm on it.

Building blocks of big data analytics

At a fundamental level, big data systems can be considered to have four major layers, each of which are indispensable. There are many such layers that are outlined in various textbooks and literature and, as such, it can be ambiguous. Nevertheless, at a high level, the layers defined here are both intuitive and simplistic:

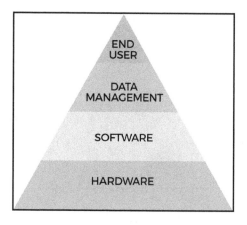

Big Data Analytics Layers

The levels are broken down as follows:

- **Hardware**: Servers that provide the computing backbone, storage devices that store the data, and network connectivity across different server components are some of the elements that define the hardware stack. In essence, the systems that provide the computational and storage capabilities and systems that support the interoperability of these devices form the foundational layer of the building blocks.

- **Software**: Software resources that facilitate analytics on the datasets hosted in the hardware layer, such as Hadoop and NoSQL systems, represent the next level in the big data stack. Analytics software can be classified into various subdivisions. Two of the primary high-level classifications for analytics software are tools that facilitate are:

  - **Data mining**: Software that provides facilities for aggregations, joins across datasets, and pivot tables on large datasets fall into this category. Standard NoSQL platforms such as Cassandra, Redis, and others are high-level, data mining tools for big data analytics.

  - **Statistical analytics**: Platforms that provide analytics capabilities beyond simple data mining, such as running algorithms that can range from simple regressions to advanced neural networks such as Google TensorFlow or R, fall into this category.

- **Data management**: Data encryption, governance, access, compliance, and other features salient to any enterprise and production environment to manage and, in some ways, reduce operational complexity form the next basic layer. Although they are less tangible than hardware or software, data management tools provide a defined framework, using which organizations can fulfill their obligations such as security and compliance.

- **End user**: The end user of the analytics software forms the final aspect of a big data analytics engagement. A data platform, after all, is only as good as the extent to which it can be leveraged efficiently and addresses business-specific use cases. This is where the role of the practitioner who makes use of the analytics platform to derive value comes into play. The term data scientist is often used to denote individuals who implement the underlying big data analytics capabilities while business users reap the benefits of faster access and analytics capabilities not available in traditional systems.

Types of Big Data

Data can be broadly classified as being structured, unstructured, or semi-structured. Although these distinctions have always existed, the classification of data into these categories has become more prominent with the advent of big data.

Structured

Structured data, as the name implies, indicates datasets that have a defined organizational structure such as Microsoft Excel or CSV files. In pure database terms, the data should be representable using a schema. As an example, the following table representing the top five *happiest* countries in the world published by the United Nations in its 2017 World Happiness Index ranking would be an atypical representation of structured data.

We can clearly define the data types of the columns--Rank, Score, GDP per capita, Social support, Healthy life expectancy, Trust, Generosity, and Dystopia are numerical columns, whereas Country is represented using letters, or more specifically, **strings**.

Refer to the following table for a little more clarity:

Rank	Country	Score	GDP per capita	Social support	Healthy life expectancy	Generosity	Trust	Dystopia
1	Norway	7.537	1.616	1.534	0.797	0.362	0.316	2.277
2	Denmark	7.522	1.482	1.551	0.793	0.355	0.401	2.314
3	Iceland	7.504	1.481	1.611	0.834	0.476	0.154	2.323
4	Switzerland	7.494	1.565	1.517	0.858	0.291	0.367	2.277
5	Finland	7.469	1.444	1.54	0.809	0.245	0.383	2.43

World Happiness Report, 2017 [Source: https://en.wikipedia.org/wiki/World_Happiness_Report#cite_note-4]

Commercial databases such as Teradata, Greenplum as well as Redis, Cassandra, and Hive in the open source domain are examples of technologies that provide the ability to manage and query structured data.

Unstructured

Unstructured data consists of any dataset that does not have a predefined organizational schema as in the table in the prior section. Spoken words, music, videos, and even books, *including this one*, would be considered **unstructured**. This by no means implies that the content doesn't have organization. Indeed, a book has a table of contents, chapters, subchapters, and an index--in that sense, it follows a definite organization.

However, it would be futile to represent every word and sentence as being part of a strict set of rules. A sentence can consist of words, numbers, punctuation marks, and so on and does not have a predefined data type as spreadsheets do. To be *structured*, the book would need to have an exact set of characteristics in every sentence, which would be both unreasonable and impractical.

Data from social media, such as posts on Twitter, messages from friends on Facebook, and photos on Instagram, are all examples of unstructured data.

Unstructured data can be stored in various formats. They can be Blobs or, in the case of textual data, freeform text held in a data storage medium. For textual data, technologies such as Lucene/Solr, Elasticsearch, and others are generally used to query, index, and other operations.

Semi-structured

Semi-structured data refers to data that has both the elements of an organizational schema as well as aspects that are arbitrary. A personal phone diary (increasingly rare these days!) with columns for name, address, phone number, and notes could be considered a semi-structured dataset. The user might not be aware of the addresses of all individuals and hence some of the entries may have just a phone number and vice versa.

Similarly, the column for notes may contain additional descriptive information (such as a facsimile number, name of a relative associated with the individual, and so on). It is an arbitrary field that allows the user to add complementary information. The columns for name, address, and phone number can thus be considered structured in the sense that they can be presented in a tabular format, whereas the notes section is unstructured in the sense that it may contain an arbitrary set of descriptive information that cannot be represented in the other columns in the diary.

In computing, **semi-structured** data is usually represented by formats, such as JSON, that can encapsulate both structured as well as schemaless or arbitrary associations, generally using key-value pairs. A more common example could be email messages, which have both a structured part, such as name of the sender, time when the message was received, and so on, that is common to all email messages and an unstructured portion represented by the body or content of the email.

Platforms such as Mongo and CouchDB are generally used to store and query semi-structured datasets.

Sources of big data

Technology today allows us to collect data at an astounding rate--both in terms of volume and variety. There are various sources that generate data, but in the context of big data, the primary sources are as follows:

- **Social networks**: Arguably, the primary source of all big data that we know of today is the social networks that have proliferated over the past 5-10 years. This is by and large unstructured data that is represented by millions of social media postings and other data that is generated on a second-by-second basis through user interactions on the web across the world. Increase in access to the internet across the world has been a self-fulfilling act for the growth of data in social networks.

- **Media**: Largely a result of the growth of social networks, media represents the millions, if not billions, of audio and visual uploads that take place on a daily basis. Videos uploaded on YouTube, music recordings on SoundCloud, and pictures posted on Instagram are prime examples of media, whose volume continues to grow in an unrestrained manner.

- **Data warehouses**: Companies have long invested in specialized data storage facilities commonly known as data warehouses. A DW is essentially collections of historical data that companies wish to maintain and catalog for easy retrieval, whether for internal use or regulatory purposes. As industries gradually shift toward the practice of storing data in platforms such as Hadoop and NoSQL, more and more companies are moving data from their pre-existing data warehouses to some of the newer technologies. Company emails, accounting records, databases, and internal documents are some examples of DW data that is now being offloaded onto Hadoop or Hadoop-like platforms that leverage multiple nodes to provide a highly-available and fault-tolerant platform.

- **Sensors**: A more recent phenomenon in the space of big data has been the collection of data from sensor devices. While sensors have always existed and industries such as oil and gas have been using drilling sensors for measurements at oil rigs for many decades, the advent of wearable devices, also known as the Internet Of Things such as Fitbit and Apple Watch, meant that now each individual could stream data at the same rate at which a few oil rigs used to do just 10 years back.

Wearable devices can collect hundreds of measurements from an individual at any given point in time. While not yet a big data problem as such, as the industry keeps evolving, sensor-related data is likely to become more akin to the kind of spontaneous data that is generated on the web through social network activities.

The 4Vs of big data

The topic of the 4Vs has become overused in the context of big data, where it has started to lose some of the initial charm. Nevertheless, it helps to bear in mind what these Vs indicate for the sake of being aware of the background context to carry on a conversation.

Broadly, the 4Vs indicate the following:

- **Volume**: The amount of data that is being generated
- **Variety**: The different types of data, such as textual, media, and sensor or streaming data
- **Velocity**: The speed at which data is being generated, such as millions of messages being exchanged at any given time across social networks
- **Veracity**: This has been a more recent addition to the 3Vs and indicates the noise inherent in data, such as inconsistencies in recorded information that requires additional validation

When do you know you have a big data problem and where do you start your search for the big data solution?

Finally, big data analytics refers to the practice of putting the data to work--in other words, the process of extracting useful information from large volumes of data through the use of appropriate technologies. There is no exact definition for many of the terms used to denote different types of analytics, as they can be interpreted in different ways and the meaning hence can be subjective.

Nevertheless, some are provided here to act as references or starting points to help you in forming an initial impression:

- **Data mining**: Data mining refers to the process of extracting information from datasets through running queries or basic summarization methods such as aggregations. Finding the top 10 products by the number of sales from a dataset containing all the sales records of one million products at an online website would be the process of mining: that is, extracting useful information from a dataset. NoSQL databases such as Cassandra, Redis, and MongoDB are prime examples of tools that have strong data mining capabilities.

- **Business intelligence**: Business intelligence refers to tools such as Tableau, Spotfire, QlikView, and others that provide frontend dashboards to enable users to query data using a graphical interface. Dashboard products have gained in prominence in step with the growth of data as users seek to extract information. Easy-to-use interfaces with querying and visualization features that could be used universally by both technical and non-technical users set the groundwork to democratize analytical access to data.

- **Visualization**: Data can be expressed both succinctly and intuitively, using easy-to-understand visual depictions of the results. Visualization has played a critical role in understanding data better, especially in the context of analyzing the nature of the dataset and its distribution prior to more in-depth analytics. Developments in JavaScript, which saw a resurgence after a long period of quiet, such as D3.js and ECharts from Baidu, are some of the prime examples of visualization packages in the open source domain. Most BI tools contain advanced visualization capabilities and, as such, it has become an indispensable asset for any successful analytics product.

- **Statistical analytics**: Statistical analytics refers to tools or platforms that allow end users to run statistical operations on datasets. These tools have traditionally existed for many years, but have gained traction with the advent of big data and the challenges that large volumes of data pose in terms of performing efficient statistical operations. Languages such as R and products such as SAS are prime examples of tools that are common names in the area of computational statistics.

- **Machine learning**: Machine learning, which is often referred to by various names such as predictive analytics, predictive modeling, and others, is in essence the process of applying advanced algorithms that go beyond the realm of traditional statistics. These algorithms inevitably involve running hundreds or thousands of iterations. Such algorithms are not only inherently complex, but also very computationally intensive.

The advancement in technology has been a key driver in the growth of machine learning in analytics, to the point where it has now become a commonly used term across the industry. Innovations such as self-driving cars, traffic data on maps that adjust based on traffic patterns, and digital assistants such as Siri and Cortana are examples of the commercialization of machine learning in physical products.

Summary

Big data is undoubtedly a vast subject that can seem overly complex at first sight. Practice makes perfect, and so it is with the study of big data--the more you get involved, the more familiar the topics and verbiage gets, and the more comfortable the subject becomes.

A keen study of the various dimensions of the topic of big data analytics will help you develop an intuitive sense of the subject. This book aims to provide a holistic overview of the topic and will cover a broad range of areas such as Hadoop, Spark, NoSQL databases as well as topics that are based on hardware design and cloud infrastructures. In the next chapter, we will introduce the concept of Big Data Mining and discuss about the technical elements as well as the selection criteria for Big Data technologies.

2
Big Data Mining for the Masses

Implementing a big data mining platform in an enterprise environment that serves specific business requirements is non-trivial. While it is relatively simple to build a big data platform, the novel nature of the tools present a challenge in terms of adoption by business-facing users used to traditional methods of data mining. This, ultimately, is a measure of how successful the platform becomes within an organization.

This chapter introduces some of the salient characteristics of big data analytics relevant for both practitioners and end users of analytics tools. This will include the following topics:

- What is big data mining?
- Big data mining in the enterprise:
  - Building a use case
  - Stakeholders of the solution
  - Implementation life cycle
- Key technologies in big data mining:
  - Selecting the hardware stack:
    - Single/multinode architecture
    - Cloud-based environments
  - Selecting the software stack:
    - Hadoop, Spark, and NoSQL
    - Cloud-based environments

What is big data mining?

Big data mining forms the first of two broad categories of big data analytics, the other being Predictive Analytics, which we will cover in later chapters. In simple terms, big data mining refers to the entire life cycle of processing large-scale datasets, from procurement to implementation of the respective tools to analyze them.

The next few chapters will illustrate some of the high-level characteristics of any big data project that is undertaken in an organization.

Big data mining in the enterprise

Implementing a big data solution in a medium to large size enterprise can be a challenging task due to the extremely dynamic and diverse range of considerations, not the least of which is determining what specific business objectives the solution will address.

Building the case for a Big Data strategy

Perhaps the most important aspect of big data mining is determining the appropriate use cases and needs that the platform would address. The success of any big data platform depends largely on finding relevant problems in business units that will deliver measurable value for the department or organization. The hardware and software stack for a solution that collects large volumes of sensor or streaming data will be materially different from one that is used to analyze large volumes of internal data.

The following are some suggested steps that, in my experience, have been found to be particularly effective in building and implementing a corporate big data strategy:

- **Who needs big data mining**: Determining which business groups will benefit most significantly from a big data mining solution is the first step in this process. This would typically entail groups that are already working with large datasets, are important to the business, and have a direct revenue impact, and optimizing their processes in terms of data access or time to analyze information would have an impact on the daily work processes.
  As an example, in a pharmaceutical organization, this could include Commercial Research, Epidemiology, Health Economics, and Outcomes. At a financial services organization, this could include Algorithmic Trading Desks, Quantitative Research, and even Back Office.

- **Determining the use cases**: The departments identified in the preceding step might already have a platform that delivers the needs of the group satisfactorily. Prioritizing among multiple use cases and departments (or a collection of them) requires personal familiarity with the work being done by the respective business groups.

  Most organizations follow a hierarchical structure where the interaction among business colleagues is likely to be mainly along **rank lines**. Determining impactful analytics use cases requires a close collaboration between both the practitioner as well as the stakeholder; namely, both the management who has oversight of a department as well as the staff members who perform the hands-on analysis. The business stakeholder can shed light on which aspects of his or her business will benefit the most from more efficient data mining and analytics environment. The practitioners provide insight on the challenges that exist at the hands-on operational level. Incremental improvements that consolidate both the operational as well as the managerial aspects to determine an optimal outcome are bound to deliver faster and better results.

- **Stakeholders' buy-in**: The buy-in of the stakeholders—in other words, a consensus among decision-makers and those who can make independent budget decisions—should be established prior to commencing work on the use case(s). In general, multiple buy-ins should be secured for redundancy such that there is a pool of primary and secondary sources that can provide appropriate support and funding for an extension of any early-win into a broader goal. The buy-in process does not have to be deterministic and this may not be possible in most circumstances. Rather, a general agreement on the value that a certain use case will bring is helpful in establishing a baseline that can be leveraged on the successful execution of the use case.

- **Early-wins and the effort-to-reward ratio**: Once the appropriate use cases have been identified, finding the ones that have an optimal effort-to-reward ratio is critical. A relatively small use case that can be implemented in a short time within a smaller budget to optimize a specific business-critical function helps in showcasing early-wins, thus adding credibility to the big data solution in question. We cannot precisely quantify these intangible properties, but we can hypothesize:

$$E\text{-}R\ Ratio = \frac{Time + Cost + Number\ of\ Resources + Criticality\ of\ Use\ Case}{Business\ Value}$$

In this case, *effort* is the time and work required to implement the use case. This includes aspects such as how long it would take to procure the relevant hardware and/or software that is part of the solution, the resources or equivalent *man-hours* it will take to implement the solution, and the overall operational overhead. An open source tool might have a lower barrier to entry relative to implementing a commercial solution that may involve lengthy procurement and risk analysis by the organization. Similarly, a project that spans across departments and would require time from multiple resources who are already engaged in other projects is likely to have a longer duration than one that can be executed by the staff of a single department. If the net effort is low enough, one can also run more than one exercise in parallel as long as it doesn't compromise the quality of the projects.

- **Leveraging the early-wins**: The successful implementation of one or more of the projects in the early-wins phase often lays the groundwork to develop a bigger strategy for the big data analytics platform that goes far beyond the needs of just a single department and has a broader organizational-level impact. As such, the early-win serves as a first, but crucial, step in establishing the value of big data to an audience, who may or may not be skeptical of its viability and relevance.

Implementation life cycle

As outlined earlier, the implementation process can span multiple steps. These steps are often iterative in nature and require a trial-and-error approach. This will require a fair amount of perseverance and persistence as most undertakings will be characterized by varying degrees of successes and failures.

In practice, a Big Data strategy will include multiple stakeholders and a collaborative approach often yields the best results. Business sponsors, business support and IT & Analytics are three broad categories of stakeholders that together create a proper unified solution, catering to the needs of the business to the extent that budget and IT capabilities will permit.

Stakeholders of the solution

The exact nature of the stakeholders of a big data solution is subjective and would vary depending on the use case and problem domain. In general, the following can be considered a high-level representation of this:

- **Business sponsor**: The individual or department that provides the support and/or funding for the project. In most cases, this entity would also be the beneficiary of the solution.
- **Implementation group**: The team that implements the solution from a hands-on perspective. This is usually the IT or Analytics department of most companies that is responsible for the design and deployment of the platform.
- **IT procurement**: The procurement department in most organizations is responsible for vetting a solution to evaluate its competitive pricing and viability from an organizational perspective. Compliance with internal IT policies and assessment of other aspects such as licensing costs are some of services provided by procurement, especially for commercial products.
- **Legal**: All products, unless developed in-house, will most certainly have associated terms and conditions of use. Open source products can have a wide range of properties that defines the permissibility and restrictiveness of use. Open source software licenses such as Apache 2.0, MIT, and BSD are generally more permissible relative to GNU **GPL** (**General Purpose License**). For commercial solutions, the process is more involved as it requires the analysis of vendor-specific agreements and can take a long time to evaluate and get approved depending on the nature of the licensing terms and conditions.

Implementing the solution

The final implementation of the solution is the culmination of the collaboration between the implementation group, business beneficiaries, and auxiliary departments. The time to undertake projects from start to end can vary anywhere from 3-6 months for most small-sized projects as explained in the section on early-wins. Larger endeavors can take several months to years to accomplish and are marked by an agile framework of product management where capabilities are added incrementally during the implementation and deployment period.

The following screenshot gives us a good understanding of the concept:

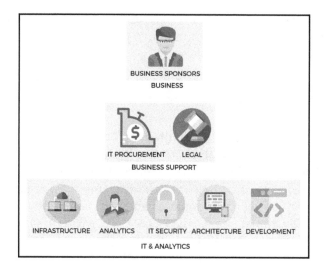

High level image showing the workflow

The images and icons have been taken from:

- https://creativecommons.org/licenses/by/3.0/us/
- Icons made by Freepik (http://www.freepik.com) from www.flaticon.com is licensed by CC 3.0 BY
- Icons made by Vectors Market (http://www.flaticon.com/authors/vectors-market) from www.flaticon.com is licensed by CC 3.0 BY
- Icons made by Prosymbols (http://www.flaticon.com/authors/prosymbols) from www.flaticon.com is licensed by CC 3.0 BY
- Vectors by Vecteezy (https://www.vecteezy.com)

Technical elements of the big data platform

Our discussion, so far, has been focused on the high-level characteristics of design and deployment of big data solutions in an enterprise environment. We will now shift attention to the technical aspects of such undertakings. From time to time, we'll incorporate high-level messages where appropriate in addition to the technical underpinnings of the topics in discussion.

At the technical level, there are primarily two main considerations:

- Selection of the hardware stack
- Selection of the software and **BI** (**business intelligence**) platform

Over the recent 2-3 years, it has become increasingly common for corporations to move their processes to cloud-based environments as a complementary solution for in-house infrastructures. As such, cloud-based deployments have become exceedingly common and hence, an additional section on on-premises versus cloud-based has been added. Note that the term *On-premises* can be used interchangeably with **In-house**, **On-site**, and other similar terminologies.

You'd often hear the term **On-premise** being used as an alternative for *On-premises*. The correct term is **On-premises**. The term **premise** is defined by the Chambers Dictionary as *premise noun 1 (also premises) something assumed to be true as a basis for stating something further.* **Premises,** on the other hand, is a term used to denote buildings (among others) and arguably makes a whole lot more sense.

Selection of the hardware stack

The choice of hardware often depends on the type of solution that is chosen and where the hardware would be located. The proper choice depends on several key metrics such as the type of data (structured, unstructured, or semi-structured), the size of data (gigabytes versus terabytes versus petabytes), and, to an extent, the frequency with which the data will be updated. The optimal choice requires a formal assessment of these variables and will be discussed later on in the book. At a high-level, we can surmise three broad models of hardware architecture:

- **Multinode architecture**: This would typically entail multiple nodes (or servers) that are interconnected and work on the principle of multinode or distributed computing. A classic example of a multinode architecture is Hadoop, where multiple servers maintain bi-directional communication to coordinate a job. Other technologies such as a NoSQL database like Cassandra and search and analytics platform like Elasticsearch also run on the principle of multinode computing architecture. Most of them leverage *commodity servers*, another name for relatively low-end machines by enterprise standards that work in tandem to provide large-scale data mining and analytics capabilities. Multinode architectures are suitable for hosting data that is in the range of terabytes and above.

- **Single-node architecture**: Single-node refers to computation done on a single server. This is relatively uncommon with the advent of multinode computing tools, but still retains a huge advantage over distributed computing architectures. The *Fallacy of Distributed Computing* outlines a set of assertions, or assumptions, related to the implementation of distributed systems such as the reliability of the network, cost of latency, bandwidth, and other considerations.
  If the dataset is structured, contains primarily textual data, and is in the order of 1-5 TB, in today's computing environment, it is entirely possible to host such datasets on single-node machines using specific technologies as has been demonstrated in later chapters.

- **Cloud-based architecture**: Over the past few years, numerous cloud-based solutions have appeared in the industry. These solutions have greatly reduced the barrier to entry in big data analytics by providing a platform that makes it incredibly easy to provision hardware resources on demand based on the needs of the task at hand. This materially reduces the significant overhead in procuring, managing, and maintaining physical hardware and hosting them at in-house data center facilities.

Cloud platforms such as Amazon Web Services, Azure from Microsoft, and the Google Compute Environment permit enterprises to provision 10s to 1000s of nodes at costs starting as low as 1 cent per hour per instance.

In the wake of the growing dominance of cloud vendors over traditional brick-and-mortar hosting facilities, several complementary services to manage client cloud environments have come into existence.

Examples include cloud management companies, such as Altiscale that provides big data as a service solutions and IBM Cloud Brokerage that facilitates selection and management of multiple cloud-based solutions.

The exponential decrease in the cost of hardware: The cost of hardware has gone down exponentially over the past few years. As a case in point, per Statistic Brain's research, the cost of hard drive storage in 2013 was approximately 4 cents per GB. Compare that with $7 per GB as recent as 2000 and over $100,000 per GB in the early 80's. Given the high cost of licensing commercial software, which can often exceed the cost of the hardware, it makes sense to allocate enough budget toward procuring capable hardware solutions. Software needs appropriate hardware to provide optimal performance and providing level importance toward hardware selection is just as important as selecting the appropriate software.

Selection of the software stack

The selection of the software stack for data mining varies based on individual circumstances. The most popular options specific to data mining are shown along with a couple of alternatives which, although not as well-known, are just as capable of managing large-scale datasets:

- **The Hadoop ecosystem**: The big data terms arguably got their start in the popular domain with the advent of Hadoop. The Hadoop ecosystem consists of multiple projects run under the auspices of the Apache Software Foundation. Hadoop supports nearly all the various types of datasets—such as structured, unstructured, and semi-structured—well-known in the big data space. Its thriving ecosystem of auxiliary tools that add new functionalities as well as a rapidly evolving marketplace where companies are vying to demonstrate the next-big-thing-in-Big-Data means that Hadoop will be here for the foreseeable future. There are four primary components of Hadoop, apart from the projects present in the large ecosystem. They are as follows:
    - **Hadoop Common**: The common utilities that support the other Hadoop modules
    - **Hadoop Distributed File System (HDFS™)**: A distributed filesystem that provides high-throughput access to application data
    - **Hadoop YARN**: A framework for job scheduling and cluster resource management
    - **Hadoop MapReduce**: A YARN-based system for parallel processing of large datasets

- **Apache Spark™**: Apache Spark was a project for a multinode computing framework first conceived at University of California at Berkeley's AMPLab as a platform that provided a seamless interface to run parallel computations and overcome limitations in the Hadoop MapReduce framework. In particular, Spark internally leverages a concept known as **DAG—directed acyclic graphs**—which indicates a functionality that optimizes a set of operations into a smaller, or more computationally efficient, set of operations. In addition, Spark exposes several **APIs—application programming interfaces**—to commonly used languages such as Python (PySpark) and Scala (natively available interface). This removes one of the barriers of entry into the Hadoop space where a knowledge of Java is essential.

Finally, Spark introduces a data structure called **Resilient Distributed Datasets** (**RDD**), which provides a mechanism to store data in-memory, thus improving data retrieval and subsequently processing times dramatically:

- **Cluster manager**: The nodes constituting a Spark cluster communicate using cluster managers, which manage the overall coordination among the nodes that are part of the cluster. As of writing this, the cluster manager can be the standalone Spark cluster manager, Apache Mesos, or YARN. There is also an additional facility of running Spark on AWS EC2 instances using spark-ec2 that automatically sets up an environment to run Spark programs.

- **Distributed storage**: Spark can access data from a range of underlying distributed storage systems such as HDFS, S3 (AWS Storage), Cassandra, HBase, Hive, Tachyon, and any Hadoop data source. It should be noted that Spark can be used as a standalone product and does *not* require Hadoop for operations. Newcomers to Spark are often under the impression that Hadoop, or more concretely an HDFS filesystem, is needed for Spark operations. This is not true. Spark can support multiple types of cluster managers as well as backend storage systems, as shown in this section.

- **NoSQL and traditional databases**: A third consideration in terms of selecting the software stack are NoSQL databases. The term NoSQL came into existence recently and is meant to distinguish databases that do not follow the traditional relational-database models. There are both open source and commercial variations of NoSQL databases and indeed even cloud-based options that have become increasingly common. There are various broad classifications of NoSQL databases and some of the more common paradigms are as follows:
  - **Key-value**: These NoSQL databases store data on a principle of hashing—a unique key identifies a set of properties about the key. An example of a key in this parlance could be the national ID number of an individual (such as the Social Security Number or SSN in the US and Aadhaar in India). This could be associated with various aspects relating to the individual such as name, address, phone number, and other variables. The end user of the database would query by the ID number to directly access information about the individual. Open source Key-Value databases such as Redis and commercial ones such as Riak are very popular.

- **In-memory**: While databases that have used in-memory facilities, such as storing caches in the memory to provide faster access relative to storing on disk, have always existed, they were adopted more broadly with the advent of big data. Accessing data in-memory is orders of magnitude faster (~ 100 nanoseconds) than accessing the same information from disk (1-10 milliseconds or 100,000 times slower). Several NoSQL databases, such as Redis and KDB+, leverage temporary in-memory **storage** in order to provide faster access to frequently used data.

- **Columnar**: These databases append multiple columns of data as opposed to rows to create a table. The primary advantage of columnar storage over row-based storage is that a columnar layout provides the means to access data faster with reduced I/O overhead and is particularly well-suited for analytics use cases. By segregating data into individual columns, the database query can retrieve data by scanning the appropriate columns instead of scanning a table on a row-by-row basis and can leverage parallel processing facilities extremely well. Well-known columnar databases include Cassandra, Google BigTable, and others.

- **Document-oriented**: In many ways considered a step up from pure key-value stores, document-oriented databases store data that do not conform to any specific schema such as unstructured text like news articles. These databases provide ways to encapsulate the information in multiple key-value pairs that do not have to be necessarily consistent in structure across all other entries. As a consequence, document databases such as MongoDB are used widely in media-related organizations such as NY Times and Forbes in addition to other mainstream companies.

- **Cloud-based solutions:** Finally, cloud-based solutions for large-scale data mining such as AWS Redshift, Azure SQL Data Warehouse, and Google Bigquery permit users to query datasets directly on the cloud-vendor's platform without having to create their own architecture. Although the end user can choose to have their own in-house specialists such as Redshift System Administrators, the management of the infrastructure, maintenance, and day-to-day routine tasks are mostly carried out by the vendor, thus reducing the operational overhead on the client side.

Summary

In this chapter, we got a high-level overview of Big Data and some of the components of implementing a Big Data solution in the Enterprise. Big Data requires selection of an optimal software and hardware stack, an effort that is non-trivial, not least because of the hundreds of solutions in the industry. Although the topic of a Big Data strategy may be deemed as a subject best left for management rather than a technical audience, it is essential to understand the nuances.

Note that without a proper, well-defined strategy and corresponding high level support, IT departments will remain limited in the extent to which they can provide successful solutions. Further, the solution, including the hardware-software stack should be such that it can be adequately managed and supported by existing IT resources. Most companies will find that it would be essential to recruit new hires for the Big Data implementation. Since such implementations require evaluation of various elements - business needs, budget, resources and other variables, a lead time, often of a few months to an year and more would be needed depending on the scale and scope.

These topics will be discussed in depth in later chapters and this section serves as a preliminary introduction to the subject.

3
The Analytics Toolkit

There are several platforms today that are used for large-scale data analytics. At a broad level, these are divided into platforms that are used primarily for data mining, such as analysis of large datasets using NoSQL platforms, and those that are used for data science—that is, machine learning and predictive analytics. Oftentimes, the solution may have both the characteristics—a robust underlying platform for storing and managing data, and solutions that have been built on top of them that provide additional capabilities in data science.

In this chapter, we will show you how to install and configure your Analytics Toolkit, a collection of software that we'll use for the rest of the chapters:

- Components of the Analytics Toolkit
- System recommendations
  - Installing on a laptop or workstation
  - Installing on the cloud
- Installing Hadoop
  - Hadoop distributions
  - Cloudera Distribution of Hadoop (CDH)
- Installing Spark
- Installing R and Python

Components of the Analytics Toolkit

This book will utilize several key technologies that are used for big data mining and more generally data science. Our Analytics Toolkit consists of Hadoop and Spark, which can be installed both locally on the user's machine as well as on the cloud; and it has R and Python, both of which can be installed on the user's machine as well as on a cloud platform. Your Analytics Toolkit will consist of:

Software/platform	Used for data mining	Used for machine learning
Hadoop	X	
Spark	X	X
Redis	X	
MongoDB	X	
Open Source R	X	X
Python (Anaconda)	X	X
Vowpal Wabbit		X
LIBSVM, LIBLINEAR		X
H2O		X

System recommendations

If you're installing Hadoop on a local machine, it is recommended that your system should have at least 4-8 GB of RAM (memory) and sufficient free disk space of at least 50 GB. Ideally, 8 GB or more memory will suffice for most applications. Below this, the performance will be lower but not prevent the user from carrying out the exercises. Please note that these numbers are estimates that are applicable for the exercises outlined in this book. A production environment will naturally have much higher requirements, which will be discussed at a later stage.

Installing analytics software, especially platforms such as Hadoop, can be quite challenging in terms of technical complexity and it is highly common for users to encounter errors that would have to be painstakingly resolved. Users spend more time attempting to resolve errors and fixing installation issues than they ideally should. This sort of additional overhead can easily be alleviated by using **virtual machines** (**VMs**), or more recently, containers such as Docker. For simpler platforms such as R and Python, we'll be using open source versions that come preinstalled with various libraries.

Installing on a laptop or workstation

The exercises in this book can be performed on any Windows, macOS, or Linux machine. The user will need Oracle VirtualBox (which can be installed from `https://www.virtualbox.org/wiki/Downloads`) to begin the process of installing the required software for the Analytics Toolkit.

Installing on the cloud

An alternative to installing the software on your physical hardware is to use Cloud-based services. Cloud services such as AWS (Amazon Web Services) and Azure from Microsoft provide an extremely agile and versatile environment to provision servers on demand at a cost of a few cents to a few dollars per hour of usage. While cloud installation is beyond the scope of this book, it is very simple to create a free AWS Account and use the same to install the different pieces of analytics software discussed in this book. Note that if you are using AWS/Azure or any of the other cloud services, you'll need to use the Docker version of Cloudera Hadoop distribution.

Installing Hadoop

There are several ways to install Hadoop. The most common ones are:

1. Installing Hadoop from the source files from `https://hadoop.apache.org`
2. Installing using open source distributions from commercial vendors such as Cloudera and Hortonworks

In this exercise, we will install the **Cloudera Distribution of Apache Hadoop** (**CDH**), an integrated platform consisting of several Hadoop and Apache-related products. Cloudera is a popular commercial Hadoop vendor that provides managed services for enterprise-scale Hadoop deployments in addition to its own release of Hadoop. In our case, we'll be installing the HDP Sandbox in a VM environment.

Installing Oracle VirtualBox

A VM environment is essentially a copy of an existing operating system that may have preinstalled software. The VM can be delivered in a single file, which allows users to replicate an entire machine by just launching a file instead of reinstalling the OS and configuring it to mimic another system. The VM operates in a self-contained environment; that is, it does not depend on the host operating system to deliver its functionalities.

To install CDH Quickstart VM, we will be using Oracle VirtualBox, which is used to launch VMs from VM files.

Steps to install CDH in VirtualBox:

1. Download the Oracle VirtualBox relevant for your system (Windows, macOS, or Linux) from `https://www.virtualbox.org/wiki/Downloads` (if this link is not accessible, go to `https://www.virtualbox.org/` and select the appropriate link to go to the **Downloads** page).
2. Double-click on the Oracle VirtualBox executable and install by following the prompts on the screen (you can accept the defaults as will be shown on screen).
3. After you have installed VirtualBox, you should also install the **Oracle VM VirtualBox Extension Pack** available at `http://www.oracle.com/technetwork/server-storage/virtualbox/downloads/index.html#extpack`.

Download the Extension Pack file relevant to your environment and click/double-click on the file. This will open the Oracle VM VirtualBox application and install the Extension Pack within the VirtualBox environment.

Downloading and installing the CDH Quickstart VM: The Quickstart VM or Docker Image for CDH can be downloaded from the Cloudera website. The steps are as follows:

4. Go to `https://www.cloudera.com` and click on Quickstart VMs from the **Download** menu at the top of the page. If the navigation has been changed, a search on Google for Cloudera Quickstart VM will usually take you directly to the Cloudera download page:

QuickStart VM Link on the Cloudera homepage

5. This will bring up the Quickstart for CDH download page. In the Select A Platform menu, select **VirtualBox**. Fill in the form that appears and click on Continue. The downloaded file will have a `.zip` extension. Unzip the file to extract the `.ova` or `.ovf` file:

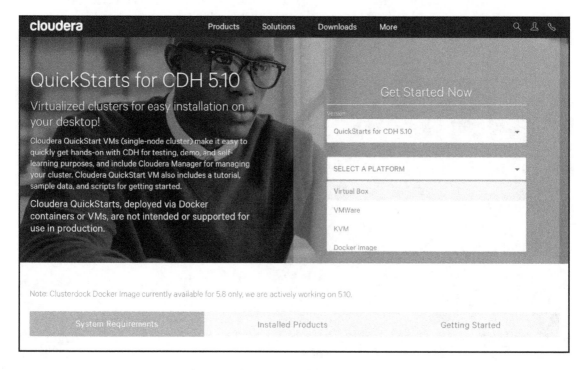

Selecting Virtualbox on the Cloudera Quickstart download options

We get the following sign in screen:

CDH Sign-up Screen

The terms and conditions are first laid out:

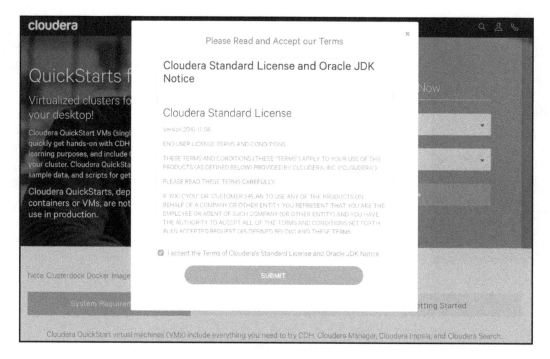

CDH License Terms Acceptance

The VM download for CDH starts:

The CDH VM is more than 5 GB and can take a while to download

Unzip the file. The folder will contain the files shown in the following image:

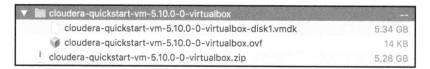

Unzip downloaded file if it is in Zip format

The download file is more than 5 GB and will take a bit of time depending on your Internet connection speed

6. After the download completes, double-click on the `.ova or .ovf` file and it will open in Oracle VirtualBox:

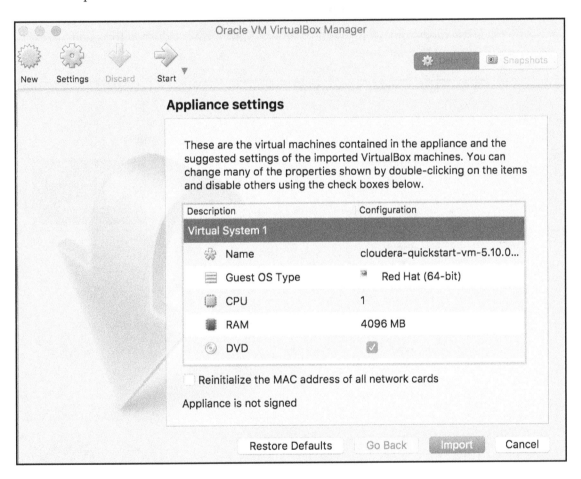

Selecting options for the VM in Virtualbox

You can also open the file manually by launching Oracle VirtualBox, going to File | Import Appliance, and selecting the `.ova/.ovf` file you downloaded as the appliance to import.

Leave all the options as default and click on the Import button, which will start the import process. At this stage, the Cloudera CDH Quickstart VM is being loaded into your Oracle VirtualBox environment.

7. Once the file is imported, you'll be able to start it by clicking on the green arrow at the top of the window:

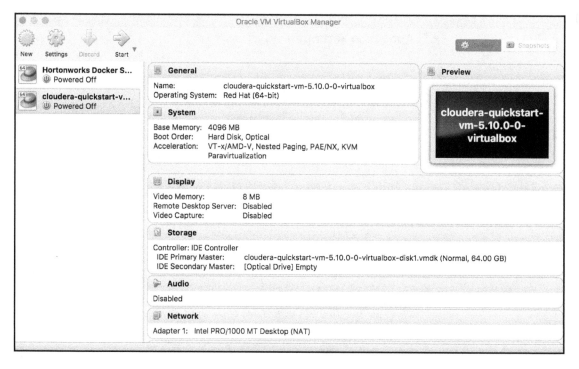

Oracle Virtualbox with CDH VM loaded

8. Leave the defaults as is when the OS initializes:

CDH Main OS page

We get the following screen as a final step of the installation:

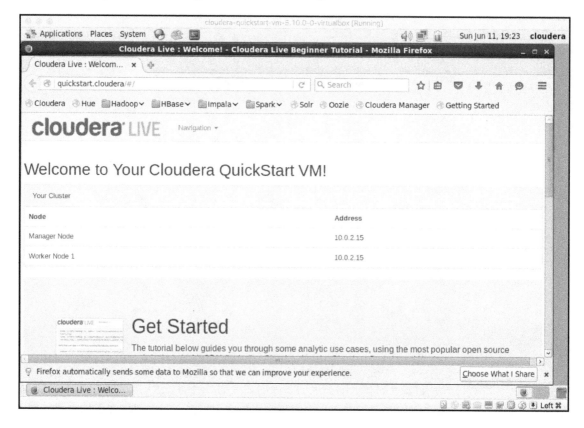

CDH Webpage to administer Hadoop and other CDH Components

This concludes the installation of the Hadoop environment using the Hortonworks Data Platform.

Installing CDH in other environments

The CDH Quickstart VM can also be installed using VMWare, Docker, and Cloud platforms. Instructions for the same are available at the links provided in the following pages.

Installing Packt Data Science Box

We have also created a separate virtual machine for some of the exercises in the book.

Download the Packt Data Science Virtual Machine Vagrant files from
`https://gitlab.com/packt_public/vm`.

To load the VM, first download **Vagrant** from
`https://www.vagrantup.com/downloads.html`.

Download page for Vagrant

Once you have completed the download, install **Vagrant** by running the downloaded Vagrant installation file. Once the installation completes, you'll get a prompt to restart the machine. Restart your system and then proceed to the next step of loading the vagrant file:

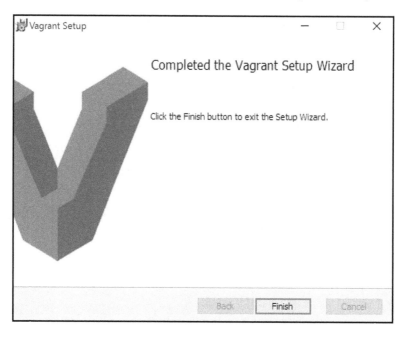

Completing the Vagrant Installation

Click confirm on the final step to restart:

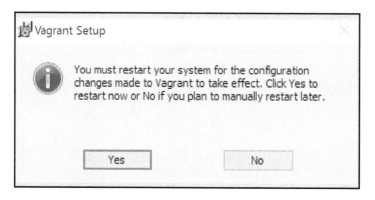

Restarting System

In the terminal or command prompt, go to the directory where you have downloaded the Packt Data Science Vagrant files and run the following commands (shown in Windows):

```
$ vagrant box add packtdatascience packtdatascience.box

==> box: Box file was not detected as metadata. Adding it directly...

==> box: Adding box 'packtdatascience' (v0) for provider:

box: Unpacking necessary files from:
file://C:/Users/packt/Downloads/packt_public_vm/packtdatascience.box

box: Progress: 100% (Rate: 435M/s, Estimated time remaining: --:--:--)

==> box: Successfully added box 'packtdatascience' (v0) for 'virtualbox'!

$ vagrant box list

packtdatascience (virtualbox, 0)

C:UsersNataraj DasguptaDownloadspackt_public_vm>vagrant up

Bringing machine 'default' up with 'virtualbox' provider...

==> default: Importing base box 'packtdatascience'...

==> default: Matching MAC address for NAT networking...

==> default: Setting the name of the VM:
packt_public_vm_default_1513453154192_57570

==> default: Clearing any previously set network interfaces...

==> default: Preparing network interfaces based on configuration...

    default: Adapter 1: nat

==> default: Forwarding ports...

    default: 22 (guest) => 2222 (host) (adapter 1)

==> default: Booting VM...
  ...
```

If all goes well, you should see a new entry in Oracle VirtualBox:

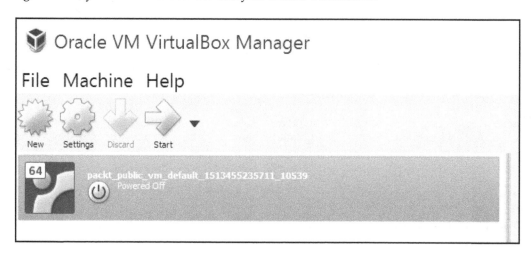

Oracle Virtualbox with Packt Data Science VM

Double-click on the name of the box to start (and test) it. Log in with id/password as
packt/packt:

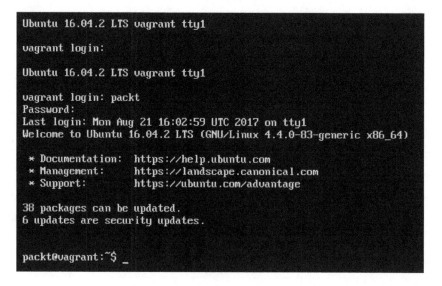

Login screen on Packt VM

Installing Spark

The CDH Quickstart VM includes Spark as one of the components, and hence it will not be necessary to install Spark separately. We'll discuss more on Spark in the chapter dedicated to the subject.

Further, our tutorial on Spark will use the Databricks Community Edition which can be accessed from `https://community.cloud.databricks.com/`. Instructions on creating an account and executing the necessary steps have been provided in the `Chapter 6`, *Spark for Big Data Analytics*.

Installing R

R is a statistical language that has become extremely popular over the last 3-5 years, especially as a platform that can be used for a wide variety of use cases, ranging from simple data mining to complex machine learning algorithms. According to an article posted in IEEE Spectrum in mid-2016, R takes the No. 5 spot among the Top 10 languages in the world.

Open source R can be downloaded from `https://www.r-project.org` via the CRAN site located at `https://cran.r-project.org/mirrors.html`.

Alternatively, you can download R from the Microsoft R Open page at `https://mran.microsoft.com/rro/`. This was earlier known as Revolution R Open, an enhanced version of open source R released by Revolution Analytics. After Microsoft acquired Revolution Analytics in 2015, it was rebranded under the new ownership.

Microsoft R Open includes all the functionalities of R, but also includes the following:

- Numerous R packages installed by default as well as a set of specialized packages released by Microsoft Corporation that complements the existing features of open source R
- Multi-threaded Math Libraries for multi-threaded computations in R
- A fixed CRAN Repository called MRAN. CRAN, the Comprehensive R Archive Network is a collection of sites that contains R binaries, packages, and associated content. Packages on CRAN can be updated on a continuous basis. MRAN takes a fixed snapshot of CRAN, which remains the same until the next release, thus allowing reproducibility and consistency.

Steps for downloading and installing Microsoft R Open

We proceed as follows:

1. Go to https://mran.microsoft.com and click on the **Download Now** button:

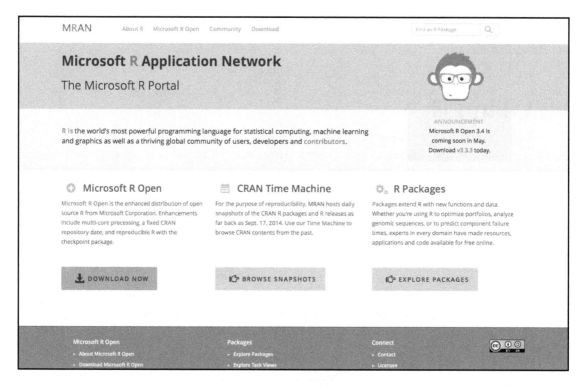

Microsoft Open R Homepage

2. Select the distribution that is appropriate for your system (Windows, macOS, or Linux):

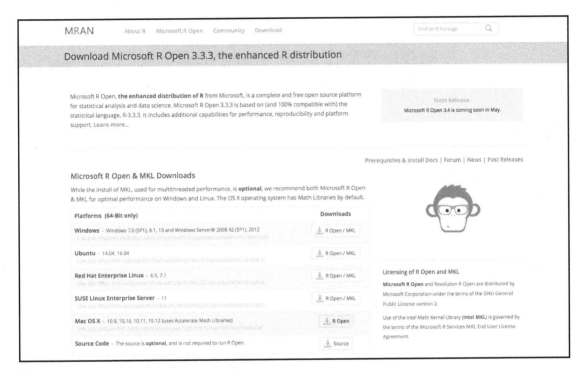

Microsoft Open R Versions

3. Once the download completes, double-click on the downloaded file to install **Microsoft R Open.**

4. Note that on a macOS, you may get an error message as follows:

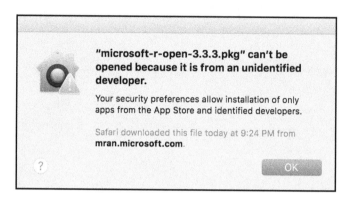

OS X message (bypass using method below)

5. If this happens, right-click on the downloaded file and select **Open** from the menu that pops up. This will let you open the file manually and install:

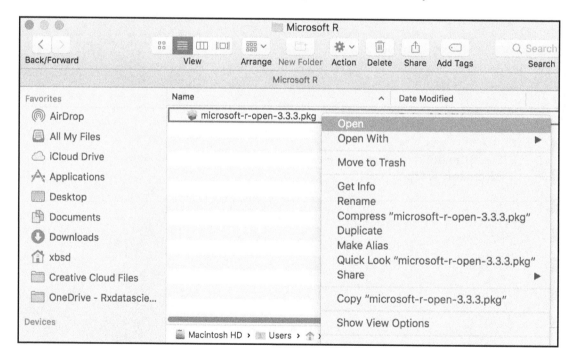

Bypassing OS X Message shown earlier

6. Once installed, double-click on **Microsoft R Open** to launch the application:

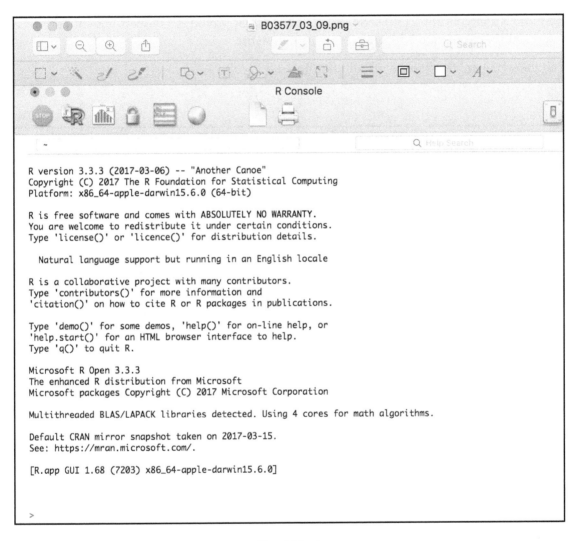

Microsoft R Console

Installing RStudio

RStudio is an application released by `rstudio.org` that provides a powerful feature-rich graphical **IDE (integrated development environment)**.

The following are the steps to install RStudio:

1. Go to `https://www.rstudio.com/products/rstudio/download`:

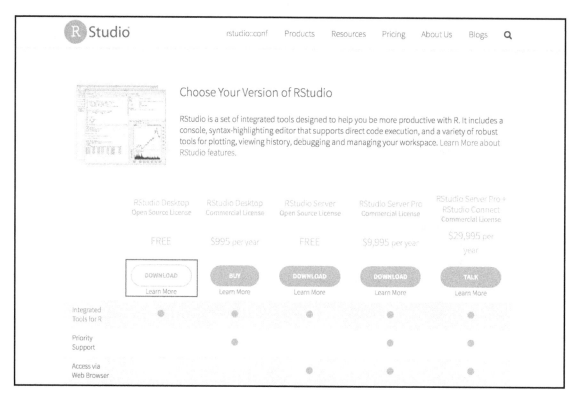

R Studio Versions

2. Click on the link relevant for your operating system, download and install the respective file:

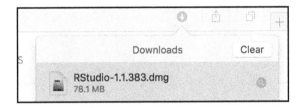

Downloading RStudio

3. Note that On a macOS, you may simply move the downloaded file to the Applications folder. On Windows and Linux operating systems, double click on the downloaded file to complete the steps to install the file:

RStudio on the Mac (copy to Applications folder)

Installing Python

We proceed with the installation as follows:

1. Similar to R, Python has gained popularity due to its versatile and diverse range of packages. Python is generally available as part of most modern Linux-based operating systems. For our exercises, we will use Anaconda from Continuum Analytics®, which enhances the base open source Python offering with many data-mining- and machine-learning-related packages that are installed natively as part of the platform. This alleviates the need for the practitioner to manually download and install packages. In that sense, it is conceptually similar in spirit to Microsoft R Open. Just as Microsoft R enhances the base open source R offering with additional functionality, Anaconda improves upon the offerings of base open source Python to provide new capabilities.

2. Steps for installing Anaconda Python

3. Go to `https://www.continuum.io/downloads:`

Python Anaconda Homepage

4. Download the distribution that is appropriate for your system. Note that we'll be downloading Python v2.7 (and not the 3.x version):

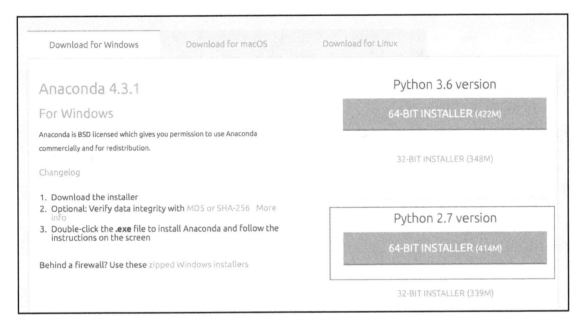

Selecting the Python Anaconda Installer

5. Once the installation is complete, you should be able to go to a Terminal Window (or the Command Window in Windows) and type in Python, which will start up Anaconda:

```
MacBook-Pro-3:~ xbsd$ python
Python 2.7.13 |Anaconda 4.3.0 (x86_64)| (default, Dec 20 2016, 23:05:08)
[GCC 4.2.1 Compatible Apple LLVM 6.0 (clang-600.0.57)] on darwin
Type "help", "copyright", "credits" or "license" for more information.
Anaconda is brought to you by Continuum Analytics.
Please check out: http://continuum.io/thanks and https://anaconda.org
>>>
```

Launching Python Anaconda in the console

This concludes the process of installing Hadoop (CDH), Spark, R, and Python. In later chapters, we will investigate these platforms in further detail.

Summary

This chapter introduced some of the key tools used for data science. In particular, it demonstrated how to download and install the virtual machine for the Cloudera Distribution of Hadoop (CDH), Spark, R, RStudio, and Python. Although the user can download the source code of Hadoop and install it on, say, a Unix system, it is usually fraught with issues and requires a fair amount of debugging. Using a VM instead allows the user to begin using and learning Hadoop with minimal effort as it is a complete preconfigured environment.

Additionally, R and Python are the two most commonly used languages for machine learning and in general, analytics. They are available for all popular operating systems. Although they can be installed in the VM, the user is encouraged to try and install them on their local machines (laptop/workstation) if feasible as it will have relatively higher performance.

In the next chapter, we will dive deeper into the details of Hadoop and its core components and concepts.

4
Big Data With Hadoop

Hadoop has become the de facto standard in the world of big data, especially over the past three to four years. Hadoop started as a subproject of Apache Nutch in 2006 and introduced two key features related to distributed filesystems and distributed computing, also known as MapReduce, that caught on very rapidly among the open source community. Today, there are thousands of new products that have been developed leveraging the core features of Hadoop, and it has evolved into a vast ecosystem consisting of more than 150 related major products. Arguably, Hadoop was one of the primary catalysts that started the big data and analytics industry.

In this chapter, we will discuss the background and core concepts of Hadoop, the components of the Hadoop platform, and delve deeper into the major products in the Hadoop ecosystem. We will learn about the core concepts of distributed filesystems and distributed processing and optimizations to improve the performance of Hadoop deployments. We'll conclude with real-world hands-on exercises using the **Cloudera Distribution of Hadoop** (**CDH**). The topics we will cover are:

- The basics of Hadoop
- The core components of Hadoop
- Hadoop 1 and Hadoop 2
- The Hadoop Distributed File System
- Distributed computing principles with MapReduce
- The Hadoop ecosystem
- Overview of the Hadoop ecosystem

- Hive, HBase, and more
- Hadoop Enterprise deployments
- In-house deployments
- Cloud deployments
- Hands-on with Cloudera Hadoop
- Using HDFS
- Using Hive
- MapReduce with WordCount

The fundamentals of Hadoop

In 2006, Doug Cutting, the creator of Hadoop, was working at Yahoo!. He was actively engaged in an open source project called Nutch that involved the development of a large-scale web crawler. A web crawler at a high level is essentially software that can browse and index web pages, generally in an automatic manner, on the internet. Intuitively, this involves efficient management and computation across large volumes of data. In late January of 2006, Doug formally announced the start of Hadoop. The first line of the request, still available on the internet at `https://issues.apache.org/jira/browse/INFRA-700`, was *The Lucene PMC has voted to split part of Nutch into a new subproject named Hadoop*. And thus, Hadoop was born.

At the onset, Hadoop had two core components : **Hadoop Distributed File System (HDFS)** and MapReduce. This was the first iteration of Hadoop, also now known as Hadoop 1. Later, in 2012, a third component was added known as **YARN (Yet Another Resource Negotiator)** which decoupled the process of resource management and job scheduling. Before we delve into the core components in more detail, it would help to get an understanding of the fundamental premises of Hadoop:

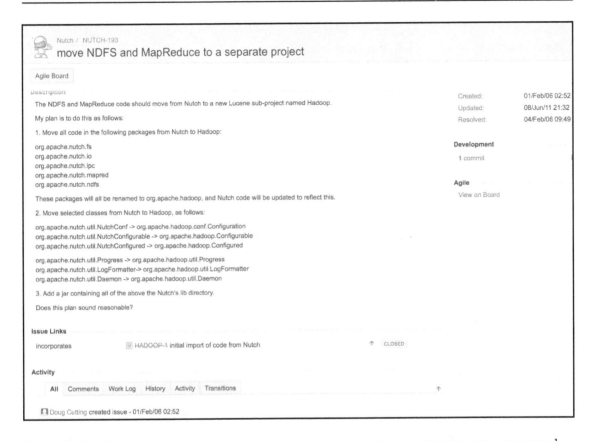

Doug Cutting's post at `https://issues.apache.org/jira/browse/NUTCH-193` announced his intent to separate **Nutch Distributed FS** (**NDFS**) and MapReduce to a new subproject called Hadoop.

The fundamental premise of Hadoop

The fundamental premise of Hadoop is that instead of attempting to perform a task on a single large machine, the task can be subdivided into smaller segments that can then be delegated to multiple smaller machines. These so-called smaller machines would then perform the task on their own portion of the data. Once the smaller machines have completed their tasks to produce the results on the tasks they were allocated, the individual units of results would then be aggregated to produce the final result.

Although, in theory, this may appear relatively simple, there are various technical considerations to bear in mind. For example:

- Is the network fast enough to collect the results from each individual server?
- Can each individual server read data fast enough from the disk?
- If one or more of the servers fail, do we have to start all over?
- If there are multiple large tasks, how should they be prioritized?

There are many more such considerations that must be considered when working with a distributed architecture of this nature.

The core modules of Hadoop

The core modules of Hadoop consist of:

- **Hadoop Common**: Libraries and other common helper utilities required by Hadoop
- **HDFS**: A distributed, highly-available, fault-tolerant filesystem that stores data
- **Hadoop MapReduce**: A programming paradigm involving distributed computing across commodity servers (or nodes)
- **Hadoop YARN**: A framework for job scheduling and resource management

Of these core components, YARN was introduced in 2012 to address some of the shortcomings of the first release of Hadoop. The first version of Hadoop (or equivalently, the first model of Hadoop) used HDFS and MapReduce as its main components. As Hadoop gained in popularity, the need to use facilities beyond those provided by MapReduce became more and more important. This, along with some other technical considerations, led to the development of YARN.

Let's now look at the salient characteristics of Hadoop as itemized previously.

Hadoop Distributed File System - HDFS

The HDFS forms the underlying basis of all Hadoop installations. Files, or more generally data, is stored in HDFS and accessed by the nodes of Hadoop.

HDFS performs two main functions:

- **Namespaces**: Provides namespaces that hold cluster metadata, that is, the location of data in the Hadoop cluster
- **Data storage**: Acts as storage for data used in the Hadoop cluster

The filesystem is termed as distributed since the data is stored in chunks across multiple servers. An intuitive understanding of HDFS can be gained from a simple example, as follows. Consider a large book that consists of Chapters A - Z. In ordinary filesystems, the entire book would be stored as a single file on the disk. In HDFS, the book would be split into smaller chunks, say a chunk for Chapters A - H, another for I - P, and a third one for Q - Z. These chunks are then stored in separate racks (or bookshelves as with this analogy). Further, the chapters are replicated three times, such that there are three copies of each of the chapters.

Suppose, further, the size of the entire book is 1 GB, and each chapter is approximately 350 MB:

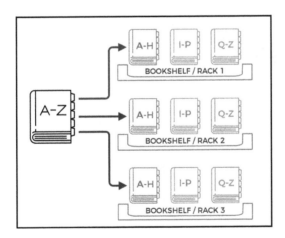

A bookshelf analogy for HDFS

Storing the book in this manner achieves a few important objectives:

- Since the book has been split into three parts by groups of chapters and each part has been replicated three times, it means that our process can read the book in parallel by querying the parts from different servers. This reduces I/O contention and is a very fitting example of the proper use of parallelism.

- If any of the racks are not available, we can retrieve the chapters from any of the other racks as there are multiple copies of each chapter available on different racks.

- If a task I have been given only requires me to access a single chapter, for example, Chapter B, I need to access only the file corresponding to Chapters A-H. Since the size of the file corresponding to Chapters A-H is a third the size of the entire book, the time to access and read the file would be much smaller.

- Other benefits, such as selective access rights to different chapter groups and so on, would also be possible with such a model.

This may be an over-simplified analogy of the actual HDFS functionality, but it conveys the basic principle of the technology - that large files are subdivided into blocks (chunks) and spread across multiple servers in a high-availability redundant configuration. We'll now look at the actual HDFS architecture in a bit more detail:

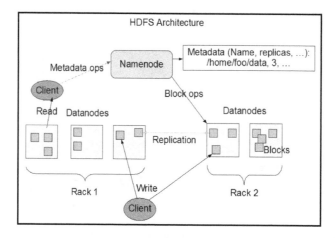

The HDFS backend of Hadoop consists of:

- **NameNode**: This can be considered the master node. The NameNode contains cluster metadata and is aware of what data is stored in which location - in short, it holds the namespace. It stores the entire namespace in RAM and when a request arrives, provides information on which servers hold the data required for the task. In Hadoop 2, there can be more than one NameNode. A secondary NameNode can be created that acts as a helper node to the primary. As such, it is not a backup NameNode, but one that helps in keeping cluster metadata up to date.

- **DataNode**: The DataNodes are the individual servers that are responsible for storing chunks of the data and performing compute operations when they receive a new request. These are primarily commodity servers that are less powerful in terms of resource and capacity than the NameNode that stores the cluster metadata.

Data storage process in HDFS

The following points should give a good idea of the data storage process:

All data in HDFS is written in blocks, usually of size 128 MB. Thus, a single file of say size 512 MB would be split into four blocks (4 * 128 MB). These blocks are then written to DataNodes. To maintain redundancy and high availability, each block is replicated to create duplicate copies. In general, Hadoop installations have a replication factor of three, indicating that each block of data is replicated three times.

This guarantees redundancy such that in the event one of the servers fails or stops responding, there would always be a second and even a third copy available. To ensure that this process works seamlessly, the DataNode places the replicas in independent servers and can also ensure that the blocks are placed on servers in different racks in a data center. This is due to the fact that even if all the replicas were on independent servers, but all the servers were on the same rack, a rack power failure would mean that no replica would be available.

The general process of writing data into HDFS is as follows:

1. The NameNode receives a request to write a new file to HDFS.
2. Since the data has to be written in blocks or chunks, the HDFS client (the entity that made the request) begins caching data into a local buffer and once the buffer reaches the allocated chunk size (for example, 128 MB), it informs the NameNode that it is ready to write the first block (chunk) of data.
3. The NameNode, based on information available to it about the state of the HDFS cluster, responds with information on the destination DataNode where the block needs to be stored.
4. The HDFS client writes data to the target DataNode and informs the NameNode once the write process for the block has completed.
5. The target DataNode, subsequently, begins copying its copy of the block of data to a second DataNode, which will serve as a replica for the current block.

6. Once the second DataNode completes the write process, it sends the block of data to the third DataNode.

7. This process repeats until all the blocks corresponding to the data (or equivalently, the file) are copied across different nodes.

Note that the number of chunks will depend on the file size. The following image illustrated the distribution of the data across 5 datanodes.

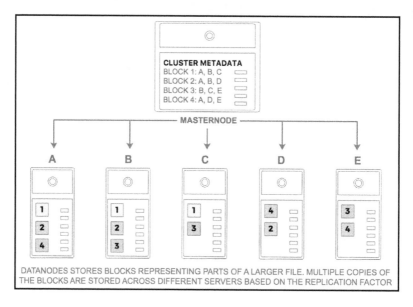

Master Node and Data Nodes

The HDFS architecture in the first release of Hadoop, also known as Hadoop 1, had the following characteristics:

- Single NameNode: Only one NameNode was available, and as a result it also acted as a single point of failure since it stored all the cluster metadata.
- Multiple DataNodes that stored blocks of data, processed client requests, and performed I/O operations (create, read, delete, and so on) on the blocks.
- The HDFS architecture in the second release of Hadoop, also known as Hadoop 2, provided all the benefits of the original HDFS design and also added some new features, most notably, the ability to have multiple NameNodes that can act as primary and secondary NameNodes. Other features included the facility to have multiple namespaces as well as HDFS Federation.

- HDFS Federation deserves special mention. The following excerpt from `http://hadoop.apache.org` explains the subject in a very precise manner:

The NameNodes are federated; the NameNodes are independent and do not require coordination with each other. The DataNodes are used as common storage for blocks by all the NameNodes. Each DataNode registers with all the NameNodes in the cluster. DataNodes send periodic heartbeats and block reports.

The secondary NameNode is not a backup node in the sense that it cannot perform the same tasks as the NameNode in the event that the NameNode is not available. However, it makes the NameNode restart process much more efficient by performing housekeeping operations.

These operations (such as merging HDFS snapshot data with information on data changes) are generally performed by the NameNode when it is restarted and can take a long time depending on the amount of changes since the last restart. The secondary NameNode can, however, perform these housekeeping operations whilst the primary NameNode is still in operation, such that in the event of a restart the primary NameNode can recover much faster. Since the secondary NameNode essentially performs a checkpoint on the HDFS data at periodic intervals, it is also known as the checkpoint node.

Hadoop MapReduce

MapReduce was one of the seminal features of Hadoop that was arguably the most instrumental in bringing it to prominence. MapReduce works on the principle of dividing larger tasks into smaller subtasks. Instead of delegating a single machine to compute a large task, a network of smaller machines can instead be used to complete the smaller subtasks. By distributing the work in this manner, the task can be completed much more efficiently relative to using a single-machine architecture.

This is not dissimilar to how we go about completing work in our day-to-day lives. An example will help to make this clearer.

An intuitive introduction to MapReduce

Let's take the example of a hypothetical organization consisting of a CEO, directors, and managers. The CEO wants to know how many new hires have joined the company. The CEO sends a request to his or her directors to report back the number of hires in their departments. The directors in turn send a request to managers in their individual departments to provide the number of new hires. The managers provide the number to the directors, who in turn send the final value back to the CEO.

This can be considered to be a real-world example of MapReduce. In this analogy, the task was finding the number of new hires. Instead of collecting all the data on his or her own, the CEO delegated it to the directors and managers who provided their own individual departmental numbers as illustrated in the following image:

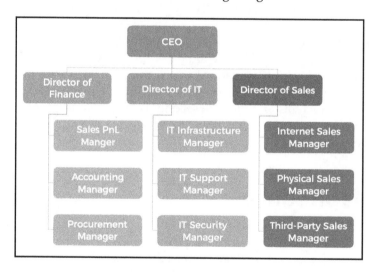

The Concept of MapReduce

In this rather simplistic scenario, the process of splitting a large task (find new hires in the entire company), into smaller tasks (new hires in each team), and then a final re-aggregation of the individual numbers, is analogous to how MapReduce works.

A technical understanding of MapReduce

MapReduce, as the name implies, has a map phase and a reduce phase. A map phase is generally a function that is applied on each element of its input, thus modifying its original value.

MapReduce generates key-value pairs as output.

 Key-value: A key-value pair establishes a relationship. For example, if John is 20 years old, a simple key-value pair could be (John, 20). In MapReduce, the map operation produces such key-value pairs that have an entity and the value assigned to the entity.

In practice, map functions can be complex and involve advanced functionalities.

The reduce phase takes the key-value input from the map function and performs a summarization operation. For example, consider the output of a map operation that contains the ages of students in different grades in a school:

Student name	Class	Age
John	Grade 1	7
Mary	Grade 2	8
Jill	Grade 1	6
Tom	Grade 3	10
Mark	Grade 3	9

We can create a simple key-value pair, taking for example the value of Class and Age (it can be anything, but I'm just taking these to provide the example). In this case, our key-value pairs would be (Grade 1, 7), (Grade 2, 8), (Grade 1, 6), (Grade 3, 10), and (Grade 3, 9).

An operation that calculates the average of the ages of students in each grade could then be defined as a reduce operation.

More concretely, we can sort the output and then send the tuples corresponding to each grade to a different server.

For example, Server A would receive the tuples (Grade 1, 7) and (Grade 1, 6), Server B would receive the tuple (Grade 2, 8), Server C would receive the tuples (Grade 3, 10) and (Grade 3, 9). Each of the servers, A, B, and C, would then find the average of the tuples and report back (Grade 1, 6.5), (Grade 2, 8), and (Grade 3, 9.5).

Observe that there was an intermediary step in this process that involved sending the output to a particular server and sorting the output to determine which server it should be sent to. And indeed, MapReduce requires a shuffle and sort phase, whereby the key-value pairs are sorted so that each reducer receives a fixed set of unique keys.

In this example, if say, instead of three servers there were only two, Server A could be assigned to computing averages for keys corresponding to Grades 1 and 2, and Server B could be assigned to computing an average for Grade 3.

In Hadoop, the following process takes place during MapReduce:

1. The client sends a request for a task.
2. NameNode allocates DataNodes (individual servers) that will perform the map operation and ones that will perform the reduce operation. Note that the selection of the DataNode server is dependent upon whether the data that is required for the operation is *local to the server*. The servers where the data resides can only perform the map operation.
3. DataNodes perform the map phase and produce key-value (k,v) pairs.

As the mapper produces the (k,v) pairs, they are sent to these reduce nodes based on the *keys* the node is assigned to compute. The allocation of keys to servers is dependent upon a partitioner function, which could be as simple as a hash value of the key (this is default in Hadoop).

Once the reduce node receives its set of data corresponding to the keys it is responsible to compute on, it applies the reduce function and generates the final output.

Hadoop maximizes the benefits of data locality. Map operations are performed by servers that hold the data locally, that is, on disk. More precisely, the map phase will be executed only by those servers that hold the blocks corresponding to the file. By delegating multiple individual nodes to perform computations independently, the Hadoop architecture can perform very large-scale data processing effectively.

Block size and number of mappers and reducers

An important consideration in the MapReduce process is an understanding of HDFS block size, that is, the size of the chunks into which the files have been split. A MapReduce task that needs to access a certain file will need to perform the map operation on each block representing the file. For example, given a 512 MB file and a 128 MB block size, four blocks would be needed to store the entire file. Hence, a MapReduce operation will at a minimum require four map tasks whereby each map operation would be applied to each subset of the data (that is, each of the four blocks).

If the file was very large, however, and required say, 10,000 blocks to store, this means we would have required 10,000 map operations. But, if we had only 10 servers, then we'd have to send 1,000 map operations to each server. This might be sub-optimal as it can lead to a high penalty due to disk I/O operations and resource allocation settings on a per-map basis.

The number of reducers required is summarized very elegantly on Hadoop Wiki (`https://wiki.apache.org/hadoop/HowManyMapsAndReduces`).

> *The ideal reducers should be the optimal value that gets them closest to:*
> ** A multiple of the block size * A task time between 5 and 15 minutes * Creates the fewest files possible*
> *Anything other than that means there is a good chance your reducers are less than great. There is a tremendous tendency for users to use a REALLY high value ("More parallelism means faster!") or a REALLY low value ("I don't want to blow my namespace quota!"). Both are equally dangerous, resulting in one or more of:*
> ** Terrible performance on the next phase of the workflow * Terrible performance due to the shuffle * Terrible overall performance because you've overloaded the namenode with objects that are ultimately useless * Destroying disk IO for no really sane reason * Lots of network transfers due to dealing with crazy amounts of CFIF/MFIF work*

Hadoop YARN

YARN was a module introduced in Hadoop 2. In Hadoop 1, the process of managing jobs and monitoring them was performed by processes known as JobTracker and TaskTracker(s). NameNodes that ran the JobTracker daemon (process) would submit jobs to the DataNodes which ran TaskTracker daemons (processes).

The JobTracker was responsible for the co-ordination of all MapReduce jobs and served as a central administrator for managing processes, handling server failure, re-allocating to new DataNodes, and so on. The TaskTracker monitored the execution of jobs local to its own instance in the DataNode and provided feedback on the status to the JobTracker as shown in the following:

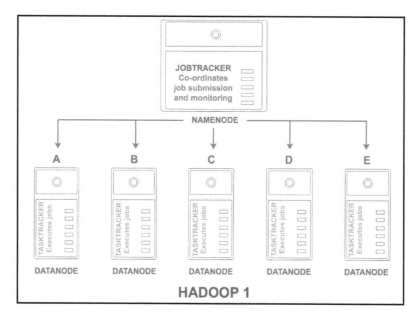

JobTracker and TaskTrackers

This design worked well for a long time, but as Hadoop evolved, the demands for more sophisticated and dynamic functionalities rose proportionally. In Hadoop 1, the NameNode, and consequently the JobTracker process, managed both job scheduling and resource monitoring. In the event the NameNode failed, all activities in the cluster would cease immediately. Lastly, all jobs had to be represented in MapReduce terms - that is, all code would have to be written in the MapReduce framework in order to be executed.

Hadoop 2 alleviated all these concerns:

- The process of job management, scheduling, and resource monitoring was decoupled and delegated to a new framework/module called YARN
- A secondary NameNode could be defined which would act as a helper for the primary NameNode
- Further, Hadoop 2.0 would accommodate frameworks beyond MapReduce
- Instead of fixed map and reduce slots, Hadoop 2 would leverage containers

In MapReduce, all data had to be read from disk, and this was fine for operations on large datasets but it was not optimal for operations on smaller datasets. In fact, any tasks that required very fast processing (low latency), were interactive in nature, or had multiple iterations (thus requiring multiple reads from the disk for the same data), would be extremely slow.

By removing these dependencies, Hadoop 2 allowed developers to implement new programming frameworks that would support jobs with diverse performance requirements, such as low latency and interactive real-time querying, iterative processing required for machine learning, different topologies such as the processing of streaming data, optimizations such as in-memory data caching/processing, and so on.

A few new terms became prominent:

- **ApplicationMaster**: Responsible for managing the resources needed by applications. For example, if a certain job required more memory, the ApplicationMaster would be responsible for securing the required resource. An application in this context refers to application execution frameworks such as MapReduce, Spark, and so on.
- **Containers**: The unit of resource allocation (for example, 1 GB of memory and four CPUs). An application may require several such containers to execute. The ResourceManager allocates containers for executing tasks. Once the allocation is complete, the ApplicationMaster requests DataNodes to start the allocated containers and takes over the management of the containers.
- **ResourceManager**: A component of YARN that had the primary role of allocating resources to applications and functioned as a replacement for the JobTracker. The ResourceManager process ran on the NameNode just as the JobTracker did.
- **NodeManagers**: A replacement for TaskTracker, NodeManagers were responsible for reporting the status of jobs to the ResourceManager (RM) and monitoring the resource utilization of containers.

The following image shows a high level view of the ResourceManager and NodeManagers in Hadoop 2.0:

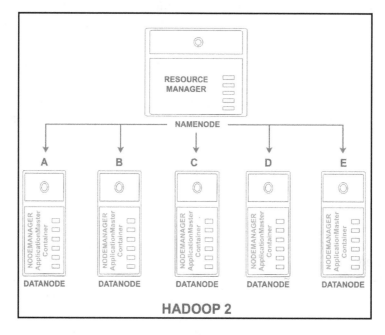

Hadoop 2.0

The prominent concepts inherent in Hadoop 2 have been illustrated in the next image:

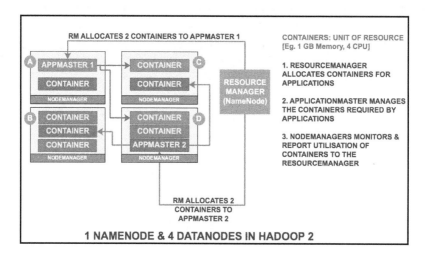

Hadoop 2.0 Concepts

Job scheduling in YARN

It is not uncommon for large Hadoop clusters to have multiple jobs running concurrently. The allocation of resources when there are multiple jobs submitted from multiple departments becomes an important and indeed interesting topic. Which request should receive priority if say, two departments, A and B, submit a job at the same time but each request is for the maximum available resources? In general, Hadoop uses a **First-In-First-Out (FIFO)** policy. That is, whoever submits the job first gets to use the resources first. But what if A submitted the job first but completing A's job will take five hours whereas B's job will complete in five minutes?

To deal with these nuances and variables in job scheduling, numerous scheduling methods have been implemented. Three of the more commonly used ones are:

- **FIFO**: As described above, FIFO scheduling uses a queue to priorities jobs. Jobs are executed in the order in which they are submitted.
- **CapacityScheduler**: CapacityScheduler assigns a value on the number of jobs that can be submitted on a per-department basis, where a department can indicate a logical group of users. This is to ensure that each department or group can have access to the Hadoop cluster and be able to utilize a minimum number of resources. The scheduler also allows departments to scale up beyond their assigned capacity up to a maximum value set on a per-department basis if there are unused resources on the server. The model of CapacityScheduler thus provides a guarantee that each department can access the cluster on a deterministic basis.
- **Fair Schedulers**: These schedulers attempt to evenly balance the utilization of resources across different apps. While an even balance might not be feasible at a certain given point in time, balancing allocation over time such that the averages are more or less similar can be achieved using Fair Schedulers.

These, and other schedulers, provide finely grained access controls (such as on a per-user or per-group basis) and primarily utilize queues in order to prioritize and allocate resources.

Other topics in Hadoop

A few other aspects of Hadoop deserve special mention. As we have discussed the most important topics at length, this section provides an overview of some of the other subjects of interest.

Encryption

Data encryption is mandated by official regulations for various types of data. In the US, data that identifies patient information is required to be compliant with the rules set forth by HIPAA that dictate how such records should be stored. Data in HDFS can be encrypted whilst at rest (on disk) and/or while in transit. The keys that are used to decrypt the data are generally managed by **Key Management Systems (KMSs)**.

User authentication

Hadoop can use the native user-authentication methods of the server. For example, in Linux-based machines, users can be authenticated based on the IDs defined in the system's /etc/passwd files. In other words, Hadoop inherits the user authentication set up on the server side.

User authentication via Kerberos, a cross-platform authentication protocol, is also commonly used in Hadoop clusters. Kerberos works based on a concept of tickets that grant privileges to users on a temporary as-needed basis. Tickets can be invalidated using Kerberos commands, thus restricting the users' rights to access resources on the cluster as needed.

Note that even if the user is permitted to access data (user authentication), he or she can still be limited in what data can be accessed due to another feature known as authorization. The term implies that even if the user can authenticate and log in to the system, the user may be restricted to only the data the user is authorized to access. This level of authorization is generally performed using native HDFS commands to change directory and file ownerships to the named users.

Hadoop data storage formats

Since Hadoop involves storing very large-scale data, it is essential to select a storage type that is appropriate for your use cases. There are a few formats in which data can be stored in Hadoop, and the selection of the optimal storage format depends on your requirements in terms of read/write I/O speeds, how well the files can be compressed and decompressed on demand, and how easily the file can be split since the data will be eventually stored as blocks.

Some of the popular and commonly used storage formats are as follows:

- **Text/CSV**: These are plain text CSV files, similar to Excel files, but saved in plain text format. Since CSV files contain records on a per-line basis, it is naturally trivial to split the files up into blocks of data.

- **Avro**: Avro was developed to improve the efficient sharing of data across heterogeneous systems. It stores both the schema as well as the actual data in a single compact binary using data serialization. Avro uses JSON to store the schema and binary format for the data and serializes them into a single Avro Object Container File. Multiple languages such as Python, Scala, C/C++, and others have native APIs that can read Avro files and consequently, it is very portable and well suited for cross-platform data exchange.

- **Parquet**: Parquet is a columnar data storage format. This helps to improve performance, sometimes significantly by permitting data storage and access on a per-column basis. Intuitively, if you were working on a 1 GB file with 100 columns and 1 million rows, and wanted to query data from only one of the 100 columns, being able to access just the individual column would be more efficient than having to access the entire file.

- **ORCFiles**: ORC stands for Optimized Row-Columnar. In a sense, it is a further layer of optimization over pure columnar formats such as Parquet. ORCFiles store data not only by columns, but also by rows, also known as stripes. A file with data in tabular format can thus be split into multiple smaller stripes where each stripe comprises of a subset of rows from the original file. By splitting data in this manner, if a user task requires access to only a small subsection of the data, the process can interrogate the specific stripe that holds the data.

- **SequenceFiles**: In SequenceFiles, data is represented as key-value pairs and stored in a binary serialized format. Due to serialization, data can be represented in a compact binary format that not only reduces the data size but consequently also improves I/O. Hadoop, and more concretely HDFS, is not efficient when there are multiple files of a small size, such as audio files. SequenceFiles solve this problem by allowing multiple small files to be stored as a single unit or SequenceFile. They are also very well suited for parallel operations that are splittable and are overall efficient for MapReduce jobs.

- **HDFS Snapshots:** HDFS Snapshots allow users to preserve data at a given point in time in a read-only mode. Users can create snapshots—in essence a replica of the data as it is at that point time—in in HDFS, such that they can be retrieved at a later stage as and when needed. This ensures that data can be recovered in the event that there is a file corruption or any other failure that affects the availability of data. In that regard, it can be also considered to be a backup. The snapshots are available in a .snapshot directory where they have been created.

- **Handling of node failures:** Large Hadoop clusters can contain tens of thousands of nodes. Hence it is likely that there would be server failures on any given day. So that the NameNode is aware of the status of all nodes in the cluster, the DataNodes send a periodic heartbeat to the NameNode. If the NameNode detects that a server has failed, that is, it has stopped receiving heartbeats, it marks the server as failed and replicates all the data that was local to the server onto a new instance.

New features expected in Hadoop 3

At the time of writing this book, Hadoop 3 is in Alpha stage. Details on the new changes that will be available in Hadoop 3 can be found on the internet. For example, `http://hadoop.apache.org/docs/current/` provides the most up-to-date information on new changes to the architecture.

The Hadoop ecosystem

This chapter should be titled as the Apache ecosystem. Hadoop, like all the other projects that will be discussed in this section, is an Apache project. Apache is used loosely as a short form for the open source projects that are supported by the Apache Software Foundation. It originally has its roots in the development of the Apache HTTP server in the early 90s, and today is a collaborative global initiative that comprises entirely of volunteers who participate in releasing open source software to the global technical community.

Hadoop started out as, and still is, one of the projects in the Apache ecosystem. Due to its popularity, many other projects that are also part of Apache have been linked directly or indirectly to Hadoop as they support key functionalities in the Hadoop environment. That said, it is important to bear in mind that these projects can in most cases exist as independent products that can function without a Hadoop environment. Whether it would provide optimal functionality would be a separate topic.

In this section, we'll go over some of the Apache projects that have had a great deal of influence as well as an impact on the growth and usability of Hadoop as a standard IT enterprise solution, as detailed in the following figure:

Product	Functionality
Apache Pig	Apache Pig, also known as Pig Latin, is a language specifically designed to represent MapReduce programs through concise statements that define workflows. Coding MapReduce programs in the traditional methods, such as with Java, can be quite complex, and Pig provides an easy abstraction to express a MapReduce workflow and complex **Extract-Transform-Load** (ETL) through the use of simple semantics. Pig programs are executed via the Grunt shell.
Apache HBase	Apache HBase is a distributed column-oriented database that sits on top of HDFS. It was modelled on Google's BigTable whereby data is represented in a columnar format. HBase supports low-latency read-write across tables with billions of records and is well suited to tasks that require direct random access to data. More concretely, HBase indexes data in three dimensions - row, column, and timestamp. It also provides a means to represent data with an arbitrary number of columns as column values can be expressed as key-value pairs within the cells of an HBase table.
Apache Hive	Apache Hive provides a SQL-like dialect to query data stored in HDFS. Hive stores data as serialized binary files in a folder-like structure in HDFS. Similar to tables in traditional database management systems, Hive stores data in tabular format in HDFS partitioned based on user-selected attributes. Partitions are thus subfolders of the higher-level directories or tables. There is a third level of abstraction provided by the concept of buckets, which reference files in the partitions of the Hive tables.
Apache Sqoop	Sqoop is used to extract data from traditional databases to HDFS. Large enterprises that have data stored in relational database management systems can thus use Sqoop to transfer data from their data warehouse to a Hadoop implementation.
Apache Flume	Flume is used for the management, aggregation, and analysis of large-scale log data.
Apache Kafka	Kafka is a publish/subscribe-based middleware system that can be used to analyze and subsequently persist (in HDFS) streaming data in real time.

Apache Oozie	Oozie is a workflow management system designed to schedule Hadoop jobs. It implements a key concept known as a **directed acyclic graph** (**DAG**), which will be discussed in our section on Spark.
Apache Spark	Spark is one of the most significant projects in Apache and was designed to address some of the shortcomings of the HDFS-MapReduce model. It started as a relatively small project at UC Berkeley and evolved rapidly to become one of the most prominent alternatives to using Hadoop for analytical tasks. Spark has seen a widespread adoption across the industry and comprises of various other subprojects that provide additional capabilities such as machine learning, streaming analytics, and others.

Hands-on with CDH

In this section, we will utilize the CDH QuickStart VM to work through some of the topics that have been discussed in the current chapter. The exercises do not have to be necessarily performed in a chronological order and are not dependent upon the completion of any of the other exercises.

We will complete the following exercises in this section:

- WordCount using Hadoop MapReduce
- Working with the HDFS
- Downloading and querying data with Apache Hive

WordCount using Hadoop MapReduce

In this exercise, we will be attempting to count the number of occurrences of each word in one of the longest novels ever written. For the exercise, we have selected the book *Artamène ou le Grand Cyrus* written by Georges and/or Madeleine de Scudéry between 1649-1653. The book is considered to be the second longest novel ever written, per the related list on Wikipedia (https://en.wikipedia.org/wiki/List_of_longest_novels). The novel consists of 13,905 pages across 10 volumes and has close to two million words.

To begin, we need to launch the Cloudera Distribution of Hadoop Quickstart VM in VirtualBox and double-click on the Cloudera Quickstart VM instance:

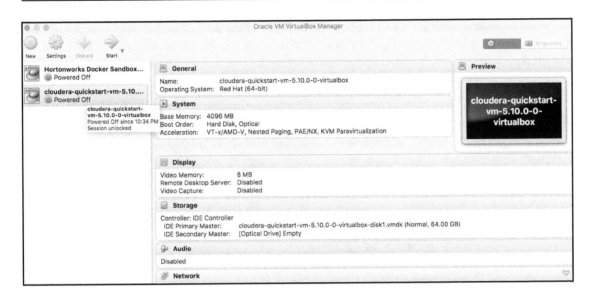

It will take some time to start up as it initializes all the CDH-related processes such as the DataNode, NameNode, and so on:

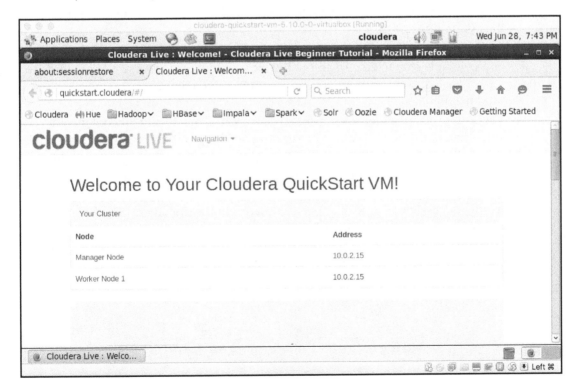

Once the process starts up, it will launch a default landing page that contains references to numerous tutorials related to Hadoop. We'll be writing our MapReduce code in the Unix terminal for this section. Launch the terminal from the top-left menu, as shown in the following screenshot:

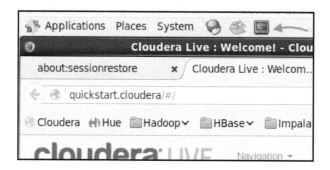

Now, we must follow these steps:

1. Create a directory named `cyrus`. This is where we will store all the files which contain the text of the book.

2. Run `getCyrusFiles.sh` as shown in step 4. This will download the book into the `cyrus` directory.

3. Run `processCyrusFiles.sh` as shown. The book contains various Unicode and non-printable characters. Additionally, we would like to change all the words to lowercase in order to ignore double-counting words that are the same but have capitalizations.

4. This will produce a file called `cyrusprint.txt`. This document contains the entire text of the book. We will be running our MapReduce code on this text file.

5. Prepare `mapper.py` and `reducer.py`. As the name implies, `mapper.py` runs the map part of the MapReduce process. Similarly, `reducer.py` runs the reduce part of the MapReduce process. The file `mapper.py` will split the document into words and assign a value of one to each word in the document. The file, `reducer.py`, will read in the sorted output of `mapper.py` and sum the occurrences of the same word (by first initializing the count of the word to one and incrementing it for each new occurrence of the word). The final output is a file containing the count of each word in the document.

The steps are as follows:

1. Create `getCyrusFiles.sh` - this script will be used to retrieve the data from the web:

```
[cloudera@quickstart ~]$ mkdir cyrus
[cloudera@quickstart ~]$ vi getCyrusFiles.sh
[cloudera@quickstart ~]$ cat getCyrusFiles.sh
for i in `seq 10`
do
curl www.artamene.org/documents/cyrus$i.txt -o cyrus$i.txt
done
```

2. Create `processCyrusFiles.sh` - this script will be used to concatenate and cleanse the files that were downloaded in the previous step:

```
[cloudera@quickstart ~]$ vi processCyrusFiles.sh
[cloudera@quickstart ~]$ cat processCyrusFiles.sh
cd ~/cyrus;
for i in `ls cyrus*.txt` do cat $i >> cyrusorig.txt; done
cat cyrusorig.txt | tr -dc '[:print:]' | tr A-Z a-z >
cyrusprint.txt
```

3. Change the permissions to 755 to make the `.sh` files executable at the command prompt:

```
[cloudera@quickstart ~]$ chmod 755 getCyrusFiles.sh
[cloudera@quickstart ~]$ chmod 755 processCyrusFiles.sh
```

4. Execute `getCyrusFiles.sh`:

```
[cloudera@quickstart cyrus]$ ./getCyrusFiles.sh
  % Total    % Received % Xferd  Average Speed   Time    Time
Time  Current
                                 Dload  Upload   Total   Spent
Left  Speed
100  908k  100  908k    0     0   372k     0  0:00:02  0:00:02 --
:--:--   421k
  % Total    % Received % Xferd  Average Speed   Time    Time
Time  Current
                                 Dload  Upload   Total   Spent
Left  Speed
100 1125k  100 1125k    0     0   414k     0  0:00:02  0:00:02 --
:--:--   471k
  % Total    % Received % Xferd  Average Speed   Time    Time
Time  Current
```

```
                                  Dload  Upload   Total    Spent
Left   Speed
100 1084k  100 1084k    0      0   186k      0  0:00:05  0:00:05 --
:--:--  236k
   % Total    % Received % Xferd  Average Speed   Time     Time
Time  Current
                                  Dload  Upload   Total    Spent
Left   Speed
100 1048k  100 1048k    0      0   267k      0  0:00:03  0:00:03 --
:--:--  291k
   % Total    % Received % Xferd  Average Speed   Time     Time
Time  Current
                                  Dload  Upload   Total    Spent
Left   Speed
100 1116k  100 1116k    0      0   351k      0  0:00:03  0:00:03 --
:--:--  489k
   % Total    % Received % Xferd  Average Speed   Time     Time
Time  Current
                                  Dload  Upload   Total    Spent
Left   Speed
100 1213k  100 1213k    0      0   440k      0  0:00:02  0:00:02 --
:--:--  488k
   % Total    % Received % Xferd  Average Speed   Time     Time
Time  Current
                                  Dload  Upload   Total    Spent
Left   Speed
100 1119k  100 1119k    0      0   370k      0  0:00:03  0:00:03 --
:--:--  407k
   % Total    % Received % Xferd  Average Speed   Time     Time
Time  Current
                                  Dload  Upload   Total    Spent
Left   Speed
100 1132k  100 1132k    0      0   190k      0  0:00:05  0:00:05 --
:--:--  249k
   % Total    % Received % Xferd  Average Speed   Time     Time
Time  Current
                                  Dload  Upload   Total    Spent
Left   Speed
100 1084k  100 1084k    0      0   325k      0  0:00:03  0:00:03 --
:--:--  365k
   % Total    % Received % Xferd  Average Speed   Time     Time
Time  Current
                                  Dload  Upload   Total    Spent
Left   Speed
100 1259k  100 1259k    0      0   445k      0  0:00:02  0:00:02 --
:--:--  486k

[cloudera@quickstart cyrus]$ ls
```

```
cyrus10.txt   cyrus3.txt   cyrus6.txt   cyrus9.txt
cyrus1.txt    cyrus4.txt   cyrus7.txt   getCyrusFiles.sh
cyrus2.txt    cyrus5.txt   cyrus8.txt   processCyrusFiles.sh
```

5. Execute `processCyrusFiles.sh`:

```
[cloudera@quickstart cyrus]$ ./processCyrusFiles.sh

[cloudera@quickstart cyrus]$ ls
cyrus10.txt   cyrus3.txt   cyrus6.txt   cyrus9.txt
getCyrusFiles.sh
cyrus1.txt    cyrus4.txt   cyrus7.txt   cyrusorig.txt
processCyrusFiles.sh
cyrus2.txt    cyrus5.txt   cyrus8.txt   cyrusprint.txt

[cloudera@quickstart cyrus]$ ls -altrh cyrusprint.txt
-rw-rw-r-- 1 cloudera cloudera 11M Jun 28 20:02 cyrusprint.txt

[cloudera@quickstart cyrus]$ wc -w cyrusprint.txt
1953931 cyrusprint.txt
```

6. Execute the following steps to copy the final file, named `cyrusprint.txt`, to
   HDFS, create the `mapper.py` and `reducer.py` scripts.

   The files, `mapper.py` and `reducer.py`, are referenced on Glenn
   Klockwood's website
   (`http://www.glennklockwood.com/data-intensive/hadoop/streaming.html`), which provides a wealth of
   information on MapReduce and related topics.

   The following code shows the contents of `mapper.py`:

```
[cloudera@quickstart cyrus]$ hdfs dfs -ls /user/cloudera

[cloudera@quickstart cyrus]$ hdfs dfs -mkdir /user/cloudera/input

[cloudera@quickstart cyrus]$ hdfs dfs -put cyrusprint.txt
/user/cloudera/input/
[cloudera@quickstart cyrus]$ vi mapper.py

[cloudera@quickstart cyrus]$ cat mapper.py
#!/usr/bin/env python
#the above just indicates to use python to intepret this file
#This mapper code will input a line of text and output <word, 1> #
```

```
import sys
sys.path.append('.')

for line in sys.stdin:
    line = line.strip()
    keys = line.split()
    for key in keys:
            value = 1
            print ("%s\t%d" % (key,value))
```

[cloudera@quickstart cyrus]$ vi reducer.py # Copy-Paste the content
of reducer.py as shown below using the vi or nano Unix editor.

[cloudera@quickstart cyrus]$ cat reducer.py
#!/usr/bin/env python

```
import sys
sys.path.append('.')

last_key = None
running_total = 0

for input_line in sys.stdin:
    input_line = input_line.strip()
    this_key, value = input_line.split("\t", 1)
    value = int(value)

    if last_key == this_key:
        running_total += value
    else:
        if last_key:
            print("%s\t%d" % (last_key, running_total))
        running_total = value
        last_key = this_key

if last_key == this_key:
    print( "%s\t%d" % (last_key, running_total) )
```

[cloudera@quickstart cyrus]$ chmod 755 *.py

7. Execute the mapper and reducer scripts that will perform the MapReduce operations in order to produce the word count. You may see error messages as shown here, but for the purpose of this exercise (and for generating the results), you may disregard them:

```
[cloudera@quickstart cyrus]$ hadoop jar /usr/lib/hadoop-
mapreduce/hadoop-streaming.jar -input /user/cloudera/input -output
/user/cloudera/output -mapper /home/cloudera/cyrus/mapper.py -
reducer /home/cloudera/cyrus/reducer.py

packageJobJar: [] [/usr/lib/hadoop-mapreduce/hadoop-
streaming-2.6.0-cdh5.10.0.jar]
/tmp/streamjob1786353270976133464.jar tmpDir=null
17/06/28 20:11:21 INFO client.RMProxy: Connecting to
ResourceManager at /0.0.0.0:8032
17/06/28 20:11:21 INFO client.RMProxy: Connecting to
ResourceManager at /0.0.0.0:8032
17/06/28 20:11:22 INFO mapred.FileInputFormat: Total input paths to
process : 1
17/06/28 20:11:22 INFO mapreduce.JobSubmitter: number of splits:2
17/06/28 20:11:23 INFO mapreduce.JobSubmitter: Submitting tokens
for job: job_1498704103152_0002
17/06/28 20:11:23 INFO impl.YarnClientImpl: Submitted application
application_1498704103152_0002
17/06/28 20:11:23 INFO mapreduce.Job: The url to track the job:
http://quickstart.cloudera:8088/proxy/application_1498704103152_000
2/
17/06/28 20:11:23 INFO mapreduce.Job: Running job:
job_1498704103152_0002
17/06/28 20:11:30 INFO mapreduce.Job: Job job_1498704103152_0002
running in uber mode : false
17/06/28 20:11:30 INFO mapreduce.Job:  map 0% reduce 0%
17/06/28 20:11:41 INFO mapreduce.Job:  map 50% reduce 0%
17/06/28 20:11:54 INFO mapreduce.Job:  map 83% reduce 0%
17/06/28 20:11:57 INFO mapreduce.Job:  map 100% reduce 0%
17/06/28 20:12:04 INFO mapreduce.Job:  map 100% reduce 100%
17/06/28 20:12:04 INFO mapreduce.Job: Job job_1498704103152_0002
completed successfully
17/06/28 20:12:04 INFO mapreduce.Job: Counters: 50
    File System Counters
            FILE: Number of bytes read=18869506
            FILE: Number of bytes written=38108830
            FILE: Number of read operations=0
            FILE: Number of large read operations=0
            FILE: Number of write operations=0
            HDFS: Number of bytes read=16633042
            HDFS: Number of bytes written=547815
```

```
        HDFS: Number of read operations=9
        HDFS: Number of large read operations=0
        HDFS: Number of write operations=2
Job Counters
        Killed map tasks=1
        Launched map tasks=3
        Launched reduce tasks=1
        Data-local map tasks=3
        Total time spent by all maps in occupied slots (ms)=39591
        Total time spent by all reduces in occupied slots
(ms)=18844
        Total time spent by all map tasks (ms)=39591
        Total time spent by all reduce tasks (ms)=18844
        Total vcore-seconds taken by all map tasks=39591
        Total vcore-seconds taken by all reduce tasks=18844
        Total megabyte-seconds taken by all map tasks=40541184
        Total megabyte-seconds taken by all reduce tasks=19296256
Map-Reduce Framework
        Map input records=1
        Map output records=1953931
        Map output bytes=14961638
        Map output materialized bytes=18869512
        Input split bytes=236
        Combine input records=0
        Combine output records=0
        Reduce input groups=45962
        Reduce shuffle bytes=18869512
        Reduce input records=1953931
        Reduce output records=45962
        Spilled Records=3907862
        Shuffled Maps =2
        Failed Shuffles=0
        Merged Map outputs=2
        GC time elapsed (ms)=352
        CPU time spent (ms)=8400
        Physical memory (bytes) snapshot=602038272
        Virtual memory (bytes) snapshot=4512694272
        Total committed heap usage (bytes)=391979008
Shuffle Errors
        BAD_ID=0
        CONNECTION=0
        IO_ERROR=0
        WRONG_LENGTH=0
        WRONG_MAP=0
        WRONG_REDUCE=0
File Input Format Counters
        Bytes Read=16632806
File Output Format Counters
```

```
                     Bytes Written=547815
            17/06/28 20:12:04 INFO streaming.StreamJob: Output directory:
            /user/cloudera/output
```

8. The results are stored in HDFS under the `/user/cloudera/output` directory in files prefixed with `part-`:

```
[cloudera@quickstart cyrus]$ hdfs dfs -ls /user/cloudera/output
Found 2 items
-rw-r--r--   1 cloudera cloudera          0 2017-06-28 20:12
/user/cloudera/output/_SUCCESS
-rw-r--r--   1 cloudera cloudera     547815 2017-06-28 20:12
/user/cloudera/output/part-00000
```

9. To view the contents of the file use `hdfs dfs -cat` and provide the name of the file. In this case we are viewing the first 10 lines of the output:

```
[cloudera@quickstart cyrus]$ hdfs dfs -cat
/user/cloudera/output/part-00000 | head -10
!   1206
!)  1
!quoy,      1
'    3
''  1
'.  1
'a  32
'appelloit  1
'auoit      1
'auroit     10
```

Analyzing oil import prices with Hive

In this section, we will use Hive to analyze the import prices of oil in countries across the world from 1980-2016. The data is available from the site of the **OECD** (**Organisation for Economic Co-operation and Development**) at the URL shown in the following screenshot:

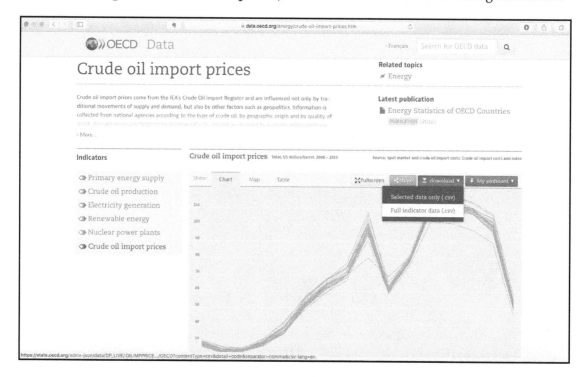

The actual CSV file is available at `https://stats.oecd.org/sdmx-json/data/DP_LIVE/.` `OILIMPPRICE.../OECD?contentType=csvamp;detail=codeamp;separator=commaamp;csv-lang=en`.

Since we'll be loading the data in Hive, it makes sense to download the file into our home directory via the terminal in our Cloudera Quickstart CDH environment. The steps we'd execute are as follows:

1. Download the CSV file into the CDH environment:

```
[cloudera@quickstart ~]$ cd /home/cloudera;
[cloudera@quickstart ~]$
[cloudera@quickstart ~]$ wget -O oil.csv "https://stats.oecd.org/sdmx-json/data/DP_LIVE/.OILIMPPRICE.../OECD?
contentType=csv&detail=code&separator=comma&csv-lang=en"
--2017-07-22 13:10:40--  https://stats.oecd.org/sdmx-json/data/DP_LIVE/.OILIMPPRICE.../OECD?contentType=csv&d
etail=code&separator=comma&csv-lang=en
Resolving stats.oecd.org... 78.41.128.136
Connecting to stats.oecd.org|78.41.128.136|:443... connected.
HTTP request sent, awaiting response... 200 OK
Length: unspecified [text/csv]
Saving to: "oil.csv"

    [                    <=>                                        ] 988,528      329K/s   in 2.9s

2017-07-22 13:10:44 (329 KB/s) - "oil.csv" saved [988528]
```

```
# Download the csv file
cd /home/cloudera;
wget -O oil.csv
"https://stats.oecd.org/sdmx-json/data/DP_LIVE/.OILIMPPRICE.../OECD
?contentType=csv&amp;detail=code&amp;separator=comma&amp;csv-
lang=en"
```

2. Clean the CSV file. Data cleansing is an area of core importance in data science. In practice, it is very common to receive files that will require some level of cleansing. This is due to the fact that there could be invalid characters or values in columns, missing data, missing or additional delimiters, and so on. We noted that various values were enclosed in double-quotes ("). In Hive, we can ignore the quotes by specifying the quoteChar property whilst creating the table. Since Linux also offers simple and easy ways to remove such characters, we used sed to remove the quotation marks:

```
[cloudera@quickstart ~]$ sed -i 's/\"//g' oil.csv
```

Moreover, in our downloaded file, oil.csv, we observed that there were non-printable characters that could cause issues. We removed them by issuing the following command:

```
[cloudera@quickstart ~]$ tr -cd '\11\12\15\40-\176' oil_.csv >
oil_clean.csv
```

(Source:
```
http://alvinalexander.com/blog/post/linux-unix/how-remove-non-prin
table-ascii-characters-file-unix)
```

Finally, we copied the new file (`oil_clean.csv`) to `oil.csv`. Since the `oil.csv` file already existed in the same folder, we were prompted with an overwrite message and we entered `yes`:

```
[cloudera@quickstart ~]$ mv oil_clean.csv oil.csv
mv: overwrite `oil.csv'? yes
```

3. Log in to Cloudera Hue:

Click on Hue on the Bookmarks bar in the browser. This will bring up the Cloudera login screen. Log in using ID `cloudera` and password `cloudera`:

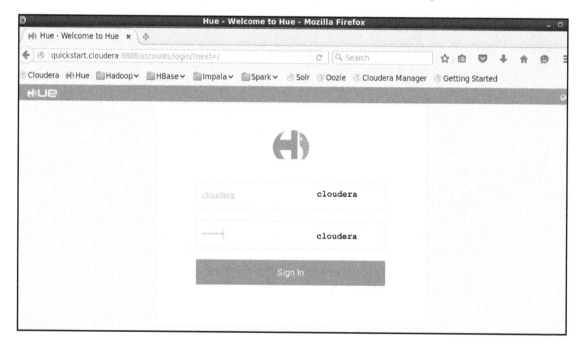

4. Click on Hue from the drop-down menu on Quick Start at the top of the Hue login window:

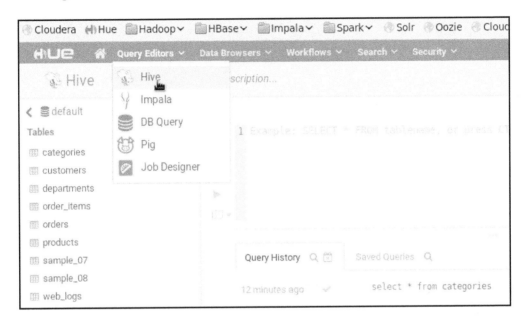

5. Create the table schema, load the CSV file, `oil.csv`, and view the records:

```
CREATE TABLE IF NOT EXISTS OIL
    (location String, indicator String, subject String, measure
String,
    frequency String, time String, value Float, flagCode String)
    ROW FORMAT DELIMITED
    FIELDS TERMINATED BY ','
    LINES TERMINATED BY '\n'
    STORED AS TEXTFILE
    tblproperties("skip.header.line.count"="1");

LOAD DATA LOCAL INPATH '/home/cloudera/oil.csv' INTO TABLE OIL;
SELECT * FROM OIL;
```

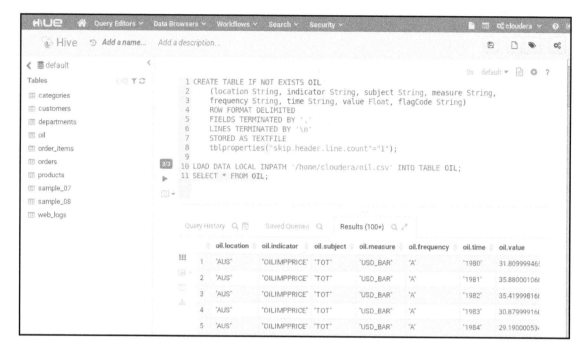

6. Load the oil file.

7. Now that the table has been loaded into Hive, you can run miscellaneous Hive commands using HiveQL. A full set of these commands is available at `https://cwiki.apache.org/confluence/display/Hive/LanguageManual`.

For instance, to find the maximum, minimum, and average value of oil prices in each country from 1980-2015 (the date range of the dataset), we can use familiar SQL operators. The query would be as follows:

```
SELECT LOCATION, MIN(value) as MINPRICE, AVG(value) as AVGPRICE,
MAX(value) as MAXPRICE
FROM OIL
WHERE FREQUENCY LIKE "A"
GROUP BY LOCATION;
```

Here is the screenshot of the same:

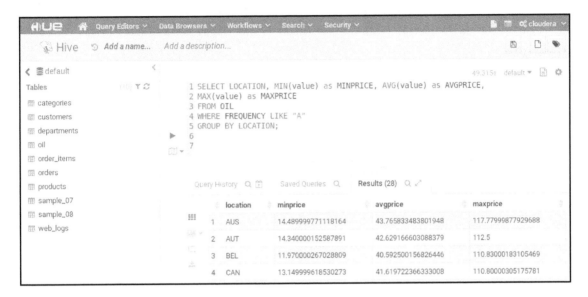

In similar ways, we can use an array of other SQL commands. The Hive Manual provides an in-depth look into these commands and the various ways data can be saved, queried, and retrieved.

Hue includes a set of useful features such as data visualization, data download, and others that allow users to perform ad hoc analysis on the data.

To access the visualization feature, click on the visualization icon underneath the grid icon in the results section, as shown in the following screenshot:

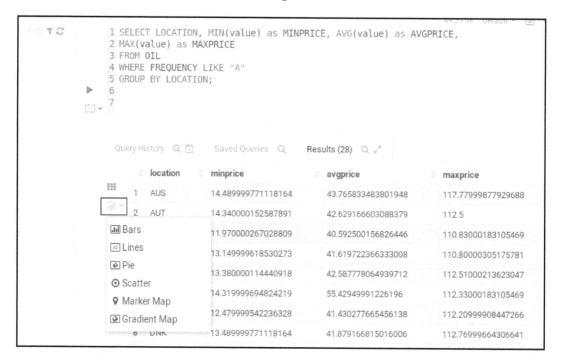

Select Scatter. In Hue, this type of chart, also known more generally as a scatterplot, allows users to create multivariate charts very easily. Different values for the x and y axes, as well as scatter size and grouping, can be selected, as shown in the following screenshot:

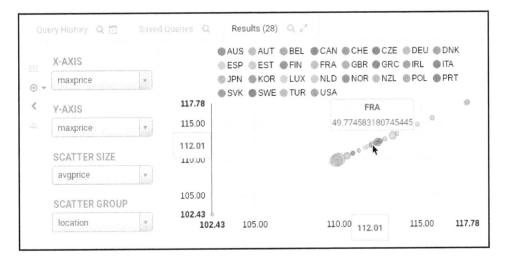

The following is a simple pie chart that can be constructed by selecting Pie in the drop-down menu:

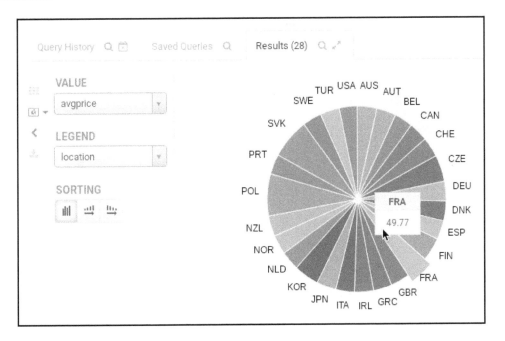

Joining tables in Hive

Hive supports advanced join functionalities. The following illustrates the process of using Left Join. As seen, the original table has data for each country represented by their three-letter country code. Since Hue supports map charts, we can add the values for latitude and longitude to overlay the oil pricing data on a world map.

To do so, we'll need to download a dataset containing the values for latitude and longitude:

```
# ENTER THE FOLLOWING IN THE UNIX TERMINAL
# DOWNLOAD LATLONG CSV FILE

cd /home/cloudera;
wget -O latlong.csv
"https://gist.githubusercontent.com/tadast/8827699/raw/7255fdfbf292c592b75c
f5f7a19c16ea59735f74/countries_codes_and_coordinates.csv"

# REMOVE QUOTATION MARKS
sed -i 's/\"//g' latlong.csv
```

Once the file has been downloaded and cleansed, define the schema and load the data in Hive:

```
CREATE TABLE IF NOT EXISTS LATLONG
    (country String, alpha2 String, alpha3 String, numCode Int, latitude
Float, longitude Float)
    ROW FORMAT DELIMITED
    FIELDS TERMINATED BY ','
    LINES TERMINATED BY '\n'
    STORED AS TEXTFILE
    TBLPROPERTIES("skip.header.line.count"="1");

LOAD DATA LOCAL INPATH '/home/cloudera/latlong.csv' INTO TABLE LATLONG;
```

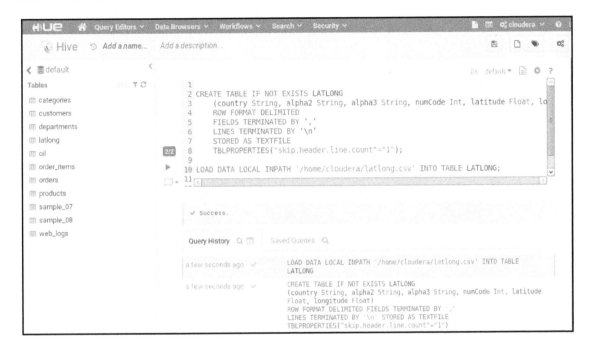

Join the oil data with the lat/long data:

```
SELECT DISTINCT * FROM
(SELECT location, avg(value) as AVGPRICE from oil GROUP BY location) x
LEFT JOIN
(SELECT TRIM(ALPHA3) AS alpha3, latitude, longitude from LATLONG) y
ON (x.location = y.alpha3);
```

```
                                                    2m, 12s   default ▼   📄  ⚙  ?
1 SELECT DISTINCT * FROM
2     (SELECT location, avg(value) as AVGPRICE from oil GROUP BY location) x
3     LEFT JOIN
4     (SELECT TRIM(ALPHA3) AS alpha3, latitude, longitude from LATLONG) y
5     ON
6     (x.location = y.alpha3);
7
```

		y.alpha3	y.latitude	y.longitude	x.location	x.avgprice
	1	AUS	-27	133	AUS	43.655062157137991
	2	AUT	47.333301544189453	13.33329963684082	AUT	25.300277796658602
	3	BEL	50.833301544189453	4	BEL	40.222350115907446
	4	CAN	60	-95	CAN	41.546758076452441
	5	CHE	47	8	CHE	37.297826310862668
	6	CZE	49.75	15.5	CZE	75.050954674955591

Query History 🔍 📅   Saved Queries 🔍   Results (28) 🔍 ↗

We can now proceed with creating geospatial visualizations. It would be useful to bear in mind that these are preliminary visualizations in Hue that provide a very convenient means to view data. More in-depth visualizations can be developed on geographical data using shapefiles, polygons, and other advanced charting methods.

Select Gradient Map from the drop-down menu and enter the appropriate values to create the chart, as shown in the following figure:

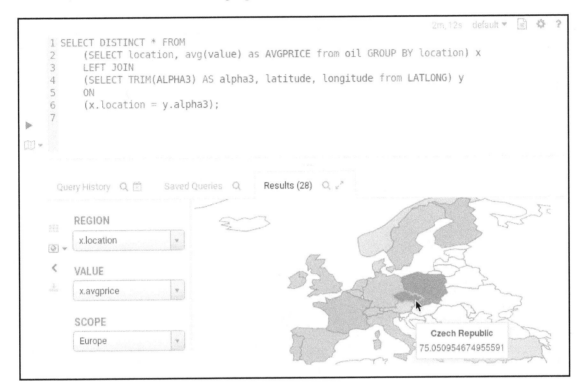

The next chart was developed using the Marker Map option in the drop-down menu. It uses the three-character country code in order to place markers and associated values on the respective regions, as shown in the following figure:

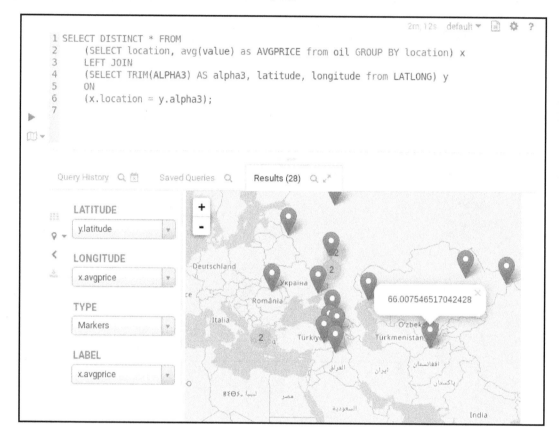

Summary

This chapter provided a technical overview of Hadoop. We discussed the core components and core concepts that are fundamental to Hadoop, such as MapReduce and HDFS. We also looked at the technical challenges and considerations of using Hadoop. While it may appear simple in concept, the inner workings and a formal administration of a Hadoop architecture can be fairly complex. In this chapter we highlighted a few of them.

We concluded with a hands-on exercise on Hadoop using the Cloudera Distribution. For this tutorial, we used the CDH Virtual Machine downloaded earlier from Cloudera's website.

In the next chapter, we will look at NoSQL, an alternative or a complementary solution to Hadoop depending upon your individual and/or organization al needs. While Hadoop offers a far richer set of capabilities, if your intended use case(s) can be done with simply NoSQL solutions, the latter may be an easier choice in terms of the effort required.

5
Big Data Mining with NoSQL

The term **NoSQL** was first used by Carlo Strozzi, who, in 1998, released the Strozzi NoSQL opensource relational database. In the late 2000s, new paradigms in database architecture emerged, many of which did not adhere to the strict constraints required of relational database systems. These databases, due to their non-conformity with standard database conventions such as ACID compliance, were soon grouped under a broad category known as NoSQL.

Each NoSQL database claims to be optimal for certain use cases. Although few of them would fit the requirements to be a general-purpose database management system, they all leverage a few common themes across the spectrum of NoSQL systems.

In this chapter, we will visit some of the broad categories of NoSQL database management systems. We will discuss the primary drivers that initiated the migration to NoSQL database systems and how such databases solved specific business needs that led to their widespread adoption, and conclude with a few hands-on NoSQL exercises.

The topics covered in this chapter include:

- Why NoSQL?
- NoSQL databases
- In-memory databases
- Columnar databases
- Document-oriented databases
- Key-value databases
- Graph databases
- Other NoSQL types and summary
- Hands-on exercise on NoSQL systems

Why NoSQL?

The term NoSQL generally means *Not Only SQL*: that is, the underlying database has properties that are different to those of common and traditional database systems. As such, there is no clear distinction that qualifies a database as NoSQL, other than the fact that they do not provide the characteristics of ACID compliance. As such, it would be helpful to understand the nature of ACID properties that have been the mainstay of database systems for many decades, as well as discuss, in brief, the significance of BASE and CAP, two other terminologies central to databases today.

The ACID, BASE, and CAP properties

Let's first proceed with ACID and SQL.

ACID and SQL

ACID stands for atomicity, consistency, isolation, and durability:

- **Atomicity**: This indicates that database transactions either execute in full or do not execute at all. In other words, either all transactions should be committed, that is, persisted in their entirety, or not committed at all. There is no scope for a partial execution of a transaction.
- **Consistency**: The constraints on the data, that is, the rules that determine data management within a database, will be consistent throughout the database. Different instances will not abide by rules that are any different to those in other instances of the database.
- **Isolation**: This property defines the rules of how concurrent operations (transactions) will read and write data. For example, if a certain record is being updated while another process reads the same record, the isolation level of the database system will determine which version of the data would be returned back to the user.
- **Durability**: The durability of a database system generally indicates that committed transactions will remain persistent even in the event of a system failure. This is generally managed by the use of transaction logs that databases can refer to during recovery.

The reader may observe that all the properties defined here relate primarily to database transactions. A **transaction** is a unit of operation that abides by the aforementioned rules and makes a change to the database. For example, a typical cash withdrawal from an ATM may have the following logical pathway:

1. User withdraws cash from an ATM
2. The bank checks the current balance of the user
3. The database system deducts the corresponding amount from the user's account
4. The database system updates the amount in the user's account to reflect the change

As such, most databases in popular use prior to the mid-1990s, such as Oracle, Sybase, DB2, and others, were optimized for recording and managing transactional data. Until this time, most databases were responsible for managing transactional data. The rapid growth of the internet in the mid-90s led to new types of data that did not necessarily require the strict ACID compliance requirements. Videos on YouTube, music on Pandora, and corporate email records are all examples of use cases where a a transactional database does not add value beyond simply functioning as a technology layer for storing data.

The BASE property of NoSQL

By the late 2000s, data volume had surged and it was apparent that a new alternative model was required in order to manage the data. This new model, called BASE, became a foundational topic that replaced ACID as the preferred model of database management systems.

BASE stands for **B**asically **A**vailable **S**oft-state **E**ventually consistency. This implies that the database is *basically* available for use most of the time; that is, there can be periods during which the services are unavailable (and hence additional redundancy measures should be implemented). *Soft-state* means that the state of the system cannot be guaranteed - different instances of the same data might have different content as it may not have yet captured recent updates in another part of the cluster. Finally, *eventually* consistent implies that although the database might not be in the same state at all times, it will eventually get to the same state; that is, become *consistent*.

The CAP theorem

First introduced in the late 1990s by Eric Allen Brewer, the CAP theorem categorizes the constraints, or more generally the characteristics, of distributed database systems. In brief, the CAP theorem postulates that strictly speaking, database systems can guarantee only two of the three properties defined by CAP, as follows:

- **Consistency**: The data should be consistent across all instances of the database and hence, when queried, should provide a coherent result across all nodes
- **Availability**: Irrespective of the state of any individual node, the system will always respond with a result upon a query being executed (whether or not it is the most recent commit)
- **Partition tolerance**: This implies that when nodes are separated across a network, the system should continue to function normally even if any node loses interconnectivity to another node

It might be evident from this that, since in a cluster nodes will be connected over a *network* which, by nature can be disrupted, partition tolerance has to be guaranteed in order for the system to continue performing normally. In this case, the contention lies with choosing between consistency and availability. For example, if the system has to be consistent; that is, show the most recent commit across all nodes, all the nodes cannot be *available* all at the same time as some nodes might not have the most recent commit. In this case, a query on a new update will not execute until all nodes have been updated with the new data. In case of availability, in similar terms, we cannot guarantee consistency, since to be available at all times means that some nodes will not have the same data as another node if a new update has not been written onto the respective node.

There is a great deal of confusion as well as contention between deciding on whether to ensure consistency or to ensure availability, and as such databases have been categorized as being either **CP** or **AP**. For the purpose of this exercise, we need not get caught up in the terminologies as that would lead to a rather abstract and philosophical discussion. The information on the aforementioned terminologies has been primarily provided to reflect upon some of the foundational theories driving the development of databases.

The need for NoSQL technologies

While most database systems were initially designed to manage transactions, the growth of internet-related technologies and new types of data that did not require the strict puritan nature of transactional systems necessitated the development of alternative frameworks.

For instance, storing the following types of data does not necessarily require a complex *transactional database*:

- Emails
- Media such as audio/video files
- Social network messages
- Website HTML pages
- Many others

Additionally, the increase in users, and as a consequence, data volume, signaled the need for developing more robust architectures with the following characteristics:

- Scalable to manage ever increasing data volume
- Leverage commodity hardware to decrease dependency on expensive hardware
- Provide distributed processing capability across multiple nodes to process large-scale datasets
- Be fault-tolerant/provide high availability to handle node and site failures

Scalable implies that the system can accommodate the increase in data volume by increasing the number of nodes, namely, by scaling horizontally. Further, increasing the number of nodes should have minimal impact on the performance of the system.

Fault-tolerant implies that the system should be able to handle node failures, which won't be uncommon in a large distributed system with hundreds if not thousands of nodes.

This led to the development of various groundbreaking and influential systems, of which perhaps the most notable were Google Bigtable and Amazon Dynamo.

Google Bigtable

Bigtable was a project that was initiated in 2004 to manage both scalability and performance of the data used for various projects at Google. The seminal paper that describes the characteristics of the system was released in 2006 (`https://static.googleusercontent.com/media/research.google.com/en//archive/bigtable-osdi06.pdf`) titled *Bigtable: A Distributed Storage System for Structured Data*. In essence, Bigtable was a *column-store* (more on this later) where each value could be uniquely identified using a row key, a column key, and a timestamp. It was one of the first mainstream databases that epitomized the benefits of storing data in a columnar format rather than using the more common row-based layout. Although columnar databases such as kdb+ and Sybase IQ existed prior to Bigtable, the use of the method by an industry leader to manage petabyte-scale information brought the concept into the limelight.

The official site of Bigtable summarizes the key-value proposition:

> *Bigtable is designed to handle massive workloads at consistent low latency and high throughput, so it's a great choice for both operational and analytical applications, including IoT, user analytics, and financial data analysis.*

Since the introduction of Bigtable, several other NoSQL databases adopted the convention of columnar data layout; most notably HBase and Accumulo, which are both Apache projects.

The Bigtable solution is today available for use at `https://cloud.google.com/bigtable/` where it can be purchased on a subscription basis. The fee for smaller amounts of data is quite nominal and reasonable, whereas larger installations would require more extensive implementations.

Amazon Dynamo

Shortly after Google announced Bigtable, Amazon followed with the announcement of its internal Dynamo database at the 21st ACM Symposium on Operating Systems Principles held in October, 2007 (`http://www.sosp2007.org`).

In the paper, now available on Werner Vogels' site at `http://www.allthingsdistributed.com/files/amazon-dynamo-sosp2007.pdf`, Amazon described a key-value store called Dynamo that was used to power some of Amazon's most critical internal services such as S3 on AWS. The paper brought to bear some key concepts such as key-value storage, consistent hashing, and vector clocks, among others, that were implemented in Dynamo.

Thus, Dynamo offered an alternative to Bigtable's columnar storage for large-scale datasets by introducing a fundamentally different method that leveraged key-value associations.

In the next few sections, we will discuss the various types of NoSQL technologies and how each of them has characteristics that make them optimal for certain use cases. NoSQL has ushered in a paradigm shift in how we treat databases, and has provided a much-needed alternative view to data management at a scale that was not feasible previously.

NoSQL databases

In our discussion of NoSQL types and databases, we will primarily focus on the following characteristics of NoSQL databases:

- In-memory databases
- Columnar databases
- Document-oriented databases
- Key-value databases
- Graph databases
- Other NoSQL types and summary

Most types of NoSQL used in the industry today fall into one or more of these categories. The next few sections will discuss the high-level properties of each of these NoSQL offerings, their main advantages, and products in the market that fall into the respective categories.

In-memory databases

In-memory databases, as the name implies, leverage the computer memory; that is, the RAM, to store datasets. Before we look into how in-memory databases work, it would be worthwhile to recollect how data transfer happens in a typical computer:

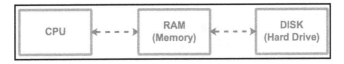

Simple Data Flow Computer Hierarchy

As shown in the preceding image, data traverses from disk to memory to the CPU. This is a very high-level generalization of the exact process as there are conditions under which the CPU does not need to send an instruction to read data from memory (such as when the data is already present in the CPU L2 Cache - a part of the CPU that contains memory reserved for caching data), but fundamentally the process is linear between the CPU, RAM, and disk.

Data that is stored on disk can be transferred to the memory at a certain rate that is dependent on the I/O (Input/Output) throughput of the disk. It takes approximately 10-20 milliseconds (ms) to access data from disk. While the exact number varies depending on the size of the data, the minimum seek time (time for the disk to find the location of the data) in itself is approximately 10-15 ms. Compare this with the time it takes to fetch data from memory, which is approximately 100 nanoseconds. Finally, it takes approximately 7 ns to read data from the CPU L2 Cache.

To put this into perspective, the disk access time of 15 milliseconds, namely, 15,000,000 nanoseconds is 150,000 times *slower* than the time it takes to access data from memory. In other words, data that is already present in memory can be read at an astounding 150 thousand times faster relative to disk. This is essentially true of reading random data. The time to read sequential data is arguably less sensational, but still nearly an order of magnitude faster.

If the disk and RAM were represented as cars, the RAM *car* would have gone all the way to the moon and be on its way back in the time it would take the disk car to go barely two miles. That is how large the difference is.

Hence, it is natural to conclude from this that if the data were stored in RAM, especially in the case of larger datasets, the access time would be dramatically lower, and consequently the time to process the data (at least on the I/O level) would be significantly reduced.

Traditionally, all data in terms of databases was stored on disk. With the advent of the internet, the industry started leveraging *memcached,* which provided a means to store data in key-value pairs in memory via an API. For example, it was, and still is, common for MySQL databases to leverage the memcached API to cache objects in memory to optimize read speeds as well as reduce the load on the primary (MySQL) database.

However, as data volumes started to increase, the complexity of using the database and memcached method started to take it's toll, and databases that were exclusively designed to store data in memory (and sometimes both on disk and in memory) were being developed at a rapid pace.

As a result, in-memory databases such as Redis started replacing memcached as the fast cache store for driving websites. In the case of Redis, although the data would be held in memory as key-value pairs, there was an option to persist the data on disk. This differentiated it from solutions such as memcached that were strictly memory caches.

The primary drivers of the move towards in-memory databases can be summarized as follows:

- Complexity of managing increasing volumes of data such as web traffic by the traditional, for example, MySQL + memcached combination
- Reduced RAM costs, making it more affordable to purchase larger sizes
- Overall industry drive towards NoSQL technologies that led to increased focus and community participation towards the development of newer, innovative database platforms
- Faster data manipulation in memory provided a means to reduce I/O overhead in situations that demanded ultra-fast, low-latency processing of data

Today, some of the leading options for databases that provide in-memory capabilities in the industry include:

Open source	Commercial
Redis	Kdb+
memcacheDB	Oracle TimesTen
Aerospike	SAP HANA
VoltDB	HP Vertica
Apache Ignite	Altibase
Apache Geode	Oracle Exalytics
MonetDB	MemSQL

Note that some of these support hybrid architectures whereby data can reside in memory as well as on disk. In general, data would be transferred from memory to disk for persistence. Also, note that some commercial in-memory databases offer community editions that can be downloaded and used at no charge within the terms of the licenses applicable to the respective solution. In these cases, they are both open source as well as commercial.

Columnar databases

Columnar databases have existed since the 90s, but came to prominence after the release of Google Bigtable as mentioned earlier. They are, in essence, a method of storing data that is optimized for querying very large volumes of data in a fast and efficient manner relative to row-based/tuple-based storage.

The benefits of columnar databases, or more concretely storing each column of data independently, can be illustrated with a simple example.

Consider a table consisting of 100 million household addresses and phone numbers. Consider also a simple query that requires the user to find the number of households in the state of New York, in the city of Albany, built after 1990. We'll create a hypothetical table to illustrate the difference in querying the data row by row versus column by column.

Hardware characteristics:

Average disk read speed: 200 MB per second

Database characteristics:

Table name: `housedb`

- Total rows = 100 million
- Total rows with State NY = Two million
- Total rows with State NY and City Albany = 10,000
- Total rows with State NY and City Albany and YearBuilt > 1990 = 500

Data size:

Let us assume that the size of each of the data of each row is as follows:

- PlotNumber, YearBuilt each = 8 bytes = total 16 bytes
- Owner, Address, State and City each = 12 bytes = Total 48 bytes
- Net size in bytes of each row = 16 + 48 = 64 bytes

Note that the actual size will be higher, as there are several other considerations such as indexing and other table optimizations and related overheads that we won't consider here for the sake of simplicity.

We will also assume that the columnar database maintains an implicit row index that permits querying the data at certain indices in each column *vector*.

The following table shows the first 4 records:

PlotNumber	Owner	Address	State	City	YearBuilt
1	John	1 Main St.	WA	Seattle	1995
2	Mary	20 J. Ave.	NY	Albany	1980
3	Jane	5 45th St.	NY	Rye Brook	2001
4	John	10 A. Blvd.	CT	Stamford	2010

In total, the table has 100 million records. The last few are shown as follows:

PlotNumber	Owner	Address	State	City	YearBuilt
99999997	Jim	23 B. Lane	NC	Cary	1995
99999998	Mike	5 L. Street	NY	Syracuse	1993
99999999	Tim	10 A. Blvd.	NY	Albany	2001
100000000	Jack	10 A. Blvd.	CT	Stamford	2010

The query we will run against this dataset is as follows:

```
select * from housedb where State like 'NY' and City like 'Albany' and
YearBuilt > 1990
```

Scenario A: Searching row by row

In the first scenario, if we did a naïve row-by-row search, since the data for each column is not stored separately, but the data for each row is scanned, we would have to query across:

100 million * 64 bytes (size of each row in bytes) = 6,400 million bytes = approximately 6000 MB of data

At a disk read speed of say, 200 MBps, this means it would take approximately 6000 / 200 = 30 seconds to read all the records to find the matching entries.

Scenario B: Searching column by column

Assuming each column of data resides in individual files representing the respective columns, we will look each where clause individually:

```
select * from housedb where State like 'NY' and City like 'Albany' and
YearBuilt > 1990
```

1. **Where clause part 1**: `where State like 'NY'`

   The State column, as described earlier, has 100 million entries each of size 12 bytes.

   In this case, we only need to search across:

   100 million * 12 bytes = 1,200 million bytes = 1,000 MB of data.

   At a data read rate of 200 MBps, this would take 200 MB, and it would take 1000 / 200 = 5 seconds to read the column of data.

   This returns two million records (as noted earlier database characteristics)

2. **Where clause part 2**: `City like 'Albany'`

   In the preceding step, we had narrowed our window of search to two million records that satisfied the criteria of State NY. In the second where clause step, now, we need not query across all 100 million records. Instead, we can simply look at the two million records that satisfied the criteria to determine which ones belong to City Albany.

   In this case, we only need to search across:

   *2 million * 12 bytes = 24 million bytes = approximately 20 MB of data.*

   At a data read rate of 200 MBps, this would take 0.1 seconds.

   This returns 10,000 records (as noted earlier in Database Characteristics).

3. **Where clause part 3**: `YearBuilt > 1990`

In the preceding step, we further narrowed our window of search to 10,000 records fulfilling both the criteria of State NY and City Albany. In this step, we will query 10,000 records in the YearBuilt column to find which ones fulfil the criteria of YearBuilt > 1990.

In this case, we only need to search across:

*10,000 * 16 bytes = 160,000 bytes = approximately 150 KB of data.*

At a data read rate of 200 MBps, this would take 0.00075 seconds, which we can round to zero seconds.

Hence, the net time spent in querying across the data was:

- Where clause part 1: `where State like 'NY'` - five seconds
- Where clause part 2: `City like 'Albany'` - 0.1 seconds
- Where clause part 3: `YearBuilt > 1990` - zero seconds

Net time taken to read the data = 5.1 seconds.

Important: Note that the actual read or more specifically, scan performance, depends on various other factors. The **size of the tuple** (row), the time to reconstruct the tuple (**tuple reconstruction**), **bandwidth of memory** (how fast data can be read into the CPU from Main Memory, and so on), **cache line size** and other factors. In practice, there would be various levels of abstractions due to which the actual performance may be slower. Further there are other considerations such as hardware architecture and parallel operations that can affect positively or otherwise the overall performance. These topics are more advanced and require dedicated reading. The analysis here focuses exclusively on the disk I/O, which is one of the critical aspects of overall performance at a high-level.

The preceding example demonstrates the benefits of querying data that has been stored in columns from a query performance or efficiency perspective based on the size of the data. There is also another benefit offered by columnar data, which is that it allows storage of tables that may have arbitrary schema in columns.

Consider the first four rows of the prior table. If, for example, we had missing information in some of the rows, that would lead to sparse columns:

PlotNumber	Owner	Address	State	City	YearBuilt
1	John	1 Main St.	*NULL*	Seattle	1995
2	Mary	20 J. Ave.	NY	*NULL*	*NULL*
3	Jane	*NULL*	NY	Rye Brook	*NULL*
4	John	10 A. Blvd.	CT	*NULL*	*NULL*

Instead of populating NULL values, we can instead create a `Column Family` called `Complete_Address` that can contain an arbitrary number of key-value pairs corresponding to only those fields that have corresponding data:

PlotNumber	Owner	Complete_Address		YearBuilt
1	John	Address: 1 Main St.	City: Seattle	1995
2	Mary	Address: 20 J. Ave.	State: NY	*NULL*
3	Jane	State: NY	City: Rye Brook	*NULL*
4	John	Address: 10 A. Blvd.	State: CT	*NULL*

A third and very important benefit offered by columnar databases is the ability to retrieve data based on three keys: a row key, a column key, and a timestamp that uniquely identifies each record, permitting very fast access to the data in question.

For example, since the Owner field can change when the property (PlotNumber) is sold, we can add another field that denotes the date of the record; that is, the date that the record corresponds to. This would allow us to distinguish among properties that had a change of ownership whilst all the other data remained the same:

PlotNumber	Owner	Address	State	City	YearBuilt	RecordDate
1	John	1 Main St.	WA	Seattle	1995	2001.04.02
2	Mary	20 J. Ave.	NY	Albany	1980	2007.05.30
3	Jane	5 45th St.	NY	Rye Brook	2001	2001.10.24
4	John	10 A. Blvd.	CT	Stamford	2010	2003.07.20

Since there can be multiple records for each PlotNumber to accommodate change of ownership, we can now define three keys that could uniquely identify each cell of data in each record, as follows:

- Row key: `PlotNumber`
- Column key: The column name
- Timestamp key: `RecordDate`

Each cell in each record in the table will thus have a unique three-value pair that distinguishes it from the other cells.

Databases such as Bigtable, Cassandra, and others employ this method to perform data analysis at scale both expeditiously and efficiently.

Some of the popular columnar databases are listed as follows. Note that there may be repetitions as databases can have multiple NoSQL properties (such as both in-memory and columnar):

Open source	Commercial
Apache Parquet	Kdb+
MonetDB	Teradata
MariaDB	SAP HANA
Druid	HP Vertica
HBase	Oracle Exadata
Apache Kudu	ParAccel
Apache Arrow	Actian Vector

Document-oriented databases

Document-based or document-oriented databases became prominent as a means of storing data that had variable structures; that is, there was no fixed schema that each record would fit into all the time. Additionally, the document may have both a structured as well as an *unstructured* part.

Structured data is, in essence, data that can be stored in a tabular format such as in a spreadsheet. Data stored in Excel spreadsheets or MySQL tables all belong to the class of structured datasets. Data that cannot be represented in a strict tabular format such as books, audio files, video files, or social network messages are considered unstructured data. As such, in document-oriented databases, we will primarily work with structured and unstructured text data.

An intuitive explanation of data that can contain both structured and unstructured text can be found in the example of a **phone diary**. Although these have become increasingly rare with the growth of digital data storage, many of us would remember a time when phone numbers were written in pocketbooks. The following image shows how we store data in a phone diary:

Address Book (Semi-Structured Dataset)

In the preceding example, the following fields can be considered as structured:

- Name
- Address
- Tel and Fax

There is a line underneath the Address field where the user can enter arbitrary information, for example, **met at a conference in 2015**, **works at company abc**. This is essentially a note that the diary keeper wrote when entering the specific information. Since there is no defining characteristic of a free-form field such as this, it could also contain information such as a second phone number, or an alternative address and other information. This would qualify as an unstructured text.

Further, since the other fields are not interdependent, a user may write the address but not the phone number, or the name and phone number but not the address.

A document-oriented database, by virtue of its ability to store schema-free data; that is, data that does not conform to any fixed schema such as fixed columns with fixed datatypes, would hence be an appropriate platform to store this information.

As such, since a phone diary contains a much smaller volume of data, in practice, we could store it in other formats, but the necessity for document-oriented datasets becomes apparent when we are working with large-scale data containing both structured and unstructured information.

Using the example of a phone diary, the data could be stored in a document-oriented dataset in JSON format, as follows:

```
(
  {
    "name": "John",
    "address": "1 Main St.",
    "notes": "Met at conference in 2015",
    "tel": 2013249978,
  },
  {
    "name": "Jack",
    "address": "20 J. Blvd",
    "notes": "Gym Instructor",
    "tel": 2054584538,
    "fax": 3482274573
  }
)
```

JSON, which stands for **J**ava**S**cript **O**bject **N**otation, provides a means of representing data in a portable text-based key-value pair format. Today, data in JSON is ubiquitous across the industry and has become the standard in storing data that does not have a fixed schema. It is also a great medium to exchange structured data, and as such is used for such datasets frequently.

The preceding illustration provides a basic example to convey how document-oriented databases work. As such, it is a very simple and hopefully intuitive example. In practice, document-oriented databases such as MongoDB and CouchDB are used to store gigabytes and terabytes of information.

For example, consider a website that stores data on users and their movie preferences. Each user may have multiple movies they have watched, rated, recommended, movies that they have added to their wishlist, and other such artifacts. In such a case, where there are various arbitrary elements in the dataset, many of which are optional and many of which might contain multiple values (for example, multiple movies recommended by a user), a JSON format to capture information becomes optimal. This is where document-oriented databases provide a superior and optimal platform to store and exchange data.

More concretely, databases such as MongoDB store information in BSON format - a binary version of JSON documents that have additional optimizations to accommodate datatypes, Unicode characters, and other features to improve upon the performance of basic JSON documents.

A more comprehensive example of a JSON document stored in MongoDB could be data stored about airline passengers that contains information on numerous attributes specific to individual passengers, for example:

```
{
    "_id" : ObjectId("597cdbb193acc5c362e7ae96"),
    "firstName" : "Rick",
    "age" : 66,
    "frequentFlyer" : (
        "Delta"
    ),
    "milesEarned" : (
        88154
    )
}
{
    "_id" : ObjectId("597cdbb193acc5c362e7ae97"),
    "firstName" : "Nina",
    "age" : 53,
    "frequentFlyer" : (
        "Delta",
        "JetBlue",
        "Delta"
    ),
    "milesEarned" : (
        59226,
        62025,
        27493
    )
}
```

Each entry is uniquely identified by the _id field, which allows us to directly query information relevant to the specific user and retrieve data without having to query across millions of records.

Today, document-oriented databases are used to store a diverse range of datasets. Examples include the use of such the following:

- Log files and log file-related information
- Articles and other text-based published materials

- Geolocation data
- User/user account-related information
- Many more use cases that are optimal for document/JSON based storage

Well-known document-oriented databases include the following:

Open source	Commercial
MongoDB	Azure Cosmos DB
CouchDB	OrientDB
Couchbase Server	Marklogic

Key-value databases

Key-value databases operate on the principle of structuring data as pairs of values corresponding to keys. To highlight the benefits of key-value databases, it would help to revisit the significance of hash maps, a common term prevalent in computer science to specify a unique data-structure that provides a constant-time lookup for key pairs.

An intuitive example for a hash table is as follows:

Consider a collection of 500 books and five bookcases. Each bookcase has five shelves. The books can be placed in an arbitrary order, but that would make it incredibly difficult to find a specific book and you may need to go through hundreds of books before locating the one you need. One method of categorizing the books would be to assign ranges of letters to each of the bookshelves, for example, A-E, F-J, K-O, P-T, U-Z, and use the first letter of the name of the book to assign it to a specific shelf. However, suppose you have a disproportionate number of books that start with the letters A-E. This means that the case assigned for A-E would have a much higher number of books relative to the other ones.

A more elegant alternative could be to assign a value to each of the books and use the respective value to determine which bookcase or bookshelf the book belongs to. To assign a number, a specific value to each book, we could sum up the numbers corresponding to each letter of the title of the book using a range of 1-26 for the letters A-Z respectively:

```
A : 1    B : 2    C : 3    D : 4    E : 5    F : 6
G : 7    H : 8    I : 9    J : 10   K : 11   L : 12
M : 13   N : 14   O : 15   P : 16   Q : 17   R : 18
S : 19   T : 20   U : 21   V : 22   W : 23   X : 24
Y : 25   Z : 26
```

Our Simple Hash Map

Since we have five bookcases, each with five shelves, we have a total of 25 shelves. One method of allocating a book to a specific shelf would be to take the numeric value of the book obtained by summing the letters in the title and dividing the value by 26. Any number, when divided by 25, will yield a remainder between 0-25; that is, 26 unique values. We can use this value then to assign the book to a particular shelf. This then becomes our self-created hash function.

Of the 25 shelves, each of them is now assigned a numeric value corresponding to the values 0-25 respectively, with the last shelf being assigned the values 24 and 25. For example, shelf zero is assigned to store books whose numeric value divided by 26 yields zero, shelf one is assigned to store books whose numeric value divided by 26 yields one, and shelf 25 is assigned to store books whose numeric value divided by 26 yields 24 or 25.

An example will help to illustrate this concept more concretely.

Book name: **HAMLET**

Numeric value of title:

Hash values

Sum total of the numeric value = 8 + 1 + 13 + 12 + 5 + 20 = 59

Divide number by 26 = 2, remainder seven

Hence, the book is assigned to shelf number seven.

We have essentially found a way to methodically assign a shelf to each individual book, and because we have a fixed rule, when a new request for a book arrives, we can find it almost instantaneously since we will know the shelf corresponding to the book.

The preceding method illustrates the concept of hashing, and in practice, we would use a hash function that would find a unique value for each book, and assuming we could get an arbitrary number of bookshelves and slots in which we can place the books, we could simply use the plain numeric value of the book to identify which shelf it would belong to.

There would be cases where two books would have the same numeric value, and in those cases we could stack the books in the slot corresponding to the number. In computer science, this effect of multiple values corresponding to a key is known as a collision, and in those cases we would assign multiple items by means of a list or similar datatype.

In real-life use cases, we have much more complex items to work with than the simple example of books. Generally, we'd use more complex hash functions that lower the chance of collision and accordingly assign the key-value pair. The data would be stored in a contiguous array in memory and hence, when a request for a certain key arrived, we could instantaneously find the value by using the hash function to identify the location in memory where the data resides.

Hence, using key-value pairs to store data can be immensely powerful because the time to retrieve information corresponding to a key can be very fast as there is no need to search through a long list to identify a matching key.

Key-value databases employ the same principle of assigning unique keys to each record, and the data corresponding to each key is stored in the corresponding location. In our discussion of MongoDB, we saw that records were assigned a certain key identified by the _id value in each record. In practice, we could use this value to retrieve the corresponding data in constant time.

As mentioned before, memcached used to be the preferred method to store data in key-value pairs for web services that required very fast access to frequently used data. In essence, it served as a memory cache to store temporary information. With the advent of NoSQL databases, new platforms that extended the limited use case of memcached became prominent. Solutions such as Redis offered not only the ability to store data in key-value pairs in memory, but also the ability to persist the data on disk. In addition, these key-value stores supported horizontal scaling, which permitted the distribution of key-value pairs across hundreds of nodes.

The disadvantage of key-value storage was that the data could not be queried with the same flexibility as standard databases, which supported multiple levels of indexing and a more richer set of SQL commands. Nevertheless, the benefits of constant time lookup implied that for use cases that required a key-value structure, there were few other solutions that were comparable in both performance and efficiency. For instance, a shopping website with thousands of users could store user profile information in a key-value database and be able to look up individual information by simply applying a hash function corresponding to, for example, the user ID.

Today, key-value databases use a variety of methods to store data:

- **SSTables**: A file of sorted key-value pairs represented as strings (and directly mapped to the **Google File System** (**GFS**)).
- **B-trees**: Balanced trees where values are identified by traversing along leaves/nodes.
- **Bloom filters**: A more optimal key-value method used when the number of keys is high. It uses multiple hash functions to set the bit-value to one in an array corresponding to keys.
- **Shards**: A process involving partitioning data across multiple nodes.

Well known key-value databases include:

Open source	Commercial
Redis	Amazon DynamoDB
Cassandra	Riak
Aerospike	Oracle NoSQL
Apache Ignite	Azure Cosmos DB
Apache Accumulo	Oracle Berkeley DB

Graph databases

Graph databases provide an efficient representation of data with records that have inter-relationships. Typical examples are your social network friend list, LinkedIn contacts, Netflix movie subscribers. By leveraging optimized algorithms for searching on tree-based/graph data structures, graph databases can locate information in a novel manner relative to other NoSQL solutions. In such a structure, discrete information and properties are represented as leaves, edges, and nodes.

The following image shows an atypical representation of a network that can be queried to discover or find complex inter-relationships using a graph database. In practice, production graph databases contain millions of nodes:

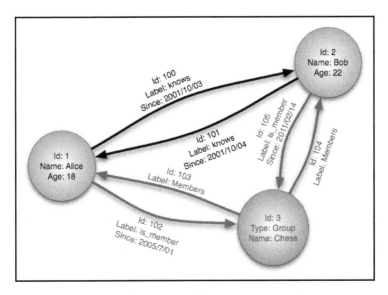

Graph Database

Although they are not as prevalent as other types of NoSQL database, graph-based platforms are used for business-critical areas. For instance, credit card companies use graph databases to find new products that an individual cardholder may be interested in by querying across millions of datapoints to assess purchasing behavior of other cardholders with similar purchasing patterns. Social network websites use graph databases to compute similarity scores, provide friend suggestions, and other related metrics.

Well-known graph databases include the following:

Open source	Commercial
Apache Giraph	Datastax Enterprise Graph
Neo4j	Teradata Aster
JanusGraph	Oracle Spatial and Graph
Apache Ignite	

Other NoSQL types and summary of other types of databases

This section described some of the commonly known NoSQL paradigms in use today. There are several other emerging platforms that have their own strengths and unique characteristics. A brief overview of some of them is given here:

Type	Feature
Object-oriented databases	Databases that leverage concepts in object-oriented programming to store data represented as objects.
Cloud databases	Databases offered by cloud vendors such as Amazon, Microsoft, and Google that are only available on their respective cloud platforms such as Amazon Redshift, Azure SQL Database, and Google BigQuery.
GPU databases	A more recent entrant in the world of databases that leverage GPU (graphic processing unit) cards to process data. Examples include MapD, Kinetica, and others.
FPGA-accelerated databases	With Intel soon announcing the release of new chips that would have embedded FPGAs, companies such as Baidu have started developing FPGA-accelerated systems that leverage FPGA processing power to improve SQL query performance.
Stream processing/IoT databases	Databases, or more generally platforms, that are optimized for processing streaming data such as from medical devices and sensors. One of the most popular examples of such a system is Apache Storm.

A question often asked is whether there is one NoSQL database that is optimal for all use cases. While the databases can have multiple features that support numerous elements of NoSQL systems (generally known as multi-modal databases), in practice, a single solution that performs universally well across a broad set of use cases is rare. In real-world use cases, companies generally implement more than one solution to meet data mining needs. In the next section, we will complete a few hands-on exercises with real-world datasets using NoSQL solutions discussed in this chapter.

Analyzing Nobel Laureates data with MongoDB

In the first exercise, we will use **MongoDB**, one of the leading document-oriented databases, to analyze Nobel Laureates from 1902-present. MongoDB provides a simple and intuitive interface to work with JSON files. As discussed earlier, JSON is a flexible format that allows representing data using a structured approach.

JSON format

Consider the following table:

Firstname	Lastname	Information
John	15	Subject: History, Grade B
Jack	18	Subject: Physics, Grade A
Jill	17	Subject: Physics, Grade A+

The Information field contains a column containing multiple values categorized under Subject and Grade. Such columns that contain multiple data are also known as columns with nested data.

Portability has been an important aspect of transferring data from one system to another. In general, ODBC connectors are used to transfer data between database systems. Another common format is CSV files with the data represented as comma-separated values. CSV files are optimal for structured data that doesn't contain more complex data structures such as nested values. In such cases, JSON provides an optimal and structured way to capture and preserve information using a key-value pair syntax.

In JSON representation, the table can be defined as follows:

```
(
    {
        "Firstname":"John",
        "Age":15,
        "Information":{
            "Subject":"History",
            "Grade":"B"
        }
    },
```

```
{
    "Firstname":"Jack",
    "Age":18,
    "Information":{
        "Subject":"Physics",
        "Grade":"A"
    }
},
{
    "Firstname":"Jill",
    "Age":17,
    "Information":{
        "Subject":"Physics",
        "Grade":"A+"
    }
}
)
```

Notice that the `Information` key contains two keys, `Subject` and `Grade`, with each having a corresponding value.

Today, most product developers and vendors accommodate the ingestion of JSON-formatted data. Also, due to the simple manner in which complex relationships can be expressed as well as exchanged in text format, JSON has become immensely popular across the world in the developer community.

MongoDB captures data in JSON format. It internally stores them in BSON—an optimized binary representation of the JSON data.

Installing and using MongoDB

MongoDB is supported on all major platforms such as Windows, Linux, and OS X platforms.

> The details for installing MongoDB can be found on their official website at https://docs.mongodb.com/manual/installation/. Note that we will be using the MongoDB Community Edition.

For our exercise, we will re-use the Linux CentOS environment from our Cloudera Hadoop Distribution VM.

The exercise is however not dependent on the platform on which you install MongoDB. Once the installation has been completed, you can execute the commands indicated in this chapter on any other supported platform. If you have access to a separate Linux machine, you can use that as well.

We will visit some of the common semantics of MongoDB and also download two datasets to compute the highest number of Nobel Prizes grouped by continent. The complete dump of the Nobel Prize data on Nobel Laureates is available from nobelprize.org. The data contains all the primary attributes of Laureates. We wish to integrate this data with demographic information on the respective countries to extract more interesting analytical information:

1. **Download MongoDB**: MongoDB can be downloaded from https://www.mongodb.com/download-center#community.

   To determine which version is applicable for us, we checked the version of Linux installed on the CDH VM:

   ```
   (cloudera@quickstart ~)$ lsb_release -a
   LSB Version:        :base-4.0-amd64:base-4.0-noarch:core-4.0-
   amd64:core-4.0-noarch
   Distributor ID:   CentOS
   Description:       CentOS release 6.7 (Final)
   Release:   6.7
   Codename: Final
   ```

2. Based on the information, we have to use the CentOS version of MongoDB, and accordingly, following the instructions at https://docs.mongodb.com/manual/tutorial/install-mongodb-on-red-hat/, we installed the software, shown as follows:

   ```
   The first step involved adding the repo as follows. Type in sudo
   nano /etc/yum.repos.d/mongodb-org-3.4.repo on the command line and
   enter the text as shown.


   (root@quickstart cloudera)# sudo nano /etc/yum.repos.d/mongodb-
   org-3.4.repo

   ### Type in the information shown below and press CTRL-X
   ### When prompted to save buffer, type in yes

   (mongodb-org-3.4)
   name=MongoDB Repository
   baseurl=https://repo.mongodb.org/yum/redhat/$releasever/mongodb-org
   ```

```
/3.4/x86_64/
gpgcheck=1
enabled=1
gpgkey=https://www.mongodb.org/static/pgp/server-3.4.asc
```

The following screenshot shows the contents of the file:

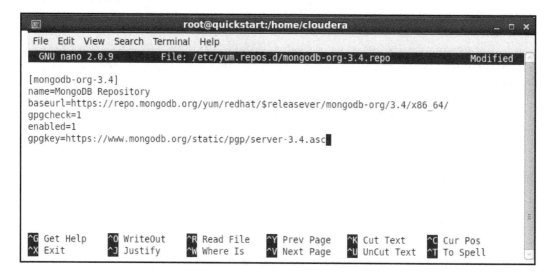

Setting up MongoDB repository

As seen in the following screenshot, type Y for Yes:

Saving the .repo file

Save the file as shown in the image as follows. This will now allow us to install `mongo-db`:

Writing and Saving the .repo file

```
# Back in terminal, type in the following

(cloudera@quickstart ~)$ sudo yum install -y mongodb-org
```

```
(...)

Installing:
 mongodb-org                    x86_64          3.4.6-1.el6
mongodb-org-3.4        5.8 k
Installing for dependencies:
 mongodb-org-mongos             x86_64          3.4.6-1.el6
mongodb-org-3.4        12 M
  mongodb-org-server            x86_64          3.4.6-1.el6
mongodb-org-3.4        20 M
  mongodb-org-shell             x86_64          3.4.6-1.el6
mongodb-org-3.4        11 M
  mongodb-org-tools             x86_64          3.4.6-1.el6
mongodb-org-3.4        49 M

Transaction Summary
=====================================================================
==
Install      5 Package(s)

Total download size: 91 M
Installed size: 258 M
Downloading Packages:
(1/5): mongodb-org-3.4.6-1.el6.x86_64.rpm
| 5.8 kB      00:00
(...)

Installed:
  mongodb-org.x86_64 0:3.4.6-1.el6

Dependency Installed:
  mongodb-org-mongos.x86_64 0:3.4.6-1.el6        mongodb-org-
server.x86_64 0:3.4.6-1.el6
  mongodb-org-shell.x86_64 0:3.4.6-1.el6         mongodb-org-
tools.x86_64 0:3.4.6-1.el6

Complete!


### Attempting to start mongo without first starting the daemon
will produce an error message ###
### You need to start the mongo daemon before you can use it ###

(cloudera@quickstart ~)$ mongo
MongoDB shell version v3.4.6
connecting to: mongodb://127.0.0.1:27017
2017-07-30T10:50:58.708-0700 W NETWORK  (thread1) Failed to connect
to 127.0.0.1:27017, in(checking socket for error after poll),
```

```
reason: Connection refused
2017-07-30T10:50:58.708-0700 E QUERY    (thread1) Error: couldn't
connect to server 127.0.0.1:27017, connection attempt failed :
connect@src/mongo/shell/mongo.js:237:13
@(connect):1:6
exception: connect failed

### The first step is to create the MongoDB dbpath - this is where
MongoDB will store all data

### Create a folder called, mongodata, this will be the mongo
dbpath ###
```

(cloudera@quickstart ~)$ mkdir mongodata

```
### Start mongod ###

(cloudera@quickstart ~)$ mongod --dbpath mongodata
2017-07-30T10:52:17.200-0700 I CONTROL    (initandlisten) MongoDB
starting : pid=16093 port=27017 dbpath=mongodata 64-bit
host=quickstart.cloudera
(...)
2017-07-30T10:52:17.321-0700 I INDEX      (initandlisten) build index
done.  scanned 0 total records. 0 secs
2017-07-30T10:52:17.321-0700 I COMMAND    (initandlisten) setting
featureCompatibilityVersion to 3.4
2017-07-30T10:52:17.321-0700 I NETWORK    (thread1) waiting for
connections on port 27017
```

Open a new terminal and download the JSON data files as shown in the following screenshot:

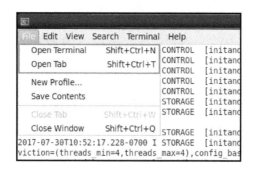

Selecting Open Terminal from Terminal App on Mac OS X

```
# Download Files
# laureates.json and country.json ###
```

```
# Change directory to go to the mongodata folder that you created earlier
(cloudera@quickstart ~)$ cd mongodata

(cloudera@quickstart mongodata)$ curl -o laureates.json
"http://api.nobelprize.org/v1/laureate.json"
  % Total    % Received % Xferd  Average Speed   Time    Time     Time
Current
                                 Dload  Upload   Total   Spent    Left
Speed
100  428k    0   428k    0     0   292k        0 --:--:--  0:00:01 --:--:--
354k



### Clean the file laureates.json
### Delete content upto the first ( on the first line of the file
### Delete the last } character from the file
### Store the cleansed dataset in a file called laureates.json
```

Note that the file needs to be slightly modified. The code is shown in the following image:

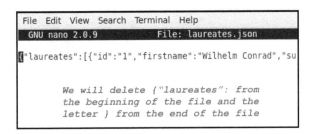

Modifying the .json file for our application

```
(cloudera@quickstart mongodata)$ cat laureates.json | sed
's/^{"laureates"://g' | sed 's/}$//g' > mongofile.json



### Import the file laureates.json into MongoDB
### mongoimport is a utility that is used to import data into MongoDB
### The command below will import data from the file, mongofile.json
### Into a db named nobel into a collection (i.e., a table) called
laureates

(cloudera@quickstart mongodata)$ mongoimport --jsonArray --db nobel --
collection laureates --file mongofile.json
2017-07-30T11:06:35.228-0700    connected to: localhost
2017-07-30T11:06:35.295-0700    imported 910 documents
```

In order to combine the data in `laureate.json` with country-specific information, we need to download the `countryInfo.txt` from `geonames.org` We will now download the second file that we need for the exercise, `country.json`. We will use both `laureates.json` and `country.json` for the exercise.

`### country.json:` Download it from `http://www.geonames.org` (license: `https://creativecommons.org/licenses/by/3.0/`). Modify the start and end of the JSON string to import into MongoDB as shown as follows:

```
# The file country.json contains descriptive information about all
countries
# We will use this file for our tutorial

### Download country.json
```

```
(cloudera@quickstart mongodata)$ curl -o country.json
"https://raw.githubusercontent.com/xbsd/packtbigdata/master/country.json"
  % Total    % Received % Xferd  Average Speed   Time    Time     Time
Current
                                 Dload  Upload   Total   Spent    Left
Speed
100  113k  100  113k    0     0   360k      0 --:--:-- --:--:-- --:--:--
885k
```

```
### The file, country.json has already been cleaned and can be imported
directly into MongoDB
(cloudera@quickstart mongodata)$ mongoimport --jsonArray --db nobel --
collection country --file country.json
2017-07-30T12:10:35.554-0700   connected to: localhost
2017-07-30T12:10:35.580-0700   imported 250 documents
```

```
### MONGO SHELL ###
(cloudera@quickstart mongodata)$ mongo
MongoDB shell version v3.4.6
connecting to: mongodb://127.0.0.1:27017
MongoDB server version: 3.4.6
Server has startup warnings:
(...)

2017-07-30T10:52:17.298-0700 I CONTROL  (initandlisten)

### Switch to the database nobel using the 'use <databasename>' command
> use nobel
switched to db nobel

### Show all collections (i.e., tables)
```

```
### This will show the tables that we imported into MongoDB - country and
laureates
> show collections
country
laureates
>

### Collections in MongoDB are the equivalent to tables in SQL

### 1. Common Operations

### View collection statistics using db.<dbname>.stats()
> db.laureates.stats()

   "ns" : "nobel.laureates",  # Name Space
   "size" : 484053,           # Size in Bytes
   "count" : 910,             # Number of Records
   "avgObjSize" : 531,        # Average Object Size
   "storageSize" : 225280,    # Data size


# Check space used (in bytes)
> db.laureates.storageSize()
225280


# Check number of records
> db.laureates.count()
910


### 2. View data from collection
###
### There is an extensive list of commands that can be used in MongoDB. As
such discussing them all is outside the scope of the text. However, a few
of the familiar commands have been given below as a marker to help the
reader get started with the platform.


### See first record for laureates using findOne()
### findOne() will show the first record in the collection
> db.laureates.findOne()

{
   "_id" : ObjectId("597e202bcd8724f48de485d4"),
   "id" : "1",
   "firstname" : "Wilhelm Conrad",
   "surname" : "Röntgen",
```

```
        "born" : "1845-03-27",
        "died" : "1923-02-10",
        "bornCountry" : "Prussia (now Germany)",
        "bornCountryCode" : "DE",
        "bornCity" : "Lennep (now Remscheid)",
        "diedCountry" : "Germany",
        "diedCountryCode" : "DE",
        "diedCity" : "Munich",
        "gender" : "male",
        "prizes" : (
                {
                        "year" : "1901",
                        "category" : "physics",
                        "share" : "1",
                        "motivation" : "\"in recognition of the extraordinary
services he has rendered by the discovery of the remarkable rays
subsequently named after him\"",
                        "affiliations" : (
                                {
                                        "name" : "Munich University",
                                        "city" : "Munich",
                                        "country" : "Germany"
                                }
                        )
                }
        )
}


### See all records for laureates
> db.laureates.find()

{ "_id" : ObjectId("597e202bcd8724f48de485d4"), "id" : "1", "firstname" :
"Wilhelm Conrad", "surname" : "Röntgen", "born" : "1845-03-27", "died" :
"1923-02-10", "bornCountry" : "Prussia (now Germany)", "bornCountryCode" :
"DE", "bornCity" : "Lennep (now Remscheid)"
(...)


...


### MongoDB functions accept JSON formatted strings as parameters to
options
### Some examples are shown below for reference
### Query a field - Find all Nobel Laureates who were male
> db.laureates.find({"gender":"male"})

(...)
{ "_id" : ObjectId("597e202bcd8724f48de485d5"), "id" : "2", "firstname" :
"Hendrik Antoon", "surname" : "Lorentz", "born" : "1853-07-18", "died" :
```

```
"1928-02-04", "bornCountry" : "the Netherlands", "bornCountryCode" : "NL",
"bornCity" : "Arnhem", "diedCountry" : "the Netherlands", "diedCountryCode"
: "NL", "gender" : "male", "prizes" : ( { "year" : "1902", "category" :
"physics", "share" : "2", "motivation" : "\"in recognition of the
extraordinary service they rendered by their researches into the influence
of magnetism upon radiation phenomena\"", "affiliations" : ( { "name" :
"Leiden University", "city" : "Leiden", "country" : "the Netherlands" } ) }
) }
(...)
```

Query a field - find all Nobel Laureates who were born in the US and received a Nobel Prize in Physics. Note that here we have a nested field (category is under prizes as shown). Hence, we will use the dot notation as shown in the coming image.

Image illustrating `category`, one of the nested fields:

Nested JSON Fields

```
> db.laureates.find({"bornCountryCode":"US", "prizes.category":"physics",
"bornCity": /Chicago/})

{ "_id" : ObjectId("597e202bcd8724f48de48638"), "id" : "103", "firstname" :
"Ben Roy", "surname" : "Mottelson", "born" : "1926-07-09", "died" :
"0000-00-00", "bornCountry" : "USA", "bornCountryCode" : "US", "bornCity" :
"Chicago, IL",
...


### Check number of distinct prize categories using distinct
> db.laureates.distinct("prizes.category")
(
    "physics",
    "chemistry",
    "peace",
    "medicine",
    "literature",
    "economics"
)
```

```
### Using Comparison Operators
### MongoDB allows users to chain multiple comparison operators
### Details on MongoDB operators can be found at:
https://docs.mongodb.com/manual/reference/operator/

# Find Nobel Laureates born in either India or Egypt using the $in operator
> db.laureates.find ( { bornCountryCode: { $in: ("IN","EG") } } )

{ "_id" : ObjectId("597e202bcd8724f48de485f7"), "id" : "37", "firstname" :
"Sir Chandrasekhara Venkata", "surname" : "Raman", "born" : "1888-11-07",
"died" : "1970-11-21", "bornCountry" : "India", "bornCountryCode" : "IN",
"bornCity" : "Tiruchirappalli", "diedCountry" : "India", "diedCountryCode"
: "IN", "diedCity" : "Bangalore", "gender" : "male", "prizes" : ( { "year"
: "1930", "category" : "physics", "share" : "1", "motivation" : "\"for his
work on the scattering of light and for the discovery of the effect named
after him\"", "affiliations" : ( { "name" : "Calcutta University", "city" :
"Calcutta", "country" : "India" } ) } ) }
...


### Using Multiple Comparison Operators

### Find Nobel laureates who were born in either US or China and won prize
in either Physics or Chemistry using the $and and $or operator
> db.laureates.find( {
$and : ({ $or : ( { bornCountryCode : "US" }, { bornCountryCode : "CN" } )
},
{ $or : ( { "prizes.category" : "physics" }, { "prizes.category" :
"chemistry" } ) }
    )
} )

{ "_id" : ObjectId("597e202bcd8724f48de485ee"), "id" : "28", "firstname" :
"Robert Andrews", "surname" : "Millikan", "born" : "1868-03-22", "died" :
"1953-12-19", "bornCountry" : "USA", "bornCountryCode" : "US", "bornCity" :
"Morrison, IL", "diedCountry" : "USA", "diedCountryCode" : "US", "diedCity"
: "San Marino, CA", "gender" : "male", "prizes" : ( { "year" : "1923",
"category" : "physics", "share" : "1", "motivation" : "\"for his work on
the elementary charge of electricity and on the photoelectric effect\"",
"affiliations" : ( { "name" : "California Institute of Technology
(Caltech)", "city" : "Pasadena, CA", "country" : "USA" } ) } ) }
...


### Performing Aggregations is one of the common operations in MongoDB
queries
### MongoDB allows users to perform pipeline aggregations, map-reduce
aggregations and single purpose aggregations

### Details on MongoDB aggregations can be found at the URL
```

```
### https://docs.mongodb.com/manual/aggregation/

### Aggregation Examples

### Count and aggregate total Nobel laureates by year and sort in
descending order
### Step 1: Use the $group operator to indicate that prize.year will be the
grouping variable
### Step 2: Use the $sum operator (accumulator) to sum each entry under a
variable called totalPrizes
### Step 3: Use the $sort operator to rank totalPrizes

> db.laureates.aggregate(
  {$group: {_id: '$prizes.year', totalPrizes: {$sum: 1}}},
  {$sort: {totalPrizes: -1}}
);

{ "_id" : ( "2001" ), "totalPrizes" : 15 }
{ "_id" : ( "2014" ), "totalPrizes" : 13 }
{ "_id" : ( "2002" ), "totalPrizes" : 13 }
{ "_id" : ( "2000" ), "totalPrizes" : 13 }

(...)

### To count and aggregate total prizes by country of birth
> db.laureates.aggregate(
  {$group: {_id: '$bornCountry', totalPrizes: {$sum: 1}}},
  {$sort: {totalPrizes: -1}}
);

{ "_id" : "USA", "totalPrizes" : 257 }
{ "_id" : "United Kingdom", "totalPrizes" : 84 }
{ "_id" : "Germany", "totalPrizes" : 61 }
{ "_id" : "France", "totalPrizes" : 51 }
...

### MongoDB also supports PCRE (Perl-Compatible) Regular Expressions
### For more information, see
https://docs.mongodb.com/manual/reference/operator/query/regex

### Using Regular Expressions: Find count of nobel laureates by country of
birth whose prize was related to 'radiation' (as indicated in the field
motivation under prizes)

> db.laureates.aggregate(
  {$match : { "prizes.motivation" : /radiation/ }},
  {$group: {_id: '$bornCountry', totalPrizes: {$sum: 1}}},
  {$sort: {totalPrizes: -1}}
```

```
);

{ "_id" : "USA", "totalPrizes" : 4 }
{ "_id" : "Germany", "totalPrizes" : 2 }
{ "_id" : "the Netherlands", "totalPrizes" : 2 }
{ "_id" : "United Kingdom", "totalPrizes" : 2 }
{ "_id" : "France", "totalPrizes" : 1 }
{ "_id" : "Prussia (now Russia)", "totalPrizes" : 1 }
```

Result: We see that the highest number of prizes (in which radiation was mentioned as a key-word) was the US

Interestingly, we can also do joins and other similar operations that allow us to combine the data with other data sources
In this case, we'd like to join the data in laureates with the data from country information obtained earlier
The collection country contains many interesting fields, but for this exercise, we will show how to find the total number of nobel laureates by continent

The Left Join

Step 1: Use the $lookup operator to define the from/to fields, collection names and assign the data to a field named countryInfo

We can join the field bornCountryCode from laureates with the field countryCode from the collection country
> **db.laureates.aggregate(**
  {$lookup: { from: "country", localField: "bornCountryCode", foreignField: "countryCode", as: "countryInfo" }})

```
{ "_id" : ObjectId("597e202bcd8724f48de485d4"), "id" : "1", "firstname" :
"Wilhelm Conrad", "surname" : "Röntgen", "born" : "1845-03-27", "died" :
"1923-02-10", "bornCountry" : "Prussia (now Germany)", "bornCountryCode" :
"DE", "bornCity" : "Lennep (now (..) "country" : "Germany" } ) } ),
"countryInfo" : ( { "_id" : ObjectId("597e2f2bcd8724f48de489aa"),
"continent" : "EU", "capital" : "Berlin", "languages" : "de", "geonameId" :
2921044, "south" : 47.2701236047002, ...
```

With the data joined, we can now perform combined aggregations

Find the number of Nobel laureates by continent
> **db.laureates.aggregate(**
  {$lookup: { from: "country", localField: "bornCountryCode", foreignField: "countryCode", as: "countryInfo" }},
  {$group: {_id: '$countryInfo.continent', totalPrizes: {$sum: 1}}},
  {$sort: {totalPrizes: -1}}

```
);

... );
{ "_id" : ( "EU" ), "totalPrizes" : 478 }
{ "_id" : ( "NA" ), "totalPrizes" : 285 }
{ "_id" : ( "AS" ), "totalPrizes" : 67 }
...
This indicates that Europe has by far the highest number of Nobel
Laureates.
```

There are many other operations that can be performed, but the intention of the prior section was to introduce MongoDB at a high level with a simple use case. The URLs given in this chapter contain more in-depth information on using MongoDB.

There are also several visualization tools in the industry that are used to interact with and visualize data stored in MongoDB collections using a point-and-click interface. A simple yet powerful tool called MongoDB Compass is available at `https://www.mongodb.com/download-center?filter=enterprise?jmp=nav#compass`.

Navigate to the previously mentioned URL and download the version of Compass that is appropriate for your environment:

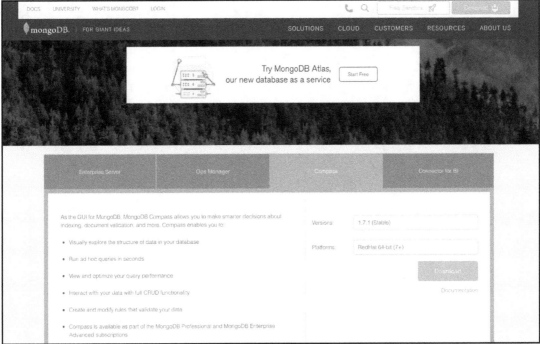

Downloading MongoDB Compass

After installation, you'll see a welcome screen. Click on **Next** until you see the main dashboard:

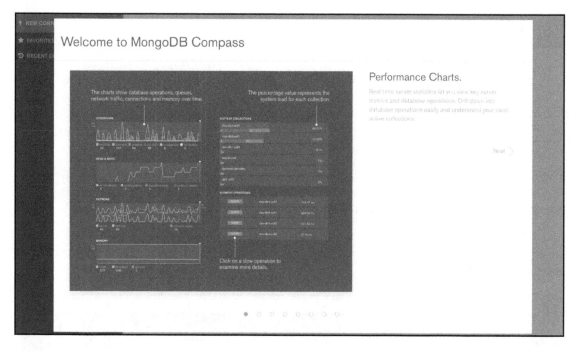

MongoDB Compass Screenshot

Click on **Performance** to view the current status of MongoDB:

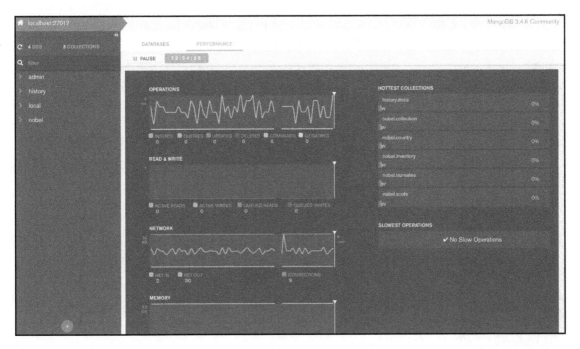

MongoDB Performance Screen

Expand the nobel database by clicking on the arrow next to the word on the left sidebar. You can click and drag on different parts of the bar charts and run ad hoc queries. This is very useful if you want to get an overall understanding of the dataset without necessarily having to run all queries by hand, as shown in the following screenshot:

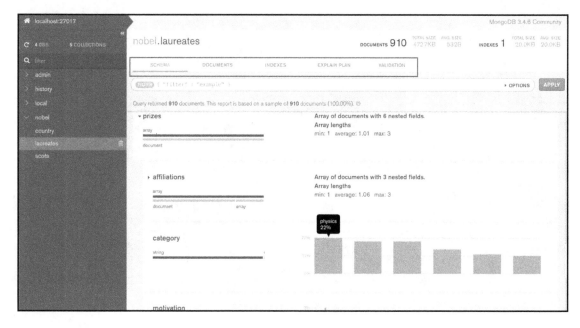

Viewing our file in MongoDB Compass

Tracking physician payments with real-world data

Physicians and hospitals alike receive payments from various external organizations, such as pharmaceutical companies who engage sales representatives to not only educate practitioners on their products, but also provide gifts or payments in kind or otherwise. In theory, gifts or payments made to physicians are not intended to influence their prescribing behavior, and pharmaceutical companies adopt careful measures to maintain checks and balances on payments being made to healthcare providers.

In 2010, President Obama's signature **Affordable Care Act** (**ACA**), also known in popular parlance as Obamacare, went into effect. Alongside the ACA, a separate legislation known as the Sunshine Act made reporting items of monetary value (directly or indirectly) mandatory for pharmaceutical companies and other organizations. While such rules existed in the past, rarely were such rules available in the public domain. By making detailed payment records made to all physicians available publicly, the Sunshine Act introduced an unprecedented level of transparency in monetary dealings involving healthcare providers.

The data is freely available on the website of CMS Open Payments at `https://openpaymentsdata.cms.gov`.

The site provides an interface to query the data, but does not have any means to perform large-scale data aggregation. For example, if a user wanted to find the total payments made in the state of CT, there is no simple and easy way to run the query through the default web-based tool. An API that provides the functionality is available, but requires a degree of familiarity and technical knowledge to use effectively. There are third-party products that provide such facilities, but in most cases they are expensive, and end users cannot modify the software to their particular needs.

In this tutorial, we will develop a fast, highly efficient web-based application to analyze tens of millions of records that capture payments made to physicians in 2016. We will be using a combination of a NoSQL database, R, and RStudio to create the final product - the web-based portal through which end users can query the database in real time.

The technologies we will use to develop the application are as follows:

- Kdb+ NoSQL database: `http://www.kx.com`
- R
- RStudio

For the tutorial, I will be using the VM image we downloaded for our Hadoop exercise. The tools can also be installed on Windows, Mac, and other Linux machines. The choice of the VM is mainly to provide a consistent and local OS independent platform.

Installing kdb+, R, and RStudio

A Packt Data Science VM download has been provided, which contains all the necessary software required for this chapter. However, if you prefer to install the software on your local machine instead, instructions, have been provided in the following sections. You can skip the installation sections and proceed directly to the section on *Developing the Open Payment Application*.

Installing kdb+

kdb+ is a time-series, in-memory, columnar database that has been used in the financial industry for almost 20 years. It is one of the fastest database platforms available for performing large-scale data mining, but one that is not as well-known as other NoSQL tools due to the fact that it has been used almost exclusively by hedge funds and investment banks for most of its existence. In particular, due to its speed and low overhead in processing vast amounts of data, it is used by algorithmic trading desks that engage in high-frequency trading.

With kdb+, it is fairly simple to analyze tens of millions and even hundreds of millions of records on a laptop. The main constraints would be at a hardware level - such as the amount of memory, disk space, and CPU that is available to process the data. In this tutorial, we will install the free 32-bit edition of kdb+ available for non-commercial use.

kdb+ is not open source, but academic institutes can use the 64-bit license at no charge by writing to `academic@kx.com`.

There are certain key characteristics of kdb+ that make it very well suited to large-scale data analysis:

- **Low-level implementation**: The database is written in C, thus reducing common causes of performance issues with most contemporary NoSQL databases that rely heavily on Java, which implements multiple layers of abstraction to provide processing capabilities
- **Architectural simplicity**: The entire binary for the kdb+ database is about 500-600 KB. This is a fraction of the size of an MP3 song and can be easily downloaded even on a dial-up connection
- **MapReduce**: The database implements an internal MapReduce process that allows queries to execute across multiple cores simultaneously
- **No installation**: The database requires no system-level privileges and users can start using kdb+ with their user account on most systems
- **Enterprise-ready**: The database has been used for nearly 20 years and is a very mature product used in global enterprise environments for analysis of high-frequency trading data among other applications
- **Wide availability of interfaces**: The database has a wide range of interfaces for languages such as C, C++,C#, Java, R, Python, MATLAB, and others to allow easy integration with existing software

The steps to install kdb+ are given as follows. Please note that if you are using the Packt Data Science VM, no additional installation is necessary. The instructions have been provided primarily for users who would like to install the software afresh.

Although the instructions are for Linux, the installation process is also quite simple for both Windows and Macs. The instructions herein are geared towards the Packt Data Science VM. The instructions for downloading the Packt Data Science VM was provided in Chapter 3, *The Analytics Toolkit*

1. Visit www.kx.com and click on the **Download** drop-down option from the **Connect with us** menu item. You may also directly go to the download page located at https://kx.com/download/:

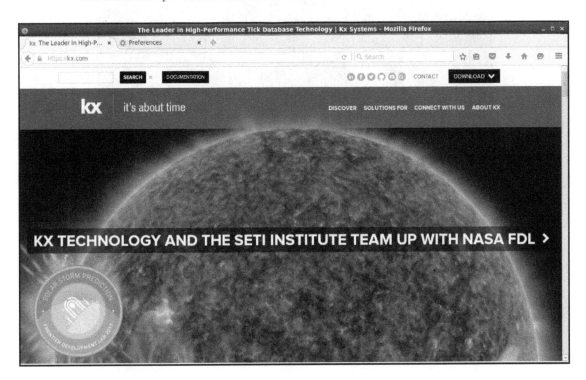

Kx Systems Homepage

The download page is as shown in the following screenshot:

Downloading KDB+

2. Click on Download on the next page.
3. You'll be taken to `https://kx.com/download/` where you can select the respective download of your choice after agreeing to the terms. If you are using the VM, download the *Linux-86 version*.
4. Select **Save File** to save the downloaded ZIP file in your Downloads folder:

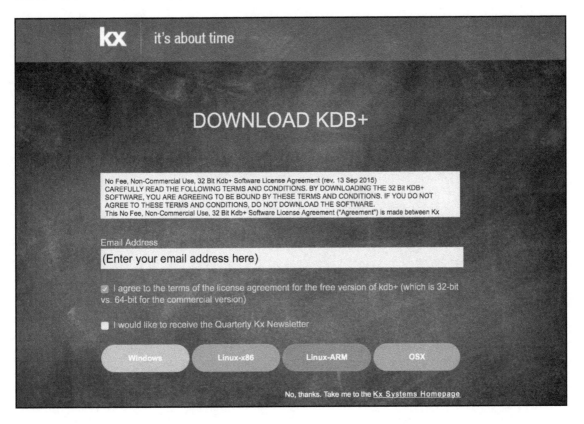

KDB+ 32-bit license terms

Go to the folder where the file was downloaded and copy the ZIP file under your home directory:

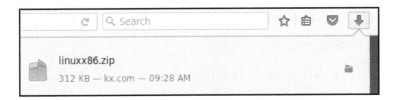

KDB+ Zip file download

For Mac or Linux systems, this will be the ~/ folder. In Windows, copy the ZIP file under C:\ and unzip to extract the q folder. The following instructions are mainly for Linux-based systems:

```
$ cd Downloads/ # cd to the folder where you have downloaded the zip file

$ unzip linuxx86.zip
Archive:  linuxx86.zip
  inflating: q/README.txt
  inflating: q/l32/q
  inflating: q/q.q
  inflating: q/q.k
  inflating: q/s.k
  inflating: q/trade.q
  inflating: q/sp.q

$ mv ~/Downloads/q ~/
$ cd ~/q
$ cd l32
$ ./q
KDB+ 3.5 2017.06.15 Copyright (C) 1993-2017 Kx Systems
l32/ 1()core 3830MB cloudera quickstart.cloudera 10.0.2.15 NONEXPIRE

Welcome to kdb+ 32bit edition
For support please see http://groups.google.com/d/forum/personal-kdbplus
Tutorials can be found at http://code.kx.com/wiki/Tutorials
To exit, type \\
To remove this startup msg, edit q.q
q)\\

/NOTE THAT YOU MAY NEED TO INSTALL THE FOLLOWING IF YOU GET AN ERROR
MESSAGE STATING THAT THE FILE q CANNOT BE FOUND. IN THAT CASE, INSTALL THE
REQUISITE SOFTWARE AS SHOWN BELOW

$ sudo dpkg --add-architecture i386
$ sudo apt-get update
$ sudo apt-get install libc6:i386 libncurses5:i386 libstdc++6:i386
```

Installing R

The frontend of the application will be developed using R. There are three options for installing R to complete the tutorial:

1. If you have installed Microsoft R from `Chapter 3`, *The Analytics Toolkit*, and will be using your local machine for the tutorial, no further installation is necessary.
2. Alternatively, if you will be using the Packt Data Science Virtualbox VM, no further installation will be needed.
3. If you plan to install R from the official R website, the binary can be downloaded from any of the download sites (mirrors) listed at `https://cran.r-project.org/mirrors.html`:

The Comprehensive R Archive Network

Download and Install R

Precompiled binary distributions of the base system and contributed packages, **Windows and Mac** users most likely want one of these versions of R:

- Download R for Linux
- Download R for (Mac) OS X
- Download R for Windows

R is part of many Linux distributions, you should check with your Linux package management system in addition to the link above.

Installing Open Source R

Installing RStudio

We will use RStudio in order to build our web-based application. You can either download the binary for RStudio from the website or install it from the terminal. RStudio is available in two versions - RStudio Desktop and RStudio Server. Both versions can be used to build the application. The Server version provides an interface that can be used by multiple users, whereas the Desktop version is generally used locally on the user's machine.

 The instructions also appear in `Chapter 3`, *The Analytics Toolkit*. They have been provided here for reference.

There are two methods to complete the installation for the R tutorial:

1. If you will be using the Packt Data Science VM, no further installation is necessary.

2. If you will be using your local machine for the tutorial, you can download RStudio Desktop from `https://www.rstudio.com/products/rstudio/download/#download` or RStudio Server (only for Linux users) from `https://www.rstudio.com/products/rstudio/download-server/`.

The following instructions have been provided for users wishing to download RStudio from the vendor's website and perform a fresh installation:

Go to the website of `https://www.rstudio.com` and click on **Products** | **RStudio**:

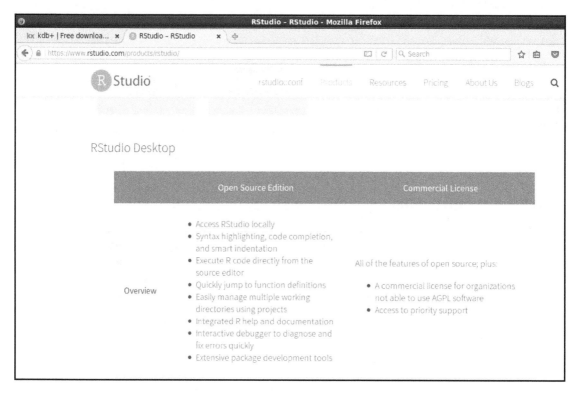

Open Source R Studio Desktop Versions

On the RStudio page, click on **Download RStudio Desktop**:

Selecting RStudio Desktop

Select the free version of RStudio Desktop:

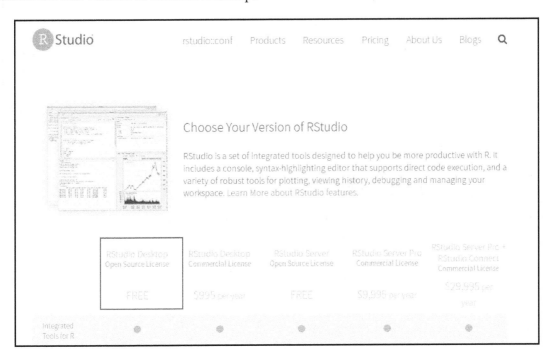

Selecting Open Source R Studio Desktop

RStudio is available for Windows, Mac, and Linux.

Download the appropriate executable for your system and proceed to perform the installation:

Installers	Size	Date	MD5
RStudio 1.0.153 - Windows Vista/7/8/10	81.9 MB	2017-07-20	b3b4bbc82865ab105c21cb70b17271b3
RStudio 1.0.153 - Mac OS X 10.6+ (64-bit)	71.2 MB	2017-07-20	8773610566b74ec3e1a88b2fdb10c8b5
RStudio 1.0.153 - Ubuntu 12.04-15.10/Debian 8 (32-bit)	85.5 MB	2017-07-20	981be44f91fc07e5f69f52330da32659
RStudio 1.0.153 - Ubuntu 12.04-15.10/Debian 8 (64-bit)	91.7 MB	2017-07-20	2d0769bea2bf6041511d6901a1cf69c3
RStudio 1.0.153 - Ubuntu 16.04+/Debian 9+ (64-bit)	61.9 MB	2017-07-20	d584cbab01041777a15d62cbef69a976
RStudio 1.0.153 - Fedora 19+/RedHat 7+/openSUSE 13.1+ (32-bit)	84.7 MB	2017-07-20	8dfee96059b05a063c49b705eca0ceb4
RStudio 1.0.153 - Fedora 19+/RedHat 7+/openSUSE 13.1+ (64-bit)	85.7 MB	2017-07-20	16c2c8334f961c65d9bfa8fb813ad7e7

Zip/Tarballs

Zip/tar archives	Size	Date	MD5
RStudio 1.0.153 - Windows Vista/7/8/10	117.6 MB	2017-07-20	024b5714fa6ef337fe0c6f5e2894cbcb
RStudio 1.0.153 - Ubuntu 12.04-15.10/Debian 8 (32-bit)	86.2 MB	2017-07-20	f8e0ffa7ec62665524f9e2477facd346
RStudio 1.0.153 - Ubuntu 12.04-15.10/Debian 8 (64-bit)	92.7 MB	2017-07-20	2077c181311d1aad6fb8d435f8f1f45f
RStudio 1.0.153 - Fedora 19+/RedHat 7+/openSUSE 13.1+ (32-bit)	85.4 MB	2017-07-20	92e1a22d14952273ec389e5a55be614f
RStudio 1.0.153 - Fedora 19+/RedHat 7+/openSUSE 13.1+ (64-bit)	86.6 MB	2017-07-20	0b71c5a7fc53c84b3fe67242240b3531

RStudio Binaries (Versions)

The CMS Open Payments Portal

In this section, we will begin developing our application for CMS Open Payments.

The Packt Data Science VM contains all the necessary software for this tutorial. To download the VM, please refer to `Chapter 3`, *The Analytics Toolkit*.

Downloading the CMS Open Payments data

The CMS Open Payments data is available directly as a web-based download from the CMS website. We'll download the data using the Unix wget utility, but first we have to register with the CMS website to get our own API key:

1. Go to `https://openpaymentsdata.cms.gov` and click on the **Sign In** link at the top-right of the page:

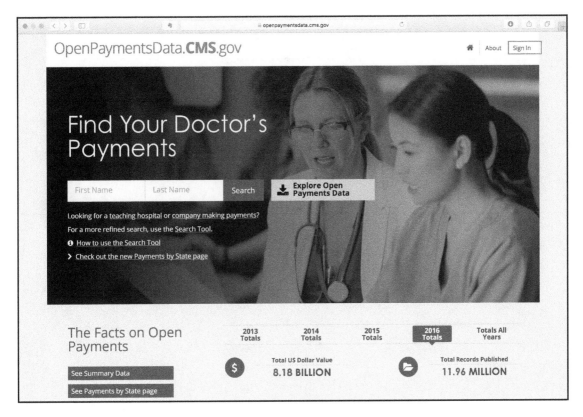

Homepage of CMS OpenPayments

Click on **Sign Up**:

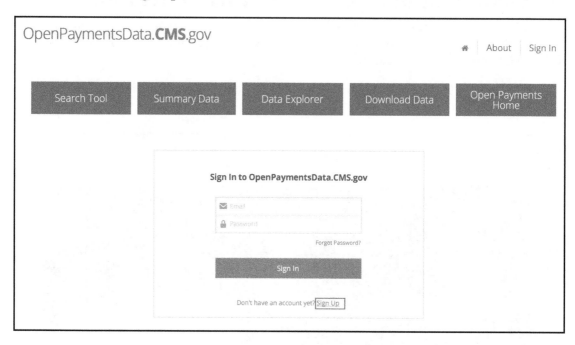

Sign-Up Page on CMS OpenPayments

Enter your information and click on the **Create My Account** button:

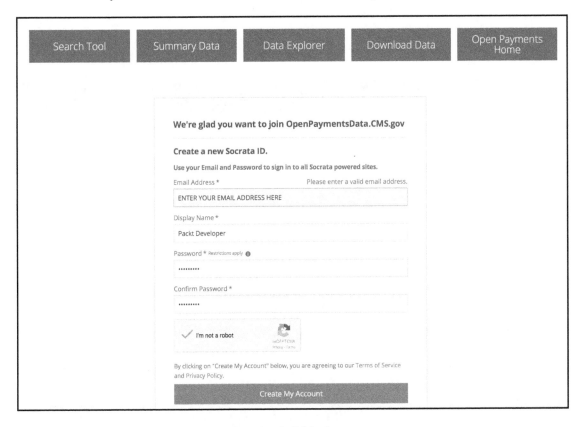

Sign-Up Form for CMS OpenPayments

Sign In to your account:

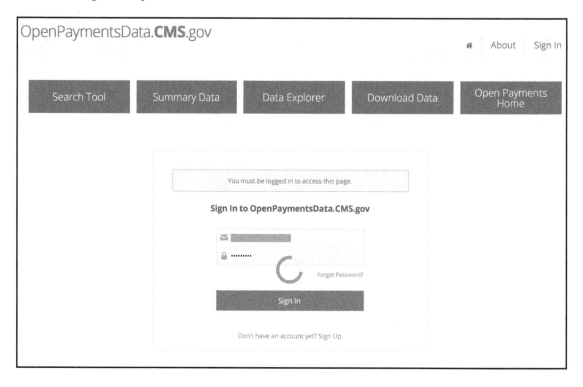

Signing into CMS OpenPayments

Click on **Manage** under **Packt Developer's Applications**. Note that Applications here refers to apps that you may create that will query data available on the CMS website:

Creating 'Applications'

Assign a name for the application (examples are shown in the following image):

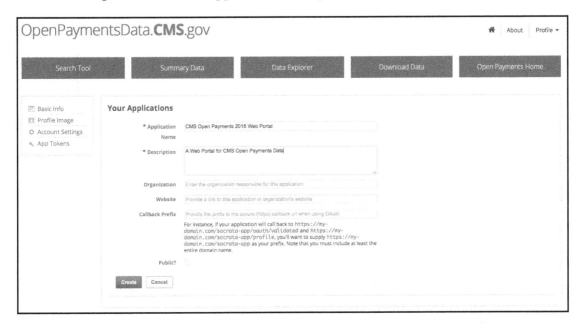

Defining an application

You'll get a notification that the **Application Token** has been created:

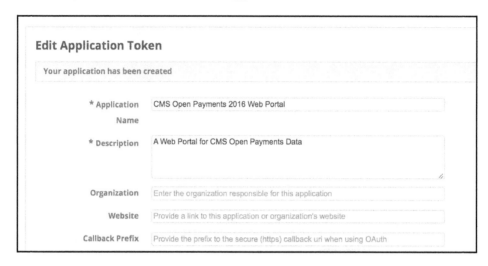

Creating the Application Token

The system will generate an **App Token**. Copy the **App Token**:

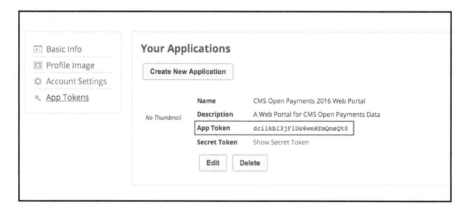

The Application Token

2. Now, log in to the Packt Data Science VM as user packt and execute the following shell command after replacing the term YOURAPPTOKEN with the one that you were assigned (it will be a long string of characters/numbers). Note that for the tutorial, we will only download a few of the columns and restrict the data to only physicians (the other option is hospitals).

You can reduce the volume of the data downloaded by reducing the value of the limit specified at the end of the command to a lower number. In the command, we have used `12000000` (12 million), which would let us download the entire 2016 dataset representing physician payments. The application will still work if, for example, you were to download only one million entries instead of the approximately 11-12 million records.

Note: Two approaches are shown below. One using the Token and the other without using the Token. Application Tokens allow users to have a higher throttling limit. More information can be found at `https://dev.socrata.com/docs/app-tokens.html`

```
# Replace YOURAPPTOKEN and 12000000 with your API Key and desired record
limit respectively

cd /home/packt;

time wget -O cms2016.csv
'https://openpaymentsdata.cms.gov/resource/vq63-hu5i.csv?$$app_token=YOURAP
PTOKEN&$query=select Physician_First_Name as firstName,Physician_Last_Name
as lastName,Recipient_City as city,Recipient_State as
state,Submitting_Applicable_Manufacturer_or_Applicable_GPO_Name as
company,Total_Amount_of_Payment_USDollars as payment,Date_of_Payment as
date,Nature_of_Payment_or_Transfer_of_Value as
paymentNature,Product_Category_or_Therapeutic_Area_1 as
category,Name_of_Drug_or_Biological_or_Device_or_Medical_Supply_1 as
product where covered_recipient_type like "Covered Recipient Physician"
limit 12000000'
```

Important: It is possible to also download the file without using an app token. However, the method should be used sparingly. The URL to download the file without using an application token is shown as follows:

```
# Downloading without using APP TOKEN

wget -O cms2016.csv
'https://openpaymentsdata.cms.gov/resource/vq63-hu5i.csv?$query=select
Physician_First_Name as firstName,Physician_Last_Name as
lastName,Recipient_City as city,Recipient_State as
state,Submitting_Applicable_Manufacturer_or_Applicable_GPO_Name as
company,Total_Amount_of_Payment_USDollars as payment,Date_of_Payment as
date,Nature_of_Payment_or_Transfer_of_Value as
paymentNature,Product_Category_or_Therapeutic_Area_1 as
category,Name_of_Drug_or_Biological_or_Device_or_Medical_Supply_1 as
product where covered_recipient_type like "Covered Recipient Physician"
limit 12000000'
```

Creating the Q application

This section describes the process of creating the kdb+/Q application, beginning with the process of loading data from the database and creating the scripts that will serve as the backend for the application.

Loading the data

Log in to the VM using the ID `packt` (**password:** `packt`):

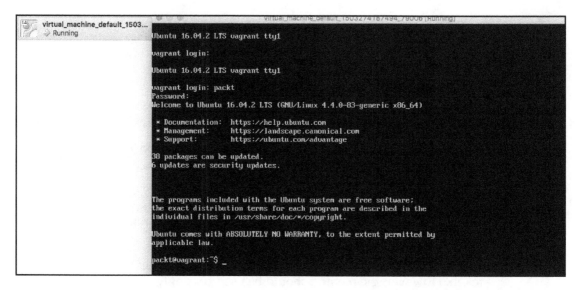

Logging into the Packt VM

```
# We will start KDB+ - the NoSQL database that we'll use for the tutorial

# Launch the Q Console by typing:

packt@vagrant:~$ rlwrap ~/q/l32/q -s 4 -p 5001

KDB+ 3.5 2017.06.15 Copyright (C) 1993-2017 Kx Systems
l32/ 1()core 3951MB packt vagrant 127.0.1.1 NONEXPIRE

Welcome to kdb+ 32bit edition
For support please see http://groups.google.com/d/forum/personal-kdbplus
Tutorials can be found at http://code.kx.com/wiki/Tutorials
To exit, type \\
To remove this startup msg, edit q.q
```

q)

```
# Enter the following at the Q console. Explanations for each of the
commands have been provided in the comments (using /):

/change to the home directory for user packt
\cd /home/packt/

/Define the schema of the cms table
d:(`category`city`company`date`firstName`lastName`payment`paymentNature`pro
duct`state)!"SSSZSSFSSS";

/Read the headersfrom the cms csv file. These will be our table column
names

columns:system "head -1 cms2016.csv";
columns:`$"," vs ssr(raze columns;"\"";"");

/Run Garbage Collection
.Q.gc();

/Load the cms csv file
\ts cms2016:(d columns;enlist",")0:`:cms2016.csv;

/Add a month column to the data
\ts cms2016: `month`date xasc update month:`month$date, date:`date$date
from cms2016

.Q.gc();

/Modify character columns to be lower case. The data contains u
\ts update lower firstName from `cms2016
\ts update lower lastName from `cms2016
\ts update lower city from `cms2016
\ts update lower state from `cms2016
\ts update lower product from `cms2016
\ts update lower category from `cms2016
\ts update lower paymentNature from `cms2016
\ts update lower company from `cms2016
.Q.gc()

cms2016:`month`date`firstName`lastName`company`state`city`product`category`
payment`paymentNature xcols cms2016

count cms2016 /11 million

/Function to save the data that was read from the CMS csv file
```

```
savedata:{show (string .z.T)," Writing: ",string x;cms::delete month from
select from cms2016 where month=x; .Q.dpft(`:cms;x;`date;`cms)}
```

```
/Save the data in monthly partitions in the current folder
```

```
savedata each 2016.01m +til 12
```

The backend code

Once the script completes, exit from the Q prompt by typing in \\ and pressing *Enter*.

Copy the following text into a file called cms.q:

```
system "p 5001"

system "l /home/packt/cms"

/firstCap: Takes a string (sym) input and capitalizes the first letter of
each word separated by a blank space
firstCap:{" " sv {@(x;0;upper)} each (" " vs string x) except enlist ""}
/VARIABLES AND HELPER TABLES

/alldata: Aggregates data from the primary cms database
alldata: distinct `company`product xasc update showCompany:`$firstCap each
company, showProduct:`$firstCap each product from ungroup select distinct
product by company from cms where not null product

/minDate: First month
minDate:exec date from select min date from cms where month=min month

/maxDate: Last month
maxDate:exec date from select max date from cms where month=max month

/companyStateCity: Cleans and normalises the· company names
(capitalisations, etc)
companyStateCity:select asc upper distinct state, asc `$firstCap each
distinct city by company from cms


/FUNCTIONS
/getShowProduct: Function to get product list from company name
getShowProduct:{$((`$"Select All") in x;raze exec showProduct from
alldata;exec showProduct from alldata where showCompany in x)}
/getShowState: Function to get state list from company name
getShowState:{$((`$"Select All") in x;raze exec state from
```

```
companyStateCity;exec state from companyStateCity where company = exec
first company from alldata where showCompany in x)}
/getShowCity: Function to get city list from company name
getShowCity:{$((`$"Select All") in x;raze exec city from
companyStateCity;exec city from companyStateCity where company = exec first
company from alldata where showCompany in x)}
/getShowInfo: Generic Function for Product, State and City
getShowInfo:{y:`$"|" vs y;:asc distinct raze raze
$(x~`product;getShowProduct each y;x~`state;getShowState each
y;x~`city;getShowCity each y;"")}

/Example: Run this after loading the entire script after removing the
comment mark (/) from the beginning
/getShowInfo(`state;"Abb Con-cise Optical Group Llc|Select All|Abbott
Laboratories")

/Convert encoded URL into a Q dictionary
decodeJSON:{.j.k .h.uh x}

/Convert atoms to list
ensym:{$(0>type x;enlist x;x)}

/Date functions

withinDates:{enlist (within;`date;"D"$x(`date))}
withinMonths:{enlist (within;`month;`month$"D"$x(`date))}
/Helper function to remove null keys
delNullDict:{kx!x kx:where {not x~0n} each x}
/If showdata=enlist 1,

/Function to process the data for displaying results only

getData:{"x is the dictionary from web";d:`$dx:lower delNullDict x;
enz:`$delete showData,date,columns from dx; ?(`cms;(withinMonths
x),(withinDates x),{(in;x 0;enlist 1_x)} each ((key enz),'value
enz);0b;(dc)!dc:ensym `$x`columns)}

/Aggregation Function

aggDict:(`$("Total Payment";"Number of Payments";"Minimum Payment";"Maximum
Payment";"Average
Payment"))!((sum;`payment);(#:;`i);(min;`payment);(max;`payment);(avg;`paym
ent))
/Function to aggregate the data
getDataGroups:{(aggDict;x) "x is the dictionary from web";d:`$dx:lower
delNullDict x; enz:`$delete showData,date,columns,aggVars,aggData from dx;
?(`cms;(withinMonths x),(withinDates x),{(in;x 0;enlist 1_x)} each ((key
enz),'value enz);xv!xv:ensym `$x`aggVars;xa!aggDict xa:ensym
```

```
`$x`aggData)}(aggDict;)

/Generic Function to create error messages

errtable:{tab:(()Time:enlist `$string .z.Z;Alert:enlist x);(tab;"Missing
Fields")}

/Validation for input

initialValidation:{$(0n~x(`company);;:errtable `$"Company must be
selected";(`aggVars in key x) and ((0=count x(`aggVars)) or
0n~x(`aggData));:errtable `$"Both Metric and Aggregate Data field should be
selected when using Aggregate Data option";x)}
/Special Handling for some variables, in this case month
specialHandling:{0N!x;$(`month in cols x; update `$string month from x;x)}

/Normalise Columns
columnFix:{(`$firstCap each cols x) xcol x}

/Use comma separator for numeric values
commaFmt: {(((x<0)#"-"),(reverse",","sv 3 cut reverse string floor
a),1_string(a:abs x)mod 1}

/Wrapper for show data and aggregate data options
getRes:{0N!x;.Q.gc();st:.z.t;x:decodeJSON x; if (not x ~
ix:initialValidation x;;:ix); res:$(`aggData in key x;getDataGroups
x;getData x);res:specialHandling res; res:columnFix res;ccms:count cms;
cres:count res; en:.z.t; .Q.gc();;:(res;`$(string en),": Processed
",(commaFmt ccms)," records in ",(string en - st)," seconds. Returned
result with ",(commaFmt cres)," rows.\n")
```

Creating the frontend web portal

R Shiny, a package intended to make development of web-based applications simple, started gaining traction since it was introduced in around 2012-2013. In general, R developers tend not to be very frontend development savvy as their main areas of work would be related to statistics or similar disciplines.

As data science, as a profession and a mainstream activity became popular, the need to create sophisticated web-based applications became necessary as a means of delivering results to end users in a dynamic environment.

JavaScript, which had all but lost its original appeal, made a surprise comeback and soon enough the web world was abuzz with the release of various leading JavaScript packages for web development and visualization, such as D3, Angular, Ember, and others ever since 2010-2011.

But these were mostly used by seasoned JavaScript developers, few of whom were also proficient in R. Developing a solution that would help bridge the gap between JavaScript web-based application development and R programming became a necessity for R developers to showcase and share their work with a broader audience.

R Shiny platform for developers

R Shiny introduced a platform for R developers to create JavaScript-based web applications without having to get involved, or, for that, matter even be proficient in JavaScript.

In order to build our application, we will leverage R Shiny and create an interface to connect to the CMS Open Payments data we set up in the prior section.

If you are using your own R installation (locally), you'll need to install a few R packages. Note that if you are using a Linux workstation, you may need to install some additional Linux packages. For example, in Ubuntu Linux, you'll need to install the following. You may already have some of the packages, in which case you'll receive a message indicating that no further changes were needed for the respective package:

```
sudo apt-get install software-properties-common libssl-dev libcurl4-
openssl-dev gdebi-core rlwrap
```

 If you are using the Packt Data Science VM, you can proceed directly to developing the application as these Linux packages have already been installed for you.

The Shiny application requires a few additional R packages to provide all its functionalities. Note that R packages are different from the Linux packages described previously. R packages, which number in the thousands, provide specialized functions for specific subject areas. For the web application, we will install a few R packages that will let us leverage some of the features in the web-based application.

The following steps outline the process of creating the web portal:

1. Log in to RStudio. If you are using the Packt Data Science VM, go to `http://localhost:8787/auth-sign-in`. Log in with the user ID **packt** and password **packt** (same as user ID).

 Note that if you had installed RStudio locally, you'll not have a separate login screen. The instruction is purely for the Packt Data Science VM:

Logging into RStudio Server (Only for Packt VM)

If you receive an error message stating that the site cannot be loaded, it may be due to the fact that the port forwarding has not been set up. To fix the issue, make the following changes:

2. In VirtualBox, right-click on the **VM** and select **Settings.**
3. Click on **Network** under **Settings** and expand the arrow next to **Advanced**:

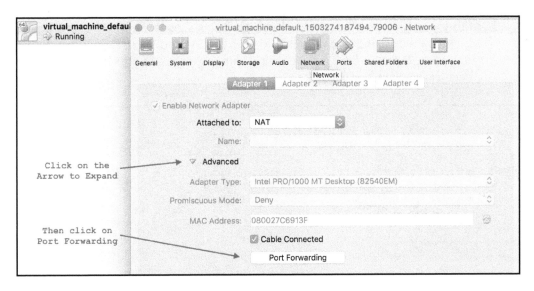

Setting up the VM parameters

4. Click on Port Forwarding and add a rule to forward port 8787 from the VM to the host. The rule marked as Packt Rule has to be added, shown as follows:

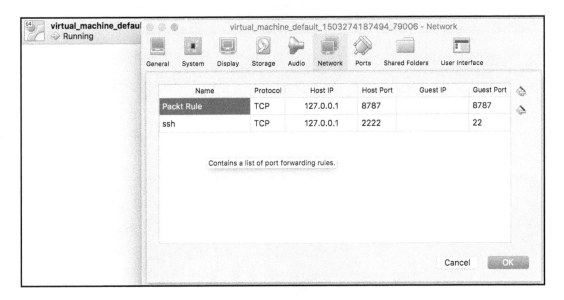

Configuring Port Forwarding

5. After logging in, you'll see the following screen. This is the interface for RStudio, which you'll be using to complete the exercise. We'll discuss R and RStudio in much more detail in later chapters, and this section illustrates the process to create the basic web application:

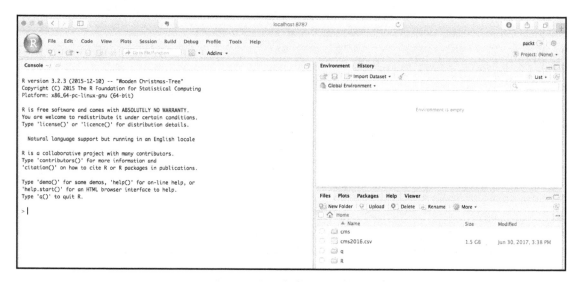

The RStudio Console

6. Install the necessary R packages. Click on **File | R Script** and copy and paste the code below.

7. Then, click on **Source** to execute the following lines:

```
install.packages(c("shiny","shinydashboard","data.table",
                "DT","rjson","jsonlite","shinyjs","devtools"))

library(devtools)
devtools::install_github('kxsystems/rkdb', quiet=TRUE)
```

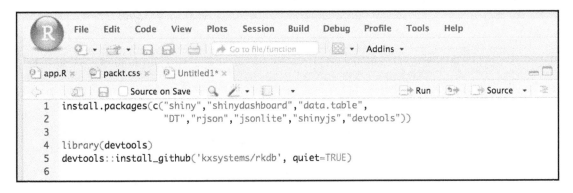

Installing required packages in R via RStudio

8. Click on **File|New File|Shiny Web App**:

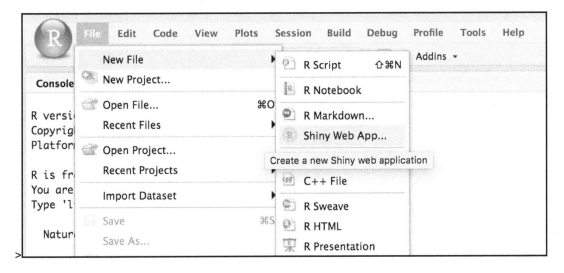

Creating a new RShiny Application

9. Type in `cmspackt` under **application name** and click on **Create:**

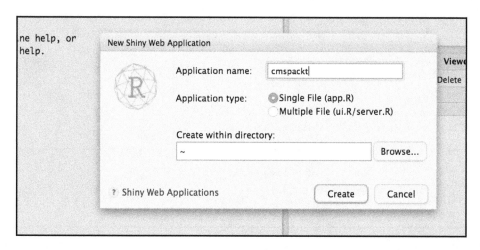

Assigning a name to the RShiny Application

This will create a `cmspackt` folder in the home directory, shown as follows:

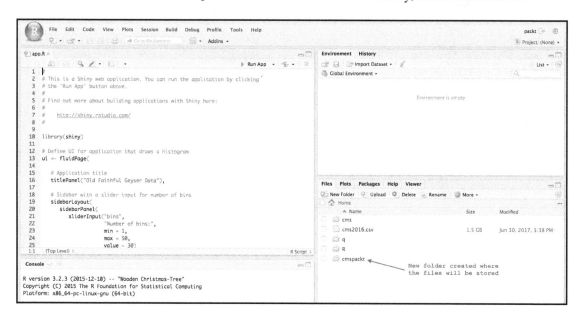

The app.R file for the R Shiny Application

10. Copy and paste the following code into the `app.R` section:

```
# # This is a Shiny web application. You can run the application by
clicking # the 'Run App' button above. # # Find out more about building
applications with Shiny here: # # http://shiny.rstudio.com/

#
# This is a Shiny web application. You can run the application by clicking
# the 'Run App' button above.
#
# Find out more about building applications with Shiny here:
#
# http://shiny.rstudio.com/
#

library(shiny)
library(shinydashboard)
library(data.table)
library(DT)
library(rjson)
library(jsonlite)
library(shinyjs)
library(rkdb)

ui <- dashboardPage (skin="purple", dashboardHeader(title = "CMS Open
Payments 2016"),
    dashboardSidebar(
    useShinyjs(),
    sidebarMenu(
    uiOutput("month"),
    uiOutput("company"),
    uiOutput("product"),
    uiOutput("state"),
    uiOutput("city"),
    uiOutput("showData"),
    uiOutput("displayColumns"),
    uiOutput("aggregationColumns"),
    actionButton("queryButton", "View Results")
    )
    ),dashboardBody(
    tags$head(tags$link(rel = "stylesheet", type = "text/css", href =
"packt.css")),
    textOutput("stats"),
    dataTableOutput("tableData")
    ),
    title = "CMS Open Payments Data Mining"
)
```

```
# Define server logic required to draw a histogram
server <- function(input, output, session) {
  h <- open_connection("localhost","5001")
  minDate <- execute(h,"minDate")
  maxDate <- execute(h,"maxDate")
  startDate <- minDate
  endDate <- startDate + 31
cmsdata <-
data.table(dbColumns=c("month","date","firstName","lastName","city","state"
,"company","product","category","payment","paymentNature"),
webColumns=c("Month","Date","First Name","Last
Name","City","State","Company","Product","Category","Payment","Payment
Nature"))
companyData <- execute(h,"exec distinct showCompany from alldata")
gbyVars <- c("Company","Product","State","City","Category","Payment
Nature")

PLACEHOLDERLIST <- list(
    placeholder = 'Please select an option below',
    onInitialize = I('function() { this.setValue(""); }')
  )

PLACEHOLDERLIST2 <- list(
    placeholder = 'Select All',
    onInitialize = I('function() { this.setValue(""); }')
  )
output$month <- renderUI({
    dateRangeInput("date", label = 'PAYMENT DATE', start = startDate, end =
endDate, min = minDate, max = maxDate)
  })
output$company <- renderUI({
    selectizeInput("company","COMPANY" , companyData, multiple =
TRUE,options = PLACEHOLDERLIST)
  })

output$product <- renderUI({
    productQuery <-
paste0("getShowInfo(`product;\"",paste(input$company,collapse="|"),"\")")
    productVals <- execute(h,productQuery)
    selectizeInput("product", "DRUG/PRODUCT" , productVals, multiple =
TRUE,options = PLACEHOLDERLIST2)
  })
output$state <- renderUI({
    stateQuery <-
paste0("getShowInfo(`state;\"",paste(input$company,collapse="|"),"\")")
    stateVals <- execute(h,stateQuery)
    selectizeInput("state", "STATE" , stateVals, multiple = TRUE,options =
PLACEHOLDERLIST2)
```

```
    })
output$city <- renderUI({
    cityQuery <-
paste0("getShowInfo(`city;\"",paste(input$company,collapse="|"),"\")")
    cityVals <- execute(h,cityQuery)
    selectizeInput("city", "CITY" , cityVals, multiple = TRUE,options =
PLACEHOLDERLIST2)
    })
output$showData <- renderUI({
    selectInput("showData", label = "DISPLAY TYPE", choices = list("Show
Data" = 1, "Aggregate Data" = 2), selected = 1)
    })
output$displayColumns <- renderUI({
    if (is.null(input$showData)) {selectInput("columns", "SHOW
DATA",cmsdata$webColumns, selectize = FALSE, multiple = TRUE, size=11)}
    else if(input$showData == 1) {selectInput("columns", "SHOW
DATA",cmsdata$webColumns, selectize = FALSE, multiple = TRUE, size=11) }
    else if(input$showData == 2) {selectInput("aggVars", "AGGREGATE
DATA",gbyVars, selectize = FALSE, multiple = TRUE, size=6) }
    })

output$aggregationColumns <- renderUI ({ conditionalPanel(
    condition = "input.showData != 1",
    selectInput("aggData", "CALCULATE METRICS" , c("Total Payment","Number
of Payments","Minimum Payment","Maximum Payment","Average Payment"),
selectize = TRUE, multiple = TRUE)
    )})
getTableData <- eventReactive(input$queryButton, {
    disable("queryButton")
    queryInfo <- (list(date=as.character(input$date),company=input$company,
product=input$product, state=input$state,
city=input$city,columns=cmsdata$dbColumns(cmsdata$webColumns %in%
input$columns),showData=input$showData))
    if (input$showData !=1) {queryInfo <- c(queryInfo,
list(aggVars=cmsdata$dbColumns(cmsdata$webColumns %in% input$aggVars),
aggData=input$aggData))} else {queryInfo <- c(queryInfo)}
    JSON <- rjson::toJSON(queryInfo)
    getQuery <- paste0("getRes \"",URLencode(JSON),"\"")
    finalResults <- execute(h,getQuery)
    enable("queryButton")
    print (finalResults)
    fres <<- finalResults
    print (class(finalResults((1))))
    print (finalResults)
    finalResults
    })
 output$tableData <- renderDataTable({ datatable(getTableData()((1)))})
 output$stats <- renderText({(getTableData())((2))})
```

```
}

# Run the application
shinyApp(ui = ui, server = server)
```

11. Click on **New Folder** in the lower-right box:

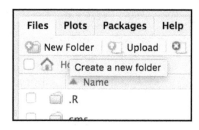

Creating a folder for CSS files

12. Rename the new folder to `cmspackt/www`, shown as follows:

Assigning a name to the folder

13. Click on **File** | **New File** | **Text File:**

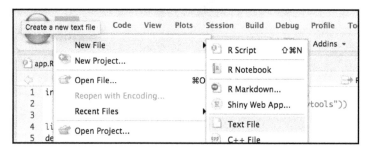

Creating the CSS File

14. Copy and paste the following code:

```
.shiny-text-output, .shiny-bount-output {
  margin: 1px;
  font-weight: bold;
}

.main-header .logo {
height: 20px;
font-size: 14px;
font-weight: bold;
line-height: 20px;
}

.main-header .sidebar-toggle {
  padding: 0px;
}

.main-header .navbar {
  min-height: 0px !important;
}

.left-side, .main-sidebar {
  padding-top: 15px !important;
}

.form-group {
  margin-bottom: 2px;
}

.selectize-input {
  min-height: 0px !important;
  padding-top: 1px !important;
  padding-bottom: 1px !important;
  padding-left: 12px !important;
  padding-right: 12px !important;
}

.sidebar {
  height: 99vh;
  overflow-y: auto;
}

section.sidebar .shiny-input-container {
    padding: 5px 15px 0px 12px;
}
```

```
.btn {
  padding: 1px;
  margin-left: 15px;
  color:#636363;
  background-color:#e0f3f8;
  border-color:#e0f3f8;
}

.btn.focus, .btn:focus, .btn:hover {
  color: #4575b4;
  background-color:#fff;
  border-color:#fff;
}

pre {
    display: inline-table;
    width: 100%;
    padding: 2px;
    margin: 0 0 5px;
    font-size: 12px;
    line-height: 1.42857143;
    color: rgb(51, 52, 53);
    word-break: break-all;
    word-wrap: break-word;
    background-color: rgba(10, 9, 9, 0.06);
    border: 1px rgba(10, 9, 9, 0.06);
    /* border-radius: 4px */
}

.skin-red .sidebar a {
    color: #fff;
}

.sidebar {
  color: #e0f3f8;
  background-color:#4575b4;
  border-color:#4575b4;
}
```

15. Click on **File** | **Save As** to save the file, as follows:

Select Save As for the CSS File

16. Save as `/home/packt/cmspackt/www/packt.css`, shown as follows:

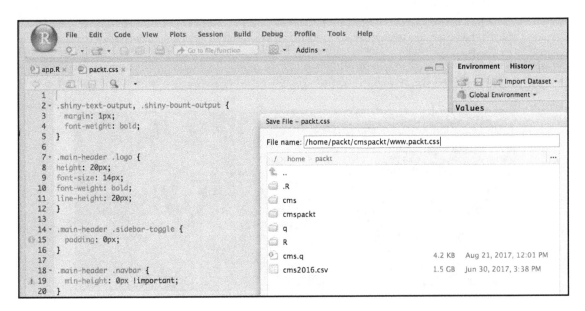

Saving the CSS File

Your application is now ready for use!

Putting it all together - The CMS Open Payments application

In the prior sections, we have learned how to:

- Download the datasets
- Create the backend database
- Create the code for the backend database
- Set up RStudio
- Create the R Shiny application

To start the application, complete the following steps:

1. Start the Q application, make sure you are in the home directory. Type pwd and hit Enter. This will show the present working directory of /home/packt as shown in the coming image.

2. Next, type q and hit **Enter.**

3. At the q prompt, type in \l cms.q.

   Note that cms.q is the file we created in our earlier section when developing the Q application.

The script will load the database and return back to the q) prompt:

```
packt@vagrant:~$
packt@vagrant:~$ pwd
/home/packt
packt@vagrant:~$ q
KDB+ 3.5 2017.06.15 Copyright (C) 1993-2017 Kx Systems
l32/ 1()core 3951MB packt vagrant 127.0.1.1 NONEXPIRE

Welcome to kdb+ 32bit edition
For support please see http://groups.google.com/d/forum/personal-kdbplus
Tutorials can be found at http://code.kx.com/wiki/Tutorials
To exit, type \\
To remove this startup msg, edit q.q
q)\l cms.q
q)
```

Putting it all together: Loading the CMS KDB+ Q Script in KDB+ Session

4. Launch the CMS Open Payment application

5. In RStudio, open the app.R file (which contains the R Code) and click on **Run App** at the top-right, shown as follows:

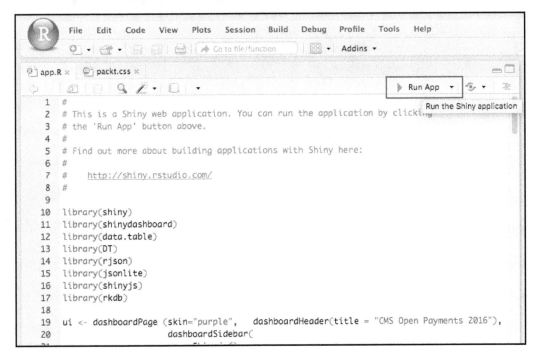

Running the RShiny Application

This will launch the web application, shown as follows:

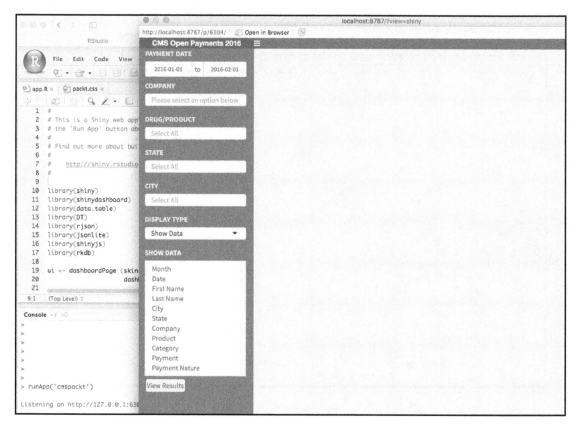

The RShiny Application

We have now finished developing a complete CMS Open Payments application that allows the end user to filter, aggregate, and analyze the data. Now, you can run queries by selecting various options on the screen. There are two functionalities in the app:

- Filtering data (default view)
- Aggregating data (you can switch to this option by selecting Aggregate Data from the Display Type menu)

Applications

A filtering example: To see payments made by a company for a certain drug in the state of NY:

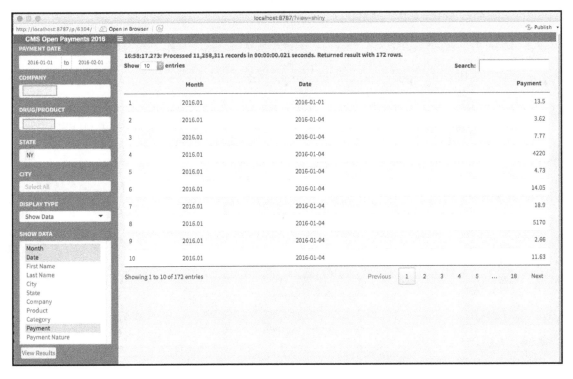

Using the RShiny Application

Note that the system processed 11 million records in 21 milliseconds, as shown in the header message. The name of the company and the product has been blanked out in the screenshot for privacy, but you are free to try out different options for both fields.

 Note that in the default VM, we are using only one core with very limited memory, and the speed with which the data is processed using kdb+ even on a laptop with very limited resources easily exceeds the performance of many well-to-do commercial solutions.

An aggregation example: To see total payments grouped by state, payment category, and payment nature for a specific company and product, select the options for the fields *Aggregate Data* and *Calculate Metrics*. Please note that the name of the company and the product have been hidden in the screenshot for privacy reasons only.

Note the message at the top that states:

16:52:46.354: Processed 11,258,311 records in 00:00:00.022 seconds. Returned result with 116 rows.

Log message indicating query and application performance

This indicates the speed with which the underlying kdb+ database processed the data. In this case, it filtered and *aggregated 11 million records in 22 milliseconds* for the given options.

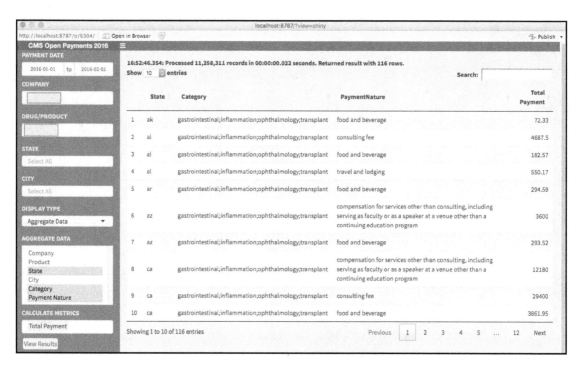

CMS OpenPayments Application Screenshot

Summary

This chapter introduced the concept of NoSQL. The term has gained popularity in recent years, especially due to its relevance and direct application to **big data** analytics. We discussed the core terminologies in NoSQL, their various types, and popular software used in the industry for such capabilities. We concluded with a couple of tutorials using MongoDB and kdb+.

We also built an application using R and R Shiny to create a dynamic web interface to interact with the data loaded in kdb+.

The next chapter will introduce another common technology in data science today, known as Spark. It is yet another toolkit that empowers data scientists across the world today.

6
Spark for Big Data Analytics

As the use of Hadoop and related technologies in the respective ecosystem gained prominence, a few obvious and salient deficiencies of the Hadoop operational model became apparent. In particular, the ingrained reliance on the MapReduce paradigm, and other facets related to MapReduce, made a truly functional use of the Hadoop ecosystem possible only for major firms that were invested deeply in the respective technologies.

At the **UC Berkeley Electrical Engineering and Computer Sciences** (**EECS**) Annual Research Symposium of 2011, a vision for a new research group at the university was announced during a presentation by Prof. Ian Stoica (`https://amplab.cs.berkeley.edu/about/`). It laid out the foundation of what was to become a pivotal unit that would profoundly change the landscape of Big Data. The **AMPLab**, launched in February 2011, aimed to deliver a scalable and unified solution by integrating Algorithms, Machines, and People that could cater to future needs without requiring any major re-engineering efforts.

The most well-known and most widely used project to evolve from the AMPLab initiative was Spark, arguably a superior alternative - or more precisely, *extension* - of the Hadoop ecosystem.

In this chapter, we will visit some of the salient characteristics of Spark and end with a real-world tutorial on how to use Spark. The topics we will cover are:

- The advent of Spark
- Theoretical concepts in Spark
- Core components of Spark
- The Spark architecture
- Spark solutions
- Spark tutorial

The advent of Spark

When the first release of Spark became available in 2014, Hadoop had already enjoyed several years of growth since 2009 onwards in the commercial space. Although Hadoop solved a major hurdle in analyzing large terabyte-scale datasets efficiently, using distributed computing methods that were broadly accessible, it still had shortfalls that hindered its wider acceptance.

Limitations of Hadoop

A few of the common limitations with Hadoop were as follows:

- **I/O Bound operations**: Due to the reliance on local disk storage for saving and retrieving data, any operation performed in Hadoop incurred an I/O overhead. The problem became more acute in cases of larger datasets that involved thousands of blocks of data across hundreds of servers. To be fair, the ability to co-ordinate concurrent I/O operations (via HDFS) formed the foundation of distributed computing in Hadoop world. However, leveraging the capability and *tuning* the Hadoop cluster in an efficient manner across different use cases and datasets required an immense and perhaps disproportionate level of expertise. Consequently, the I/O bound nature of workloads became a deterrent factor for using Hadoop against extremely large datasets. As an example, machine learning use cases that required hundreds of iterative operations meant that the system would incur an I/O overhead for each pass of the iteration.

- **MapReduce programming (MR) Model**: As discussed in the earlier parts of this book, all operations in Hadoop require expressing problems in terms of the MapReduce Programming Model - namely, the user would have to express the problem in terms of key-value pairs where each pair can be independently computed. In Hadoop, coding efficient MapReduce programs, mainly in Java, was non-trivial, especially for those new to Java or to Hadoop (or both).

- **Non-MR Use Cases**: Due to the reliance on MapReduce, other more common and simpler concepts such as filters, joins, and so on would have to also be expressed in terms of a MapReduce program. Thus, a join across two files across a primary key would have to adopt a key-value pair approach. This meant that operations, both simple and complex, were hard to achieve without significant programming efforts.

- **Programming APIs**: The use of Java as the central programming language across Hadoop meant that to be able to properly administer and use Hadoop, developers had to have a strong knowledge of Java and related topics such as JVM tuning, Garbage Collection, and others. This also meant that developers in other popular languages such as R, Python, and Scala had very little recourse for re-using or at least implementing their solution in the language they knew best.
- On the whole, even though the Hadoop world had championed the Big Data revolution, it fell short of being able to democratize the use of the technology for Big Data on a broad scale.

The team at AMPLab recognized these shortcomings early on, and set about creating Spark to address these and, in the process, hopefully develop a new, superior alternative.

Overcoming the limitations of Hadoop

We'll now look at some of the limitations discussed in the earlier section and understand how Spark addresses these areas, by virtue of which it provides a superior alternative to the Hadoop ecosystem.

A key difference to bear in mind at the onset is that Spark does NOT need Hadoop in order to operate. In fact, the underlying backend from which Spark accesses data can be technologies such as HBase, Hive and Cassandra in addition to HDFS.

This means that organizations that wish to leverage a standalone Spark system can do so without building a separate Hadoop infrastructure if one does not already exist.

The Spark solutions are as follows:

- **I/O Bound operations**: Unlike Hadoop, Spark can store and access data stored in *memory*, namely RAM - which, as discussed earlier, is 1,000+ times faster than reading data from a disk. With the emergence of SSD drives, the standard in today's enterprise systems, the difference has gone down significantly. Recent NVMe drives can deliver up to 3-5 GB (Giga Bytes) of bandwidth per second. Nevertheless, RAM, which averages about 25-30 GB per second in read speed, is still 5-10x faster compared to reading from the newer storage technologies. As a result, being able to store data in RAM provides a 5x or more improvement to the time it takes to read data for Spark operations. This is a significant improvement over the Hadoop operating model which relies on disk read for all operations. In particular, tasks that involve iterative operations as in machine learning benefit immensely from the Spark's facility to store and read data from memory.

- **MapReduce programming (MR) Model**: While MapReduce is the primary programming model through which users can benefit from a Hadoop platform, Spark does not have the same requirement. This is particularly helpful for more complex use cases such as quantitative analysis involving calculations that cannot be easily *parallelized*, such as machine learning algorithms. By decoupling the programming model from the platform, Spark allows users to write and execute code written in various languages without forcing any specific programming model as a pre-requisite.

- **Non-MR use cases**: Spark SQL, Spark Streaming and other components of the Spark ecosystem provide a rich set of functionalities that allow users to perform common tasks such as SQL joins, aggregations, and related database-like operations without having to leverage other, external solutions. Spark SQL queries are generally executed against data stored in Hive (JSON is another option), and the functionality is also available in other Spark APIs such as R and Python.

- **Programming APIs**: The most commonly used APIs in Spark are Python, Scala and Java. For R programmers, there is a separate package called SparkR that permits direct access to Spark data from R. This is a major differentiating factor between Hadoop and Spark, and by exposing APIs in these languages, Spark becomes immediately accessible to a much larger community of developers. In Data Science and Analytics, Python and R are the most prominent languages of choice, and hence, any Python or R programmer can leverage Spark with a much simpler learning curve relative to Hadoop. In addition, Spark also includes an interactive shell for ad-hoc analysis.

Theoretical concepts in Spark

The following are the core concepts in Spark:

- Resilient distributed datasets
- Directed acyclic graphs
- SparkContext
- Spark DataFrames
- Actions and transformations
- Spark deployment options

Resilient distributed datasets

Resilient distributed datasets, more commonly known as **RDDs**, are the primary data structure used in Spark. RDDs are essentially a collection of records that are stored across a Spark cluster in a distributed manner. RDDs are *immutable*, which is to say, they cannot be altered once created. RDDs that are stored across nodes can be accessed in parallel, and hence support parallel operations natively.

The user does not need to write separate code to get the benefits of parallelization but can get the benefits of *actions and transformations* of data simply by running specific commands that are native to the Spark platform. Because RDDs can be also stored in memory, as an additional benefit, the parallel operations can act on the data directly in memory without incurring expensive I/O access penalties.

Directed acyclic graphs

In computer science and mathematics parlance, a directed acyclic graph represents pairs of nodes (also known as **vertices**) connected with edges (or **lines**) that are unidirectional. Namely, given Node A and Node B, the edge can connect A à B or B à A but not both. In other words, there isn't a circular relationship between any pair of nodes.

Spark leverages the concept of DAG to build an internal workflow that delineates the different stages of processing in a Spark job. Conceptually, this is akin to creating a virtual flowchart of the series of steps needed to obtain a certain output. For instance, if the required output involves producing a count of words in a document, the intermediary steps map-shuffle-reduce can be represented as a series of actions that lead to the final result. By maintaining such a **map**, Spark is able to keep track of the dependencies involved in the operation. More specifically, RDDs are the **nodes**, and transformations, which are discussed later in this section, are the **edges** of the DAG.

SparkContext

A SparkContext is the entry point for all Spark operations and means by which the application connects to the resources of the Spark cluster. It initializes an instance of Spark and can thereafter be used to create RDDs, perform actions and transformations on the RDDs, and extract data and other Spark functionalities. A SparkContext also initializes various properties of the process, such as the application name, number of cores, memory usage parameters, and other characteristics. Collectively, these properties are contained in the object SparkConf, which is passed to SparkContext as a parameter.

`SparkSession` is the new abstraction through which users initiate their connection to Spark. It is a superset of the functionality provided in `SparkContext` prior to Spark 2.0.0. However, practitioners still use `SparkSession` and `SparkContext` interchangeably to mean one and the same entity; namely, the primary mode of interacting with Spark. `SparkSession` has essentially combined the functionalities of both SparkContext and `HiveContext`.

Spark DataFrames

A DataFrame in Spark is the raw data organized into rows and columns. This is conceptually similar to CSV files or SQL tables. Using R, Python and other Spark APIs, the user can interact with a DataFrame using common Spark commands used for filtering, aggregating, and more generally manipulating the data. The data contained in DataFrames are physically located across the multiple nodes of the Spark cluster. However, by representing them in a **DataFrame** they appear to be a cohesive unit of data without exposing the complexity of the underlying operations.

Note that DataFrames are not the same as Datasets, another common term used in Spark. Datasets refer to the actual data that is held across the Spark cluster. A DataFrame is the tabular representation of the Dataset.

Starting with Spark 2.0, the DataFrame and Dataset APIs were merged and a DataFrame in essence now represents a Dataset of Row. That said, DataFrame still remains the primary abstraction for users who want to leverage Python and R for interacting with Spark data.

Actions and transformations

There are 2 types of Spark operations:

- Transformations
- Actions

Transformations specify general data manipulation operations such as filtering data, joining data, performing aggregations, sampling data, and so on. Transformations do not return any result when the line containing the transformation operation in the code is executed. Instead, the command, upon execution, supplements Spark's internal DAG with the corresponding operation request. Examples of common transformations include: `map`, `filter`, `groupBy`, `union`, `coalesce`, and many others.

Actions, on the other hand, return results. Namely, they execute the series of transformations (if any) that the user may have specified on the corresponding RDD and produce an output. In other words, actions trigger the execution of the steps in the DAG. Common Actions include: `reduce`, `collect`, `take`, `aggregate`, `foreach`, and many others.

> Note that RDDs are immutable. They cannot be changed; transformations and actions will always produce new RDDs, but never modify existing ones.

Spark deployment options

Spark can be deployed in various modes. The most important ones are:

- **Standalone mode**: As an independent cluster not dependent upon any external cluster manager
- **Amazon EC2**: On EC2 instances of Amazon Web Services where it can access data from S3
- **Apache YARN**: The Hadoop ResourceManager

Other options include **Apache Mesos** and **Kubernetes.**

> Further details can be found at the Spark documentation website, `https://spark.apache.org/docs/latest/index.html`.

Spark APIs

The Spark platform is easily accessible through Spark APIs available in Python, Scala, R, and Java. Together they make working with data in Spark simple and broadly accessible. During the inception of the Spark project, it only supported Scala/Java as the primary API. However, since one of the overarching objectives of Spark was to provide an easy interface to a diverse set of developers, the Scala API was followed by a Python and R API.

In Python, the PySpark package has become a widely used standard for writing Spark applications by the Python developer community. In R, users interact with Spark via the SparkR package. This is useful for R developers who may also be interested in working with data stored in a Spark ecosystem. Both of these languages are very prevalent in the Data Science community, and hence, the introduction of the Python and R APIs set the groundwork for democratizing **Big Data** Analytics on Spark for analytical use cases.

Core components in Spark

The following components are quite important in Spark:

- Spark Core
- Spark SQL
- Spark Streaming
- GraphX
- MLlib

Spark Core

Spark Core provides fundamental functionalities in Spark, such as working with RDDs, performing actions, and transformations, in addition to more administrative tasks such as storage, high availability, and other topics.

Spark SQL

Spark SQL provides the user with the ability to query data stored in Apache Hive using standard SQL commands. This adds an additional level of accessibility by providing developers with a means to interact with datasets via the Spark SQL interface using common SQL terminologies. The platform hosting the underlying data is not limited to Apache Hive, but can also include JSON, Parquet, and others.

Spark Streaming

The streaming component of Spark allows users to interact with streaming data such as web-related content and others. It also includes enterprise characteristics such as high availability. Spark can read data from various middleware and data streaming services such as Apache Kafka, Apache Flume, and Cloud based solutions from vendors such as Amazon Web Services.

GraphX

The GraphX component of Spark supports graph-based operations, similar to technologies such as graph databases that support specialized data structures. These make it easy to use, access, and represent inter-connected points of data, such as social networks. Besides analytics, the Spark GraphX platform supports graph algorithms that are useful for business use cases that require relationships to be represented at scale. As an example, credit card companies use Graph based databases similar to the GraphX component of Spark to build recommendation engines that detect users with similar characteristics. These characteristics may include buying habits, location, demographics, and other qualitative and quantitative factors. Using Graph systems in these cases allows companies to build networks with nodes representing individuals and edges representing relationship metrics to find common features amongst them.

MLlib

MLlib is one of the flagship components of the Spark ecosystem. It provides a scalable, high-performance interface to perform resource intensive machine learning tasks in Spark. Additionally, MLlib can natively connect to HDFS, HBase, and other underlying storage systems supported in Spark. Due to this versatility, users do not need to rely on a pre-existing Hadoop environment to start using the algorithms built into MLlib. Some of the supported algorithms in MLlib include:

- **Classification**: logistic regression
- **Regression**: generalized linear regression, survival regression and others
- Decision trees, random forests, and gradient-boosted trees
- **Recommendation**: Alternating least squares
- **Clustering**: K-means, Gaussian mixtures and others
- **Topic modeling**: Latent Dirichlet allocation
- **Apriori**: Frequent Itemsets, Association Rules

ML workflow utilities include:

- **Feature transformations**: Standardization, normalization and others
- ML Pipeline construction
- Model evaluation and hyper-parameter tuning
- **ML persistence**: Saving and loading models and Pipelines

The architecture of Spark

Spark consists of 3 primary architectural components:

- The SparkSession / SparkContext
- The Cluster Manager
- The Worker Nodes (that hosts executor processes)

The **SparkSession/SparkContext**, or more generally the Spark Driver, is the entry point for all Spark applications as discussed earlier. The SparkContext will be used to create RDDs and perform operations against RDDs. The SparkDriver sends instructions to the worker nodes to schedule tasks.

The **Cluster manager** is conceptually similar to Resource Managers in Hadoop and indeed, one of the supported solutions is YARN. Other Cluster Managers include Mesos. Spark can also operate in a Standalone mode in which case YARN/Mesos are not required. Cluster Managers co-ordinate communications between the Worker Nodes, manage the nodes (such as starting, stopping, and so on), and perform other administration tasks.

Worker nodes are servers where Spark applications are hosted. Each application gets its own unique **executor process**, namely, processes that perform the actual action and transformation tasks. By assigning dedicated executor processes, Spark ensures that an issue in any particular application does not impact other applications. Worker Nodes consist of the Executor, the JVM, and the Python/R/other application process required by the Spark application. Note that in the case of Hadoop, the Worker Node and Data Nodes are one and the same:

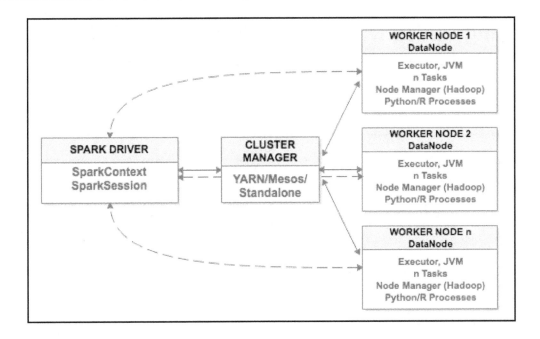

Spark solutions

Spark is directly available from `spark.apache.org` as an open-source solution. **Databricks** is the leading provider of the commercial solution of Spark. For those who are familiar with programming in Python, R, Java, or Scala, the time required to start using Spark is minimal due to efficient interfaces, such as the PySpark API that allows users to work in Spark using just Python.

Cloud-based Spark platforms, such as the Databricks Community Edition, provide an easy and simple means to work on Spark without the additional work of installing and configuring Spark. Hence, users who wish to use Spark for programming and related tasks can get started much more rapidly without spending time on administrative tasks.

Spark practicals

In this section, we will create an account on Databricks' Community Edition and complete a hands-on exercise that will walk the reader through the basics of actions, transformations, and RDD concepts in general.

Signing up for Databricks Community Edition

The following steps outline the process of signing up for the **Databricks Community Edition**:

1. Go to https://databricks.com/try-databricks:

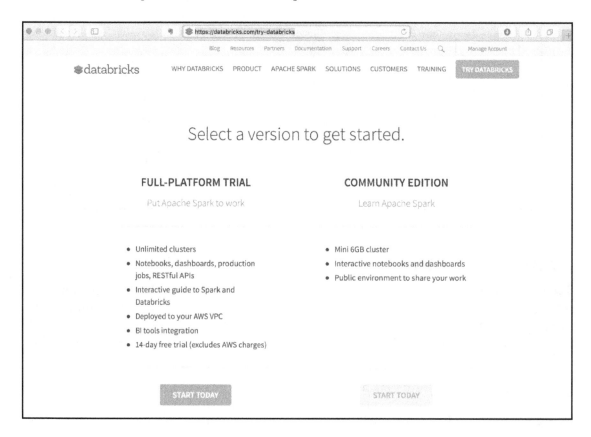

2. Click on the **START TODAY** button and enter your information:

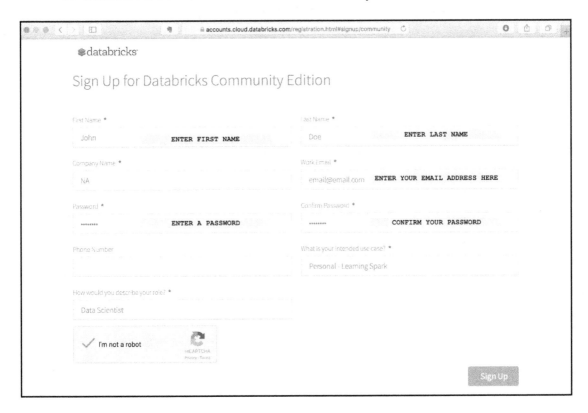

3. Confirm that you have read and agree to the terms in the popup menu (scroll down to the bottom for the **Agree** button):

Terms of Service

Read and scroll to the bottom to continue ↓

Databricks Community Edition
Terms of Service
(Posted May 24, 2016)

Welcome to Databricks Community Edition! We are pleased to provide Databricks Community Edition (**"Community Edition"**) at no charge to those interested in learning and exploring the use of Databricks' cloud-based data analytics platform, which enables data analysts and others to easily tap the power of Apache Spark™ and Databricks' other proprietary functionality. Your use of Community Edition, whether on an ongoing basis or on a temporary basis for the purposes of trialing Databricks' fee-based platform services, or your temporary, no-charge trial of our fee-based platform services apart from Community Edition (**"Free Trial"** and, together with any use of Community Edition, the **"Services"**) is governed by these Terms of Service (the **"Terms"**). By using the Services, you are agreeing to be bound by these Terms. If you are using the Services on behalf of an organization, you are agreeing to these Terms on behalf of that organization and you are confirming that you are authorized to bind it to these Terms (in which case **"you"** or **"your"** refer to that organization rather than you as an individual). Your access to the Services is contingent upon your reading these Terms carefully and, if you agree to them, clicking on the boxes at the bottom of each of the two sets of provisions below to indicate that you understand, accept and will continually abide by these Terms. If in the future Databricks agrees to add any paid upgrade or other paid services to your Community Edition or Free Trial account, these Terms shall continue to apply in full unless you and Databricks mutually agree to be bound under a superseding set of governing terms and conditions.

YOUR DATA AND USE OF COMMUNITY EDITION – RESTRICTIONS APPLY

---

4. Check your email for a confirmation email from Databricks and click on the link to confirm your account:

5. Once you click on the link to confirm your account, you'll be taken to a login screen where you can log on using the email address and password you used to sign up for the account:

6. After logging in, click on Cluster to set up a Spark cluster, as shown in the following figure:

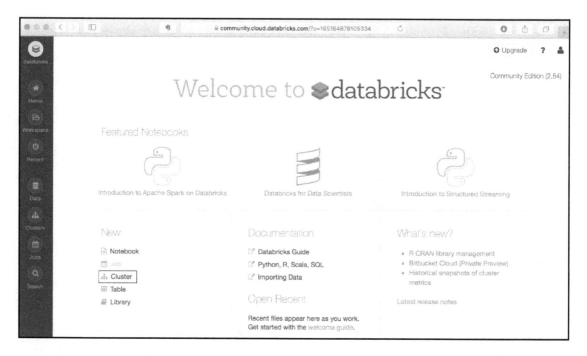

7. Enter `Packt_Exercise` as the Cluster Name and click on the Create Cluster button at the top of the page:

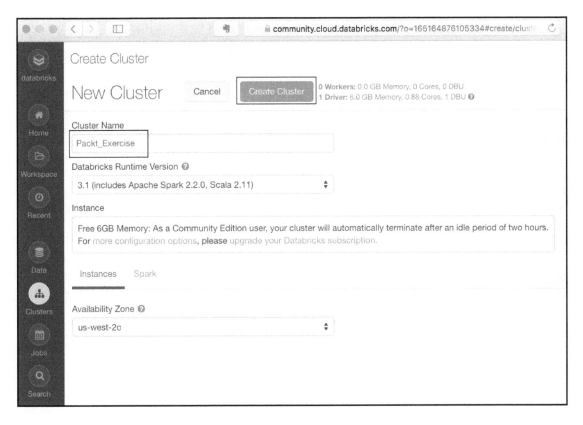

8. This will initiate the process of starting up a Spark Cluster on which we will execute our Spark commands using an iPython notebook. An iPython Notebook is the name given to a commonly used IDE - a web-based development application used for writing and testing Python code. The notebook can also support other languages through the use of **kernels**, but for the purpose of this exercise, we will focus on the Python kernel.

After a while, the Status will change from **Pending** to **Running**:

Status changes to **Running** after a few minutes:

9. Click on **Workspace** (on the left hand bar) and select **options, Users** | (Your userid) and click on the drop-down arrow next to your email address. Select **Create** | **Notebook**:

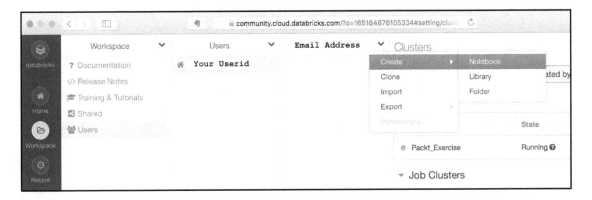

10. In the popup screen, enter `Packt_Exercise` as the name of the notebook and click on the **Create** button:

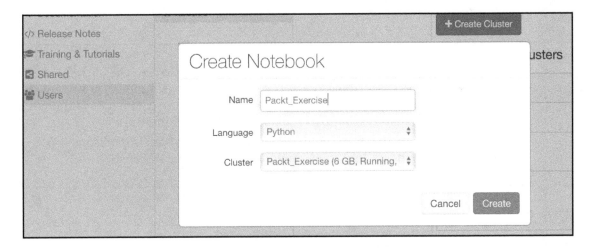

11. Once you click on the **Create** button, you'll be taken directly to the Notebook as shown in the following screenshot. This is the Spark **Notebook,** where you'll be able to execute the rest of the code given in the next few sections. The code should be typed in the **cells** of the notebook as shown. After entering your code, press *Shift + Enter* to execute the corresponding cell:

12. For the next few exercises, you can copy-paste the text into the cells of the Notebook. Alternatively, you can also import the notebook and load it directly in your workspace. If you do so, you'll not need to type in the commands (although typing in the commands will provide more hands-on familiarity).

13. An alternative approach to copy-pasting commands: You can import the notebook by clicking on Import as shown in the following screenshot:

14. Enter the following **URL** in the popup menu (select **URL** as the **Import from** option):

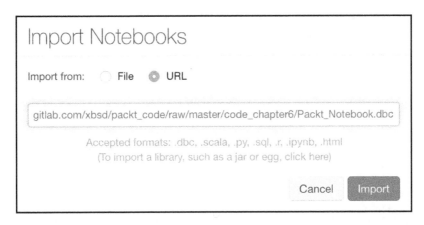

15. The notebook will then show up under your email ID. Click on the name of the notebook to load it:

Spark exercise - hands-on with Spark (Databricks)

This notebook is based on tutorials conducted by Databricks (`https://databricks.com/`). The tutorial will be conducted using the Databricks' Community Edition of Spark, available to sign up to at `https://databricks.com/try-databricks`. Databricks is a leading provider of the commercial and enterprise supported version of Spark.

In this tutorial, we will introduce a few basic commands used in Spark. Users are encouraged to try out more extensive Spark tutorials and notebooks that are available on the web for more detailed examples.

Documentation for Spark's Python API can be found at https://spark.apache.org/docs/latest/api/python/pyspark.html#pyspark.sql.

The data for this book was imported into the Databricks' Spark Platform. For more information on importing data, go to **Importing Data - Databricks** (https://docs.databricks.com/user-guide/importing-data.html).

```
# COMMAND ----------

# The SparkContext/SparkSession is the entry point for all Spark operations
# sc = the SparkContext = the execution environment of Spark, only 1 per
JVM
# Note that SparkSession is now the entry point (from Spark v2.0)
# This tutorial uses SparkContext (was used prior to Spark 2.0)

from pyspark import SparkContext
# sc = SparkContext(appName = "some_application_name") # You'd normally run
this, but in this case, it has already been created in the Databricks'
environment

# COMMAND ----------

quote = "To be, or not to be, that is the question: Whether 'tis nobler in
the mind to suffer The slings and arrows of outrageous fortune, Or to take
Arms against a Sea of troubles, And by opposing end them: to die, to sleep
No more; and by a sleep, to say we end the heart-ache, and the thousand
natural shocks that Flesh is heir to? 'Tis a consummation devoutly to be
wished. To die, to sleep, To sleep, perchance to Dream; aye, there's the
rub, for in that sleep of death, what dreams may come, when we have
shuffled off this mortal coil, must give us pause."

# COMMAND ----------
sparkdata = sc.parallelize(quote.split(' '))

# COMMAND ----------
print "sparkdata = ", sparkdata
print "sparkdata.collect = ", sparkdata.collect
print "sparkdata.collect() = ", sparkdata.collect()[1:10]

# COMMAND ----------
# A simple transformation - map
def mapword(word):
  return (word,1)

print sparkdata.map(mapword) # Nothing has happened here
print sparkdata.map(mapword).collect()[1:10] # collect causes the DAG to
execute
```

```
# COMMAND ----------
# Another Transformation

def charsmorethan2(tuple1):
 if len(tuple1[0])>2:
 return tuple1
 pass

rdd3 = sparkdata.map(mapword).filter(lambda x: charsmorethan2(x))
# Multiple Transformations in 1 statement, nothing is happening yet
rdd3.collect()[1:10]
# The DAG gets executed. Note that since we didn't remove punctuation marks
... 'be,', etc are also included

# COMMAND ----------
# With Tables, a general example
cms = sc.parallelize([[1,"Dr. A",12.50,"Yale"],[2,"Dr.
B",5.10,"Duke"],[3,"Dr. C",200.34,"Mt. Sinai"],[4,"Dr.
D",5.67,"Duke"],[1,"Dr. E",52.50,"Yale"]])

# COMMAND ----------
def findPayment(data):
 return data[2]

print "Payments = ", cms.map(findPayment).collect()
print "Mean = ", cms.map(findPayment).mean() # Mean is an action

# COMMAND ----------
# Creating a DataFrame (familiar to Python programmers)

cms_df = sqlContext.createDataFrame(cms, ["ID","Name","Payment","Hosp"])
print cms_df.show()
print cms_df.groupby('Hosp').agg(func.avg('Payment'),
func.max('Payment'),func.min('Payment'))
print cms_df.groupby('Hosp').agg(func.avg('Payment'),
func.max('Payment'),func.min('Payment')).collect()
print
print "Converting to a Pandas DataFrame"
print "-------------------------------"
pd_df = cms_df.groupby('Hosp').agg(func.avg('Payment'),
func.max('Payment'),func.min('Payment')).toPandas()
print type(pd_df)
print
print pd_df

# COMMAND ----------
wordsList = ['to','be','or','not','to','be']
wordsRDD = sc.parallelize(wordsList, 3) # Splits into 2 groups
```

```
# Print out the type of wordsRDD
print type(wordsRDD)

# COMMAND ----------
# Glom coallesces all elements within each partition into a list
print wordsRDD.glom().take(2) # Take is an action, here we are 'take'-ing
the first 2 elements of the wordsRDD
print wordsRDD.glom().collect() # Collect

# COMMAND ----------
# An example with changing the case of words
# One way of completing the function
def makeUpperCase(word):
 return word.upper()

print makeUpperCase('cat')

# COMMAND ----------
upperRDD = wordsRDD.map(makeUpperCase)
print upperRDD.collect()

# COMMAND ----------
upperLambdaRDD = wordsRDD.map(lambda word: word.upper())
print upperLambdaRDD.collect()

# COMMAND ----------

# Pair RDDs
wordPairs = wordsRDD.map(lambda word: (word, 1))
print wordPairs.collect()

# COMMAND ----------

# #### Part 2: Counting with pair RDDs
# There are multiple ways of performing group-by operations in Spark
# One such method is groupByKey()
#
# ** Using groupByKey() **
#
# This method creates a key-value pair whereby each key (in this case word)
is assigned a value of 1 for our wordcount operation. It then combines all
keys into a single list. This can be quite memory intensive, especially if
the dataset is large.

# COMMAND ----------
# Using groupByKey
wordsGrouped = wordPairs.groupByKey()
for key, value in wordsGrouped.collect():
```

```
   print '{0}: {1}'.format(key, list(value))

# COMMAND ----------
# Summation of the key values (to get the word count)
wordCountsGrouped = wordsGrouped.map(lambda (k,v): (k, sum(v)))
print wordCountsGrouped.collect()

# COMMAND ----------

# ** (2c) Counting using reduceByKey **
#
# reduceByKey creates a new pair RDD. It then iteratively applies a
function first to each key (i.e., within the key values) and then across
all the keys, i.e., in other words it applies the given function
iteratively.

# COMMAND ----------

wordCounts = wordPairs.reduceByKey(lambda a,b: a+b)
print wordCounts.collect()

# COMMAND ----------
# %md
# ** Combining all of the above into a single statement **

# COMMAND ----------

wordCountsCollected = (wordsRDD
  .map(lambda word: (word, 1))
  .reduceByKey(lambda a,b: a+b)
  .collect())
print wordCountsCollected

# COMMAND ----------

# %md
#
# This tutorial has provided a basic overview of Spark and introduced the
Databricks community edition where users can upload and execute their own
Spark notebooks. There are various in-depth tutorials on the web and also
at Databricks on Spark and users are encouraged to peruse them if
interested in learning further about Spark.
```

Summary

In this chapter, we read about some of the core features of Spark, one of the most prominent technologies in the Big Data landscape today. Spark has matured rapidly since its inception in 2014, when it was released as a Big Data solution that alleviated many of the shortcomings of Hadoop, such as I/O contention and others.

Today, Spark has several components, including dedicated ones for streaming analytics and machine learning, and is being actively developed. Databricks is the leading provider of the commercially supported version of Spark and also hosts a very convenient cloud-based Spark environment with limited resources that any user can access at no charge. This has dramatically lowered the barrier to entry as users do not need to install a complete Spark environment to learn and use the platform.

In the next chapter, we will begin our discussion on machine learning. Most of the text, until this section, has focused on the management of large scale data. Making use of the data effectively and gaining *insights* from the data is always the final aim. In order to do so, we need to employ the advanced algorithmic techniques that have become commonplace today. The next chapter will discuss the basic tenets of machine learning, and thereafter we will delve deeper into the subject area in the subsequent chapter.

7
An Introduction to Machine Learning Concepts

Machine learning has become a commonplace topic in our day-to-day lives. The advancement in the field has been so dramatic that today, even cell phones incorporate advanced machine learning and artificial intelligence-related facilities, capable of responding and taking actions based on human instructions.

A subject that was once limited to university classrooms has transformed into a full-fledged industry, pervading our daily lives in ways we could not have envisioned even just a few years ago.

The aim of this chapter is to introduce the reader to the underpinnings of machine learning and explain the concepts in simple, lucid terms that will help readers become familiar with the core ideas in the subject. We'll start off with a high-level overview of machine learning, and explain the different categories and how to distinguish them. We'll explain some of the salient concepts in machine learning, such as data pre-processing, feature engineering, and variable importance. The next chapter will go into more detail regarding individual algorithms and theoretical machine learning.

We'll conclude with exercises that leverage real-world datasets to perform machine learning operations using R.

We will cover the following topics in this chapter:

- What is machine learning?
- The popular emergence
- Machine learning, statistics, and artificial intelligence (AI)

- Categories of machine learning
- Core concepts in machine learning
- Machine learning tutorial

What is machine learning?

Machine learning is not a new subject; it has existed in academia for well over 70 years as a formal discipline, but known by different names: statistics, and more generally mathematics, then **artificial intelligence** (**AI**), and today as machine learning. While the other related subject areas of statistics and AI are just as prevalent, machine learning has carved out a separate niche and become an independent discipline in and of itself.

In simple terms, machine learning involves predicting future events based on historical data. We see it manifested in our day-to-day lives and indeed we employ, knowingly or otherwise, principles of machine learning on a daily basis.

When we casually comment on whether a movie will succeed at the box office using our understanding of the popularity of the individuals in the lead roles, we are applying machine learning, albeit subconsciously. Our understanding of the characters in the lead roles has been shaped over years of watching movies where they appeared. And, when we make a determination of the success of a future movie featuring the same person, we are using historical information to make an assessment.

As another example, if we had data on temperature, humidity, and precipitation (rain) over a period of say, 12 months, can we use that information to predict whether it will rain today, given information on temperature and humidity?

This is akin to common regression problems found in statistics. But, machine learning involves applying a much higher level of rigor to the exercise to reach a conclusive decision based not only on theoretical calculations, but verification of the calculations hundreds or thousands of times using iterative methods before reaching a conclusion.

It should be noted and clarified here that the term *machine learning* relates to algorithms or programs that are executed typically on a computing device whose objective it is to predict outcomes. The algorithms build mathematical models that can then be used to make predictions. It is a common misconception that machine learning quite literally refers to a *machine* that is *learning*. The actual implication, as just explained, is much less dramatic.

The evolution of machine learning

The timeline of machine learning, as available on Wikipedia (`https://en.wikipedia.org/wiki/Timeline_of_machine_learning`), provides a succinct and insightful overview of the evolution of the field. The roots can be traced back to as early as the mid-1700s, when Thomas Bayes presented his paper on *inverse probability* at the Royal Society of London. Inverse probability, more commonly known today as probability distribution, deals with the problem of determining the state of a system given a prior set of events. For example, if a box contained milk chocolate and white chocolate, you took out a few at random, and received two milk and three white chocolates, can we infer how many of each chocolate there are in the box?

In other words, what can we infer about the unknown given a few points of data with which we can postulate a formal theory? Bayes' work was developed further into Bayes' Theorem by Pierre-Simon Laplace in his text, *Théorie Analytique des Probabilités*.

In the early 1900s, Andrey Markov's analysis of Pushkin's Poem, Eugeny Onegin, to determine the alliteration of consonants and vowels in Russian literature, led to the development of a technique known as Markov Chains, used today to model complex situations involving random events. Google's PageRank algorithm implements a form of Markov Chains.

The first formal application of machine learning, or more generally, AI, and its eventual emergence as a discipline, should be attributed to Alan Turing. He developed the Turing Test - a way to determine whether a machine is intelligent enough to mimic human behavior. Turing presented this in his paper, *Computing Machinery and Intelligence*, which starts out with the following:

> *I propose to consider the question, "Can machines think?" This should begin with definitions of the meaning of the terms "machine" and "think." The definitions might be framed so as to reflect so far as possible the normal use of the words, but this attitude is dangerous, If the meaning of the words "machine" and "think" are to be found by examining how they are commonly used it is difficult to escape the conclusion that the meaning and the answer to the question, "Can machines think?" is to be sought in a statistical survey such as a Gallup poll. But this is absurd. Instead of attempting such a definition I shall replace the question by another, which is closely related to it and is expressed in relatively unambiguous words.[...]*

Later in the paper, Turing writes:

> *The original question, "Can machines think?" I believe to be too meaningless to deserve discussion. Nevertheless I believe that at the end of the century the use of words and general educated opinion will have altered so much that one will be able to speak of machines thinking without expecting to be contradicted. I believe further that no useful purpose is served by concealing these beliefs.*

Turing's work on AI was followed by a series of seminal events in machine learning and AI. The first neural network was developed by Marvin Misky in 1951, Arthur Samuel began his work on the first machine learning programs that played checkers in 1952, and Rosenblatt invented the perceptron, a fundamental unit of neural networks, in 1957. Pioneers such as Leo Breiman, Jerome Friedman, Vladimir Vapnik and Alexey Chervonenkis, Geoff Hinton, and YannLeCun made significant contributions through the late 1990s to bring machine learning into the limelight. We are greatly indebted to their work and contributions, which have made machine learning stand out as a distinct area of research today.

In 1997, IBM's Deep Blue beat Kasparov and it immediately became a worldwide sensation. The ability of a machine to beat the world's top chess champion was no ordinary achievement. The event gave some much-needed credibility to machine learning as a formidable contender for the intelligent machines that Turing envisaged.

Factors that led to the success of machine learning

Given machine learning, as a subject, has existed for many decades, it begs the question: why hadn't it become as popular as it is today much sooner? Indeed, the theories of complex machine learning algorithms such as neural networks were well known by the late 1990s, and the foundation had been established well before that in the theoretical realm.

There are a few factors that can be attributed to the success of machine learning:

- **The Internet**: The web played a critical role in democratizing information and connecting people in an unprecedented way. It made the exchange of information simple in a way that could not have been achieved through the pre-existing methods of print media communication. Not only did the web transform and revolutionize the dissemination of information, it also opened up new opportunities. Google's PageRank, as mentioned earlier, was one of the first large-scale and highly visible successes in the application of statistical models to develop a highly successful web enterprise.

- **Social media**: While the web provided a platform for communication, it lacked a level of flexibility akin to how people interacted with one another in the real world. There was a noticeable, but understated, and arguably unexplored gap. Tools such as IRC and Usenet were the precursors to social network websites such as Myspace, which was one of the first web-based platforms intended to create personal networks. By early-mid 2000, Facebook had emerged as the leader in social networking. These platforms provided a unique opportunity to leverage the Internet to collect data at an individual level. Each user left a trail of messages, ripe for collection and analysis using Natural Language Processing and other techniques.

- **Computing hardware**: Hardware used for computers developed at an exponential rate. Machine learning algorithms are inherently compute and resource intensive, that is, they require powerful CPUs, fast disks, and high memory depending on the size of data. The invention of new ways to store data on **solid state drives** (**SSDs**) was a leap from the erstwhile process of storing on spinning hard drives. Faster access meant that data could be delivered to the CPU at a much faster rate and reduce the I/O bottleneck that has traditionally been a weak area in computing. Faster CPUs meant it was possible to perform hundreds and thousands of iterations demanded by machine learning algorithms in a timely manner. Finally, the demand led to the reduction in prices for computing resources, allowing more people to be able to afford buying computing hardware that was prohibitively expensive. Algorithms existed, but the resources were finally able to execute them in a reasonable time and cost.

- **Programming languages and packages**: Communities such as R and Python developers seized the opportunity, and individuals started releasing packages that exposed their work to a broader community of programmers. In particular, packages that provided machine learning algorithms became immediately popular and inspired other practitioners to release their individual code repositories, making platforms such as R a truly global collaborative effort. Today there are over 10,000 packages in R, up from 2000 in 2010.

Machine learning, statistics, and AI

Machine learning is a term that has various synonyms - names that are the result of either marketing activities by corporates or just terms that have been used interchangeably. Although some may argue that they have different implications, they all ultimately refer to machine learning as a subject that facilitates the prediction of future events using historical information.

The commonly heard terms for machine learning include predictive analysis, predictive analytics, predictive modeling, and many others. As such, unless the entity that publishes material explaining their interpretation of the term and more specifically, how it is different, it is generally safe to assume that they are referring to machine learning. This is often a source of confusion among those new to the subject, largely due to the misuse and overuse of technical verbiage.

Statistics, on the other hand, is a distinct subject area that has been well known for over 200 years. The word is derived from the new Latin, *statisticum collegium* (council of state, in English) and the Italian word *statista*, meaning statesman or politician. You can visit `https://en.wikipedia.org/wiki/History_of_statistics#Etymology` for more details on this topic. Machine learning implements various statistical models, which due to the rigor of computation involved, is distinct from the branch of classical statistics.

AI is also closely related to machine learning, but is a much broader subject. It can be loosely defined as systems (software/hardware) that, in the presence of uncertainties, can arrive at a concrete decision in (usually) a responsible and socially aware manner to attain a target end objective. In other words, AI aims to produce actions by systematically processing a situation that involves both known and unknown (latent) factors.

AI conjures up images of smart and sometimes rebellious robots in sci-fi movies, just as much as it reminds us of intelligent systems, such as IBM Watson, that can parse complex questions and process ambiguous statements to find concrete answers.

Machine learning shares some of the same traits - the step-wise development of a model using training data, and measuring accuracy using test data. However, AI has existed for many decades and has been a familiar household term. Institutions in the US, such as Carnegie Mellon University, have led the way in establishing key principles and guidelines of AI.

The online resources/articles on AI versus machine learning do not seem to provide any conclusive answers on how they differ. However, the syllabus of AI courses at universities makes the differences very obvious. You can learn more about AI at `https://cs.brown.edu/courses/csci1410/lectures.html`.

AI refers to a vast array of study areas that involve:

- **Constrained optimization**: Reach best possible results given a set of constraints or limitations in a given situation
- **Game theory**: For instance, zero-sum games, equilibrium, and others - taking a measured decision based on how the decision can affect future decisions and impact desired end goals
- **Uncertainty/Bayes' rule**: Given prior information, what is the likelihood of this happening given something else has already happened
- **Planning**: Formulating a plan of action = a set of paths (graph) to tackle a situation/reach an end goal
- **Machine learning**: The implementation (realization) of the preceding goals by using algorithms that are designed to handle uncertainties and imitate human reasoning. The machine learning algorithms generally used for AI include:
    - Neural networks/deep learning (find hidden factors)
    - Natural language processing (NLP) (understand context using tenor, linguistics, and such)
    - Visual object recognition
    - Probabilistic models (for example, Bayes' classifiers)
    - Markov decision processes (decisions for random events, for example, gambling)
    - Various other machine learning Algorithms (clustering, SVM)
- **Sociology**: A study of how machine learning decisions affect society and take remedial steps to correct issues

Categories of machine learning

Arthur Samuel coined the term **machine learning** in 1959 while at IBM. A popular definition of machine learning is due to Arthur, who, it is believed, called machine learning *a field of computer science that gives computers the ability to learn without being explicitly programmed.*

> Tom Mitchell, in 1998, added a more specific definition to machine learning and called it a, *study of algorithms that improve their performance P at some task T with experience E.*

A simple explanation would help to illustrate this concept. By now, most of us are familiar with the concept of spam in emails. Most email accounts also contain a separate folder known as **Junk**, **Spam**, or a related term. A cursory check of the folders will usually indicate the presence of several emails, many of which were presumably unsolicited and contain meaningless information.

The mere task of categorizing emails as spam and moving them to a folder involves the application of machine learning. Andrew Ng highlighted this elegantly in his popular MOOC course on machine learning.

In Mitchell's terms, the spam classification process involves:

- **Task T**: Classifying emails as spam/not spam
- **Performance P**: Number of emails accurately identified as spam
- **Experience E**: The model is provided emails that have been marked as spam/not spam and uses that information to determine whether a new email is spam or not

Broadly speaking, there are two distinct types of machine learning:

- Supervised machine learning
- Unsupervised machine learning

We shall discuss them in turn here.

Supervised and unsupervised machine learning

Let us start with supervised machine learning first.

Supervised machine learning

Supervised machine learning refers to machine learning exercises that involve predicting outcomes with labelled data. Labelled data simply refers to the fact that the dataset we are using to make the predictions (as well as the outcome we will predict) has a definite value (irrespective of what it is). For instance, classifying emails as spam or not spam, predicting temperature, and identifying faces from images are all examples of supervised machine learning.

Vehicle Mileage, Number Recognition and other examples

Given a dataset containing information on miles per gallon, number of cylinders, and such of various cars, can we predict what the value for miles per gallon would be if we only had the other values available?

In this case, our outcome is mpg and we are using the other variables of cyl (Cylinders), hp (Horsepower), gear (number of gears), and others to build a model that can then be applied against a dataset where the values for mpg are marked as MISSING. The model reads the information in these columns in the first five rows of the data and, based on that information, predicts what the value for mpg would be in the other rows, as shown in the following image:

cyl	hp	wt	gear	mpg
6	110	2.620	4	21
6	110	2.875	4	21
4	93	2.320	4	22.8
6	110	3.215	3	21.4
8	175	3.440	3	18.7
6	105	3.460	3	MISSING
8	245	3.570	3	MISSING
4	62	3.190	4	MISSING
4	95	3.150	4	MISSING
6	123	3.440	4	MISSING

The reason this is considered supervised is that in the course of building our machine learning model, we provided the model with information on what the outcome was. Other examples include:

- **Recognizing letters and numbers**: In such cases, the input to the model are the images, say of letters and numbers, and the outcome is the alpha-numeric value shown on the image. Once the model is built, it can then be used against pictures to recognize and predict what numbers are shown in the picture. A simple example, but very powerful. Imagine if you were given 100,000 images of houses with house numbers. The manual way of identifying the house numbers would be to go through each image individually and write down the numbers. A machine learning model allows us to completely automate the entire operation. Instead of having to manually go through individual images, you could simply run the model against the images and get the results in a very short amount of time.

- **Self-driving autonomous cars**: The input to the algorithms are images where the objects in the image have been identified, for example, person, street sign, car, trees, shops, and other elements. The algorithm *learns* to recognize and differentiate among different elements once a sufficient number of images have been shown and thereafter given an unlabeled image, that is, an image where the objects have not been identified is able to recognize them individually. To be fair, this is a highly simplified explanation of a very complex topic, but the overall principle is the same.

MNIST Dataset used for number recognition:

Unsupervised machine learning

Unsupervised machine learning involves datasets that do not have labeled outcomes. Taking the example of predicting mpg values for cars, in an unsupervised exercise, our dataset would have looked as follows:

cyl	hp	wt	gear	mpg
6	110	2.620	4	MISSING
6	110	2.875	4	MISSING
4	93	2.320	4	MISSING
6	110	3.215	3	MISSING
8	175	3.440	3	MISSING
6	105	3.460	3	MISSING
8	245	3.570	3	MISSING
4	62	3.190	4	MISSING
4	95	3.150	4	MISSING
6	123	3.440	4	MISSING

If all the outcomes are *missing*, it would be impossible to know what the values might have been. Recall that the primary premise of machine learning is to use historical information to make predictions on datasets whose outcome is not known. But, if the historical information itself does not have any identified outcomes, then it would not be possible to build a model. Without knowing any other information, the values of mpg in the table could be all 0 or all 100; it is not possible to tell, as we do not have any data point that will help lead us to the value.

This is where *unsupervised* machine learning gets applied. In this type of machine learning, we are not trying to predict outcomes. Rather, we are trying to determine which items are most similar to one another.

A common name for such an exercise is *clustering*, that is, we are attempting to find *clusters* or groups of records that are most similar to one another. Where can we use this information and what are some examples of unsupervised learning?

There are various news aggregators on the web - sites that do not themselves publish information, but collect information from other news sources. One such aggregator is Google News. If, say, we had to search for information on the last images taken by the satellite Cassini of Saturn, we could do a simple search for the phrase on Google News `https://news.google.com/news/?gl=USamp;ned=usamp;hl=en`. An example is shown here:

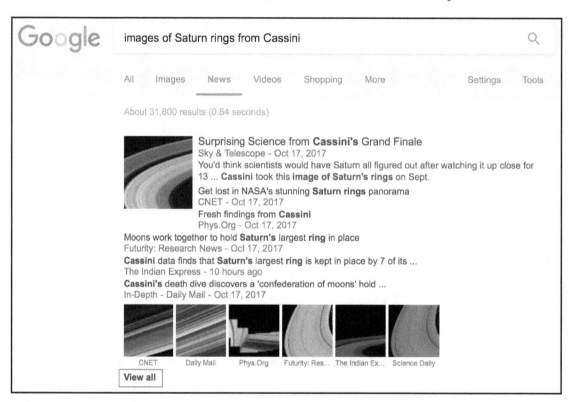

Notice that there is a link for **View all** at the bottom of the news articles. Clicking the link will take you to a page with all the other related news articles. Surely, Google didn't manually classify the articles as belonging to the specific search term. In fact, Google doesn't know in advance what the user will search for. The search term could have well been *images of Saturn rings from space*.

So, how does Google know which articles belong to a specific search term? The answer lies in the application of clustering or principles of unsupervised learning. Unsupervised learning examines the attributes of a specific dataset in order to determine which articles are most similar to one another. To do this, the algorithm doesn't even need to know the contextual background.

Suppose you were given two sets of books with no covers, a set of books on gardening and a set of books on computer programming. Although you may not know the title of the book, it would be fairly easy to distinguish books on computers from books on gardening. One set of books would have an overwhelming number of terms related to computing, while the other would have an overwhelming number of terms related to plants. To make the distinction that there were two distinct categories of books would not be difficult just by virtue of the images in the books, even for a reader who, let's assume, is not aware of either computers or gardening.

Other examples of unsupervised machine learning include detection of malignant and non-malignant tumors, and gene sequencing.

Subdividing supervised machine learning

Supervised machine learning can be further subdivided into exercises that involve either of the following:

- **Classification**
- **Regression**

The concepts are quite straightforward.

Classification involves a machine learning task that has a discrete outcome - a **categorical** outcome. All **nouns** are categorical variables, such as fruits, trees, color, and true/false.

The outcome variables in classification exercises are also known as **discrete or categorical variables**.

Some examples include:

- Identifying the fruit given size, weight, and shape
- Identifying numbers given a set of images of numbers (as shown in the earlier chapter)
- Identifying objects on the streets
- Identifying playing cards as diamonds, spades, hearts and clubs
- Identifying the class rank of a student based on the student's grade

- The last one might not seem obvious, but a rank, that is, 1st, 2nd, 3rd denotes a fixed category. A student could rank, say, 1st or 2nd, but not have a rank of 1.5!

Images of some atypical classification examples are shown below:

Classification of playing cards: diamonds, spades, hearts, and clubs

Classification of different types of fruits

Regression, on the other hand, involves calculating numeric outcomes. Any outcome on which you can perform numeric operations, such as addition, subtraction, multiplication, and division, would constitute a regression problem.

Examples of regression include:

- Predicting daily temperature
- Calculating stock prices
- Predicting the sales price of residential properties and others

Images of some atypical regression examples are shown below. In both the cases, we are dealing with quantitative numeric data that is continuous. Hence, the outcome variables of regression are also known as **quantitative or continuous variables**.

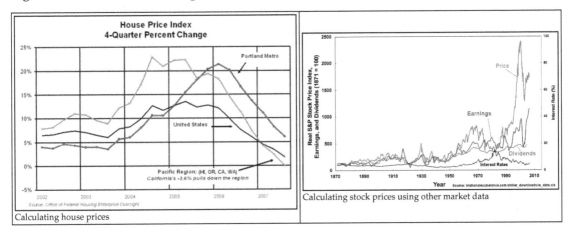

Calculating house prices

Calculating stock prices using other market data

Note that the concepts of classification or regression do not as such apply to unsupervised learning. Since there are no labels in unsupervised learning, there is no discrete classification or regression in the strict sense. That said, since unsupervised learning categories data into clusters, objects in a cluster are often said to belong to the same class (as other objects in the same cluster). This is akin to classification, except that it is created after-the-fact and no classes existed prior to the objects being classified into individual clusters.

Common terminologies in machine learning

In machine learning, you'll often hear the terms features, predictors, and dependent variables. They are all one and the same. They all refer to the variables that are used to predict an outcome. In our previous example of cars, the variables **cyl** (Cylinder), **hp** (Horsepower), **wt** (Weight), and **gear** (Gear) are the predictors and **mpg** (Miles Per Gallon) is the outcome.

In simpler terms, taking the example of a spreadsheet, the names of the columns are, in essence, known as features, predictors, and dependent variables. As an example, if we were given a dataset of toll booth charges and were tasked with predicting the amount charged based on the time of day and other factors, a hypothetical example could be as follows:

date	time	agency	type	prepaid	rate	amount
8/5/17	1:05 PM	ABTA	TOLL	Y	STANDARD	$0.78
8/12/17	5:00 PM	NCTA	TOLL	Y	STANDARD	$0.43
8/12/17	4:39 PM	NCTA	TOLL	Y	STANDARD	$0.43
8/13/17	4:00 PM	ABTA	PASS	Y	STANDARD	$0.43
8/14/17	1:52 AM	DSTC	TOLL	Y	STANDARD	$0.43
8/14/17	3:45 PM	NCTA	PASS	Y	STANDARD	$0.78
8/15/17	7:37 AM	DSTC	TOLL	Y	STANDARD	$0.78
8/17/17	8:42 PM	NCTA	TOLL	Y	STANDARD	$0.98

In this spreadsheet, the columns **date**, **time**, **agency**, **type**, **prepaid**, and **rate** are the features or predictors, whereas, the column **amount** is our outcome or dependent variable (what we are predicting).

The value of amount *depends* on the value of the other variables (which are thus known as *independent variables*).

Simple equations also reflect the obvious distinction, for example, in an equation, $y = a + b + c$, the **left hand side** (**LHS**) is the dependent/outcome variable and a, b and c are the features/predictors.

In summary:

Concept	Terminology	Meaning
Type of Variable	Continuous/Quantitative	Numbers on which you can perform arithmetic
	Discrete/Categorical	Qualitative – Alphabetical, or Numeric that simply denotes a 'category'
Variable in an equation	Dependent	The Left-Hand-Side, the y in $y = x + 1$
	Independent	The Right-Hand-Side, every variable other than the y in $y = x + 1$ (i.e., x in this case)
Type of ML	Regression	You want to predict a numeric outcome
	Classification	You want to predict a categorical outcome

The core concepts in machine learning

There are many important concepts in machine learning; we'll go over some of the more common topics. Machine learning involves a multi-step process that starts with data acquisition, data mining, and eventually leads to building the predictive models.

The key aspects of the model-building process involve:

- **Data pre-processing**: Pre-processing and feature selection (for example, centering and scaling, class imbalances, and variable importance)
- **Train, test splits and cross-validation**:
    - Creating the training set (say, 80 percent of the data)
    - Creating the test set (~ 20 percent of the data)
    - Performing cross-validation
- **Create model, get predictions**:
    - Which algorithms should you try?
    - What accuracy measures are you trying to optimize?
    - What tuning parameters should you use?

Data management steps in machine learning

Pre-processing, or more generally processing the data, is an integral part of most machine learning exercises. A dataset that you start out with is seldom going to be in the exact format against which you'll be building your machine learning models; it will invariably require a fair amount of cleansing in the majority of cases. In fact, data cleansing is often the most time-consuming part of the entire process. In this section, we will briefly highlight a few of the top data processing steps that you may encounter in practice.

Pre-processing and feature selection techniques

Data pre-processing, as the name implies, involves curating the data to make it suitable for machine learning exercises. There are various methods for pre-processing and a few of the more common ones have been illustrated here.

Note that data pre-processing should be performed as part of the cross-validation step, that is, pre-processing should not be done *before the fact*, but rather during the model-building process. This will be explained in more detail afterward.

Centering and scaling

Applying center and scale function on numeric columns is often done in order to standardize data and remove the effect of large variations in the magnitude or differences of numbers. You may have encountered this in college or university courses where students would be graded on a standardized basis, or a curve.

For instance, say an exam paper was unusually difficult and half of all the students in a class of 10 students received scores below 60 - the passing rate set for the course. The professor can either a) make a determination that 50% of the students should re-take the course, or b) standardize the scores to find how students performed relative to one another.

Say the class scores were:

45,66,66,55,55,52,61,64,65,49

With the passing score set at 60, this implies that the students who scored 45, 55, 55, 52 and 49 will not successfully complete the course.

However, this might not be a truly accurate representation of their relative merits. The professor may alternatively choose to instead use a center-and-scale method, commonly known as standardization, which involves:

- Finding the mean of all the scores
- Subtracting the mean from the scores
- Dividing the result by the standard deviation of all the scores

The operation is illustrated below for reference.

The mean of the scores is 57.8. Hence, subtracting 57.8 from each of the numbers produce the numbers shown in the second row. But, we are not done yet. We need to divide the numbers by the *standard deviation* of the scores to get the final standardized values:

Scores	45	66	66	55	55	52	61	64	65	49
Scores - Mean	-12.8	8.2	8.2	-2.8	-2.8	-5.8	3.2	6.2	7.2	-8.8
Divide by SD	-1.67	1.07	1.07	-0.4	-0.4	-0.8	0.42	0.81	0.94	-1.2

Dividing by the **SD** (**standard deviation**) shows that there were only two students whose scores were below one standard deviation across the range of all the test scores. Hence, instead of five students who do not complete the course successfully based on the raw numbers, we can narrow it down to only two students.

Although this is a truly simple operation, it is not hard to see that it is very effective in smoothing out large variations in data.

Centering and scaling can be performed very easily in R using the scale command as shown here:

```
> scores <- c(45,66,66,55,55,52,61,64,65,68)
> scale(scores)
             [,1]
 [1,] -1.9412062
 [2,]  0.8319455
 [3,]  0.8319455
 [4,] -0.6206578
 [5,] -0.6206578
 [6,] -1.0168223
 [7,]  0.1716713
 [8,]  0.5678358
 [9,]  0.6998907
[10,]  1.0960552
attr(,"scaled:center")
[1] 59.7
attr(,"scaled:scale")
[1] 7.572611
```

The near-zero variance function

The near-zero variance, available in the nearZeroVar function in the R package, caret, is used to identify variables that have little or no variance. Consider a set of 10,000 numbers with only three distinct values. Such a variable may add very little value to an algorithm. In order to use the nearZeroVar function, first install the R package, caret, in RStudio (which we had set up Chapter 3, *The Analytics Toolkit*. The exact code to replicate the effect of using nearZeroVar is shown here:

```
> library(caret)
Loading required package: lattice
Loading required package: ggplot2
Need help getting started? Try the cookbook for R:
http://www.cookbook-r.com/Graphs/

> repeated <- c(rep(100,9999),10) # 9999 values are 100 and the last value
is 10

>random<- sample(100,10000,T) # 10,000 random values from 1 - 100

>data<- data.frame(random = random, repeated = repeated)
```

```
>nearZeroVar(data)
[1] 2

> names(data)[nearZeroVar(data)]
[1] "repeated"
```

As the example shows, the function was able to correctly detect the variable that met the criteria.

Removing correlated variables

Correlated variables can produce results that over-emphasize the contribution of the variables. In regression exercises, this has the effect of increasing the value of R^2, and does not accurately represent the actual performance of the model. Although many classes of machine learning algorithms are resistant to the effects of correlated variables, it deserves some mention as it is a common topic in the discipline.

The premise of removing such variables is related to the fact that redundant variables do not add incremental value to a model. For instance, if a dataset contained height in inches and height in meters, these variables would have a near exact correlation of 1, and using one of them is just as good as using the other. Practical exercises that involve variables that we cannot judge intuitively, using methods of removing correlated variables, can greatly help in simplifying the model.

The following example illustrates the process of removing correlated variables. The dataset, **Pima Indians Diabetes**, contains vital statistics about the diet of Pima Indians and an outcome variable called `diabetes`.

During the course of the examples in successive chapters, we will refer to this dataset often. A high level overview of the meaning of the different columns in the dataset is as follows:

```
pregnant Number of times pregnant
glucose  Plasma glucose concentration (glucose tolerance test)
pressure Diastolic blood pressure (mm Hg)
triceps  Triceps skin fold thickness (mm)
insulin  2-Hour serum insulin (mu U/ml)
mass     Body mass index (weight in kg/(height in m)\^2)
pedigree Diabetes pedigree function
age            Age (years)
diabetes Class variable (test for diabetes)
```

We are interested in finding out if any of the variables, apart from diabetes (which is our outcome variable) are correlated. If so, it may be useful to remove the redundant variables.

Install the packages `mlbench` and `corrplot` in RStudio and execute the commands as shown here:

```
install.packages("mlbench")
install.packages("corrplot")

library(corrplot)
library(mlbench)

data (PimaIndiansDiabetes)
diab <- PimaIndiansDiabetes

# To produce a correlogram
corrplot(cor(diab[,-ncol(diab)]), method="color", type="upper")

# To get the actual numbers
corrplot(cor(diab[,-ncol(diab)]), method="number", type="upper")
```

The command will produce a plot as shown here using the `corrplot` package from `http:/` `/www.sthda.com/english/wiki/visualize-correlation-matrix-using-correlogram`:

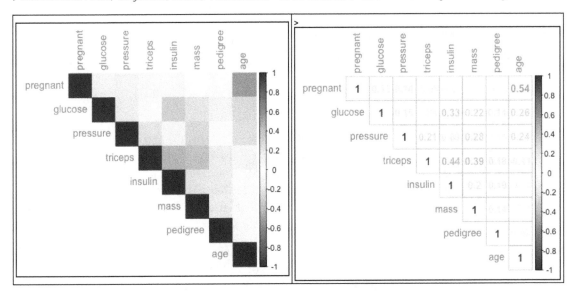

The darker the shade, the higher the correlation. In this case, it shows that age and pregnancy have a relatively high correlation. We can find the exact values by using `method="number"` as shown. You can also view the plot at `http://www.sthda.com/` `english/wiki/visualize-correlation-matrix-using-correlogram`.

We can also use functions such as the following to directly find the correlated variables without plotting the correlograms:

```
correlated_columns<- findCorrelation(cor(diab[,-ncol(diab)]), cutoff = 0.5)
correlated_columns
```

Other common data transformations

Several other data transformations are available and applicable to different situations. A summary of these transformations can be found at the documentation site for the `caret` package under **Pre-Processing** at `https://topepo.github.io/caret/pre-processing.html`.

The options available in the pre-process function of caret can be found from its help section, by running the command `?preProcess` in RStudio. The code for it is given here:

```
Method

a character vector specifying the type of processing.

Possible values are "BoxCox", "YeoJohnson", "expoTrans", "center", "scale",
"range", "knnImpute", "bagImpute", "medianImpute", "pca", "ica",
"spatialSign", "corr", "zv", "nzv", and "conditionalX" (see Details below)
```

Data sampling

You may encounter datasets that have a high level of imbalanced outcome classes. For instance, if you were working with a dataset on a rare disease, with your outcome variable being true or false, due to the rarity of the occurrence, you may find that the number of observations marked as false (that is, the person did not have the rare disease) is much higher than the number of observations marked as true (that is, the person did have the rare disease).

Machine learning algorithms attempt to maximize performance, which in many cases could be the accuracy of the predictions. Say, in a sample of 1000 records, only 10 are marked as true and the rest of the 990 observations are false.

If someone were to randomly assign *all* observations as false, the accuracy rate would be:

```
(990/1000) * 100 = 99%
```

But, the objective of the exercise was to find the *individuals who had the rare disease*. We are already well aware that due to the nature of the disease, most individuals will not belong to the category.

Data sampling, in essence, is the process of *maximizing machine learning metrics such as specificity, sensitivity, precision, recall, and kappa*. These will be discussed at a later stage, but for the purposes of this section, we'll show some ways by which you can *sample* the data so as to produce a more evenly balanced dataset.

The R package, `caret`, includes several helpful functions to create a balanced distribution of the classes from an imbalanced dataset.

In these cases, we need to re-sample the data to get a better distribution of the classes in order to build a more effective model.

Some of the general methods include:

- **Up-sample**: Increase instances of the class with lesser examples
- **Down-sample**: Reduce the instances of the class with higher examples
- **Create synthetic examples** (for example, **SMOTE (Synthetic Minority Oversampling TechniquE)**)
- Random oversampling (for example, **(ROSE) Randomly OverSampling Examples**)

We will create a simulated dataset using the same data from the prior example where 95% of the rows will be marked as negative:

```
library(mlbench)
library(caret)
diab<- PimaIndiansDiabetes

diabsim<- diab
diabrows<- nrow(diabsim)
negrows<- floor(.95 * diabrows)
posrows<- (diabrows - negrows)

negrows
[1] 729

posrows
[1] 39

diabsim$diabetes[1:729]      <- as.factor("neg")
diabsim$diabetes[-c(1:729)] <- as.factor("pos")
```

```
table(diabsim$diabetes)

neg. pos
729   39
```

```
# We observe that in this simulated dataset, we have 729 occurrences of
positive outcome and 39 occurrences of negative outcome
```

```
# Method 1: Upsampling, i.e., increasing the number of observations marked
as 'pos' (i.e., positive)
```

```
upsampled_simdata<- upSample(diabsim[,-ncol(diabsim)], diabsim$diabetes)
table(upsampled_simdata$Class)

negpos
729 729
```

```
# NOTE THAT THE OUTCOME IS CALLED AS 'Class' and not 'diabetes'
# This is because of the use of the variable separately
# We can always rename the column to revert to the original name
```

```
# Method 2: Downsampling, i.e., reducing the number of observations marked
as 'pos' (i.e., positive)
```

```
downsampled_simdata<- downSample(diabsim[,-ncol(diabsim)],
diabsim$diabetes)
```

```
table(downsampled_simdata$Class)

neg pos
39   39
```

- The **SMOTE (Synthetic Minority Over-sampling TechniquE)** is a third method that, instead of plain vanilla up-/down-sampling, creates synthetic records from the nearest neighbors of the minority class. In our simulated dataset, it is obvious that neg is the minority class, that is, the class with the lowest number of occurrences.
  The help file on the SMOTE function explains the concept succinctly:

Unbalanced classification problems cause problems to many learning algorithms. These problems are characterized by the uneven proportion of cases that are available for each class of the problem.

SMOTE (Chawla et al., 2002) is a well-known algorithm to fight this problem. The general idea of this method is to artificially generate new examples of the minority class using the nearest neighbors of these cases. Furthermore, the majority class examples are also under-sampled, leading to a more balanced dataset:

```
# Method 3: SMOTE
# The function SMOTE is available in the R Package DMwR
# In order to use it, we first need to install DmWR as follows
```

install.packages ("DMwR")

```
# Once the package has been installed, we will create a synthetic
# Dataset in which we will increase the number of 'neg' records
# Let us check once again the distribution of neg/pos in the
dataset
```

table(diabsim$diabetes)

```
negpos
729  39
```

```
# Using SMOTE we can create synthetic cases of 'pos' as follows
```

```
diabsyn<- SMOTE(diabetes ~ ., diabsim, perc.over = 500, perc.under
= 150)
```

```
# perc.over = 500 means, increase the occurrence of the minority
# class by 500%, i.e., 39 + 5*39 = 39 + 195 = 234
```

```
# perc.under = 150 means, that for each new record generated for
the
# Minority class, we will generate 1.5 cases of the majority class
# In this case, we created 195 new records (500% of 39) and hence
# we will generate 150% of 195 records = 195 * 150% = 195 * 1.5
# = 292.5, or 292 (rounded down) new records
```

```
# We can verify this by running the table command against the newly
# Created synthetic dataset, diabsyn
```

table(diabsyn$diabetes)

```
negpos
292 234
```

- **ROSE (Randomly OverSampling Examples)**, the final method in this section, is available via the ROSE package in R. Like SMOTE, it is a method for generating synthetic samples. The help file for ROSE states the high-level use of the function as follows:

  Generation of synthetic data by Randomly Over Sampling Examples creates a sample of synthetic data by enlarging the features space of minority and majority class examples. Operationally, the new examples are drawn from a conditional kernel density estimate of the two classes, as described in Menardi and Torelli (2013).

```
install.packages("ROSE")
library(ROSE)

# Loaded ROSE 0.0-3
set.seed(1)

diabsyn2 <- ROSE(diabetes ~ ., data=diabsim)

table(diabsyn2$data$diabetes)

# negpos
# 395 373
```

Data imputation

Sometimes, your data may have missing values. This could be due to errors in the data collection process, genuinely missing data, or any other reason, with the net result being that the information is not available. Real world examples of missing data can be found in surveys where the respondent did not answer a specific question on the survey.

You may have a dataset of, say, 1,000 records and 20 columns of which a certain column has 100 missing values. You may choose to discard this column altogether, but that also means discarding 90 percent of the information. You still have 19 other columns that have complete data. Another option is to simply exclude the column, but that means you cannot leverage the benefit afforded by the data that is available in the respective column.

Several methods exist for data imputation, that is, the process of filling in missing data. We do not know what the exact values are, but by looking at the other entries in the table, we may be able to make an educated and systematic assessment of what the values might be.

Some of the common methods in data imputation involve:

- **Mean, median, mode imputation**: Substituting the missing values using the mean, median, or mode value for the column. This, however, has the disadvantage of increasing the correlation among the variables that are imputed, which might not be desirable for multivariate analysis.
- **K-nearest neighbors imputation**: kNN imputation is a process of using a machine learning approach (nearest-neighbors) in order to impute missing values. It works by finding k records that are most similar to the one that has missing values and calculates the weighted average using Euclidean distance relative to k records.
- **Imputation using regression models**: Regression methods use standard regression methods in R to predict the value of the missing variables. However, as noted in the respective section on Regression-based imputation on Wikipedia `https://en.wikipedia.org/wiki/Imputation_(statistics)#Regression`, the problem (with regression imputation) is that the imputed data do not have an error term included in their estimation. Thus, the estimates fit perfectly along the regression line without any residual variance. This causes relationships to be over identified and suggests greater precision in the imputed values than is warranted.
- **Hot-deck imputation**: Another technique for filling missing values with observations from the dataset itself. This method, although very prevalent, does have a limitation in that, by assigning say, a single value, to a large range of missing values, it could add a significant bias in the observations and can produce misleading results.

A short example has been provided here to demonstrate how imputation can be done using kNN Imputation. We simulate missing data by changing a large number of values to NA in the `PimaIndiansDiabetes` dataset.

We make use of the following factors for the process:

- We use mean to fill in the NA values.
- We use kNN imputation to fill in the missing values. We then compare how the two methods performed:

```
library(DMwR)
library(caret)

diab<- PimaIndiansDiabetes
```

```
# In the dataset, the column mass represents the body mass index
# Of the individuals represented in the corresponding row

# mass: Body mass index (weight in kg/(height in m)\^2)

# Creating a backup of the diabetes dataframe
diabmiss_orig<- diab

# Creating a separate dataframe which we will modify
diabmiss<- diabmiss_orig

# Saving the original values for body mass
actual <- diabmiss_orig$mass

# Change 91 values of mass to NA in the dataset
diabmiss$mass[10:100] <- NA

# Number of missing values in mass
sum(is.na(diabmiss$mass))

# 91

# View the missing values
diabmiss[5:15,]
```

We get the output as follows:

	pregnant	glucose	pressure	triceps	insulin	mass	pedigree	age	diabetes
5	0	137	40	35	168	43.1	2.288	33	pos
6	5	116	74	0	0	25.6	0.201	30	neg
7	3	78	50	32	88	31.0	0.248	26	pos
8	10	115	0	0	0	35.3	0.134	29	neg
9	2	197	70	45	543	30.5	0.158	53	pos
10	8	125	96	0	0	NA	0.232	54	pos
11	4	110	92	0	0	NA	0.191	30	neg
12	10	168	74	0	0	NA	0.537	34	pos
13	10	139	80	0	0	NA	1.441	57	neg
14	1	189	60	23	846	NA	0.398	59	pos
15	5	166	72	19	175	NA	0.587	51	pos

```
# Test with using the mean, we will set all the missing values
# To the mean value for the column

diabmiss$mass[is.na(diabmiss$mass)] <- mean(diabmiss$mass,na.rm = TRUE)

# Check the values that have been imputed
data.frame(actual=actual[10:100], impute_with_mean=diabmiss$mass[10:100])
```

The output of the preceding code is as follows:

```
> data.frame(actual=actual[10:100], impute_with_mean=diabmiss$mass[10:100])
   actual impute_with_mean
1    0.0        32.12378
2   37.6        32.12378
3   38.0        32.12378
4   27.1        32.12378
5   30.1        32.12378
6   25.8        32.12378
7   30.0        32.12378
8   45.8        32.12378
```

```
# Check the Root-Mean-Squared-Error for the entire column
# Root Mean Squared Error provides an estimate for the
# Difference between the actual and the predicted values
# On 'average'

diabmissdf<- data.frame(actual=actual, impute_with_mean=diabmiss$mass)
rmse1 <- RMSE(diabmissdf$impute_with_mean,actual)
rmse1

# [1] 3.417476

# We will re-run the exercise using knnImputation (from package DMwR)

# Change the value of the records back to NA
diabmiss<- diabmiss_orig
diabmiss$mass[10:100] <- NA

# Perform knnImputation
diabknn<- knnImputation(diabmiss,k=25)

# Check the RMSE value for the knnImputation method
rmse2 <- RMSE(diabknn$mass,actual)
rmse2

# [1] 3.093827

# Improvement using the knnImputation methods in percentage terms

100 * (rmse1-rmse2)/rmse1

[1] 22.20689
```

While it may not represent a dramatic change, it's still better than using a naïve approach such as using simply a mean or constant value.

There are several packages in R for data imputation. A few prominent ones are as follows:

- **Amelia II**: Missing information in time-series data

    https://gking.harvard.edu/amelia

- **Hot-deck imputation with R package**: HotDeckImputation and hot.deck

    https://cran.r-project.org/web/packages/HotDeckImputation/

    https://cran.r-project.org/web/packages/hot.deck/

- **Multivariate imputation (by Chained Equations)**

    https://cran.r-project.org/web/packages/mice/index.html

- **Imputing values in a Bayesian framework with R package**: mi

    https://cran.r-project.org/web/packages/mi/index.html

The importance of variables

During model-building exercises, datasets may have tens of variables. Not all of them may add value to the predictive model. It is not uncommon to reduce the dataset to include a subset of the variables and allow the machine learning programmer to devote more time toward fine-tuning the chosen variables and the model-building process. There is also a technical justification for reducing the number of variables in the dataset. Performing machine learning modeling on very large, that is, high dimensional datasets can be very compute-intensive, that is, it may require a significant amount of time, CPU, and RAM to perform the numerical operations. This not only makes the application of certain algorithms impractical, it also has the effect of causing unwarranted delays. Hence, the methodical selection of variables helps both in terms of analysis time as well as computational requirements for algorithmic analysis.

Variable selection is also known as feature selection/attribute selection. Algorithms such as random forests and lasso regression implement variable selection as part of their algorithmic operations. But, variable selection can be done as a separate exercise.

The R package, `caret`, provides a very simple-to-use and intuitive interface for variable selection. As we haven't yet discussed the modeling process, we will learn how to find the important variables, and in the next chapter delve deeper into the subject.

We'll use a common, well-known algorithm called `RandomForest` that is used for building decision trees. The algorithm will be described in more detail in the next chapter, but the purpose of using it here is merely to show how variable selection can be performed. The example is illustrative of what the general process is.

We'll re-use the dataset we have been working with, that is, the `PimaIndiansDiabetes` data from the `mlbench` package. We haven't discussed the model training process yet, but it has been used here in order to derive the values for variable importance. The outcome variable in this case is diabetes and the other variables are used as the independent variables. In other words, can we predict if the person has diabetes using the data available:

```
diab<- PimaIndiansDiabetes

# We will use the createDataPartition function from caret to split
# The data. The function produces a set of indices using which we
# will create the corresponding training and test sets

training_index<- createDataPartition(diab$diabetes, p = 0.80, list = FALSE,
times = 1)

# Creating the training set
diab_train<- diab[training_index,]

# Create the test set
diab_test<- diab[-training_index,]

# Create the trainControl parameters for the model
diab_control<- trainControl("repeatedcv", number = 3, repeats = 2,
classProbs = TRUE, summaryFunction = twoClassSummary)

# Build the model
rf_model<- train(diabetes ~ ., data = diab_train, method = "rf", preProc =
c("center", "scale"), tuneLength = 5, trControl = diab_control, metric =
"ROC")

# Find the Variable Importance
varImp(rf_model)
rf variable importance

          Overall
glucose   100.000
mass       52.669
```

```
age        39.230
pedigree   24.885
pressure   12.619
pregnant    6.919
insulin     2.294
triceps     0.000
```

```
# This indicates that glucose levels, body mass index and age are the top 3
predictors of diabetes.
```

```
# caret also includes several useful plot functions. We can visualize the
variable importance using the command:
```

plot(varImp(rf_model))

The output of the preceding code is as shown below. It indicates that glucose, mass and age were the variables that contributed the most towards creating the model (to predict diabetes)

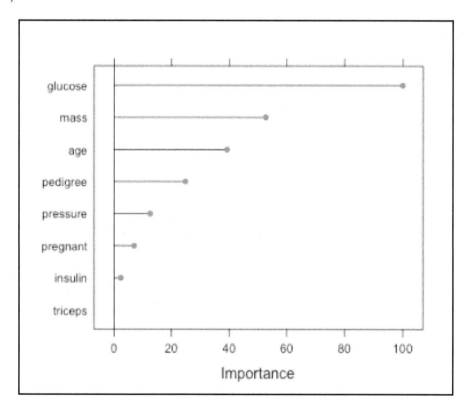

The train, test splits, and cross-validation concepts

The train, test splits, and cross-validation sets are a fundamental concept in machine learning. This is one of the areas where a pure statistical approach differs materially from the machine learning approach. Whereas in a statistical modeling task, one may perform regressions, parametric/non-parametric tests, and apply other methods, in machine learning, the algorithmic approach is supplemented with an element of iterative assessment of the results being produced and subsequent improvisation of the model with each iteration.

Splitting the data into train and test sets

Every machine learning modeling exercise begins with the process of data cleansing, as discussed earlier. The next step is to split the data into a train and test set. This is usually done by randomly selecting rows from the data that will be used to create the model. The rows that weren't selected would then be used to test the final model.

The usual split varies between 70-80 percent (training data versus test data). In an 80-20 split, 80% of the data would be used in order to create the model. The remaining 20% would be used to test the final model produced.

We applied this in the earlier section, but we can revisit the code once again. The `createDataPartition` function was used with the parameter `p = 0.80` in order to split the data. The `training_index` variable holds the training indices (of the dataset, diab) that we will use:

```
training_index<- createDataPartition(diab$diabetes, p = 0.80, list = FALSE,
times = 1)

length(training_index) # Number of items that we will select for the train
set
[1] 615

nrow(diab) # The total number of rows in the dataset
[1] 768

# Creating the training set, this is the data we will use to build our
model
diab_train<- diab[training_index,]

# Create the test set, this is the data against which we will test the
```

```
performance of our model
diab_test<- diab[-training_index,]
```

We do not have to necessarily use the `createDataPartition` function and instead, a random sample created using simple R commands as shown here will suffice:

```
# Create a set of random indices representing 80% of the data
training_index2 <- sample(nrow(diab),floor(0.80*nrow(diab)))

# Check the size of the indices just created
length(training_index2)
[1] 614

# Create the training set
diab_train2 <- diab[training_index2,]

# Create the test set
diab_test2 <- diab[-training_index2]
```

The cross-validation parameter

Cross-validation takes the train-test split concept to the next stage. The aim of the machine learning exercise is, in essence, to find what set of model parameters will provide the best performance. A model parameter indicates the arguments that the function (the model) takes. For example, for a decision tree model, parameters may include the number of levels deep the model should be built, number of splits, and so on. If, say, there are n different parameters, each having k different values, the total number of parameters would be k^n. We generally select a fixed set of combinations for each of the parameters and could easily end with 100-1000+ combinations. We will test the performance of the model (for example, accuracy in predicting the outcome correctly) for each of the parameters.

With a simple train-test split, say, if there were 500 combinations of parameters we had selected, we just need to run them against the training dataset and determine which one shows the optimal performance.

With cross-validation, we further split the training set into smaller subsets, for example, three- or five-fold is commonly used. If there are three folds, that is, we split the training set into three subsets, we keep aside one fold, say, Fold 2, and create a model using a set of parameters using Folds 1 and 3. We then test its accuracy against Fold 2. This step is repeated several times, with each iteration representing a unique set of folds on which the training-test process is being executed and accuracy measures are collected. Eventually, we would arrive at an optimal combination by selecting the parameters that showed the best overall performance.

The standard approach can be summarized as follows:

1. Create an 80-20 train-test split
2. Execute your model(s) using different combinations of model parameters
3. Select the model parameters that show the best overall performance and create the final model
4. Apply the final model on the test set to see the results

The cross-validation approach mandates that we should further split the training dataset into smaller subsets. These subsets are generally known as **folds** and collectively they are known as the **k-folds**, where *k* represents the number of splits:

1. Create an 80-20 train-test split
2. Split the training set into k-folds, say, three folds
3. Set aside Fold 1 and build a model using Fold 2 and Fold 3
4. Test your model performance on Fold 1 (for example, the percentage of accurate results)
5. Set aside Fold 2 and build a model using Fold 1 and Fold 3
6. Test your model performance on Fold 2
7. Set aside Fold 3 and build a model using Fold 1 and Fold 2
8. Test your model performance on Fold 3
9. Take the average performance of the model across all three folds
10. Repeat Step 1 for *each set of model parameters*
11. Select the model parameters that show the best overall performance and create the final model

12. Apply the final model on the test set to see the results

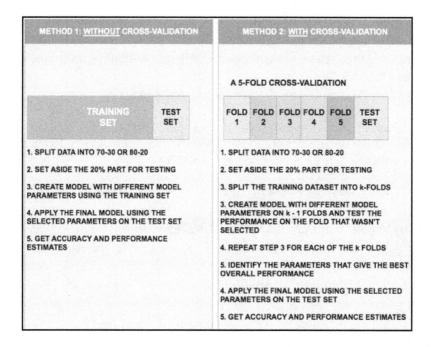

This image illustrates the difference between using an approach without cross-validation and one with cross-validation. The cross-validation method is arguably more robust and involves a rigorous evaluation of the model. That said, it is often useful to attempt creating a model initially without cross-validation to get a sense of the kind of performance that may be expected. For example, if a model built with say 2-3 training-test splits shows a performance of say, 30% accuracy, it is unlikely that any other approach, including cross-validation would somehow make that 90%. In other words the standard approach helps to get a sense of the kind of performance that may be expected. As cross-validations can be quite compute-intensive and time consuming getting an initial feedback on performance helps in a preliminary analysis of the overall process.

The caret package in R provides a very user-friendly approach to building models using cross-validation. Recall that data pre-processing must be passed or made an integral part of the cross-validation process. So, say, we had to center and scale the dataset and perform a five-fold cross-validation, all we would have to do is define the type of sampling we'd like to use in caret's `trainControl` function.

Caret's webpage on `trainControl` provides a detailed overview of the functions along with worked-out examples at `https://topepo.github.io/caret/model-training-and-tuning.html#basic-parameter-tuning`.

We have used this approach in our earlier exercise where we built a model using `RandomForest` on the `PimaIndiansDiabetes` dataset. It is shown again here to indicate where the technique was used:

```
# Create the trainControl parameters for the model
# The parameters indicate that a 3-Fold CV would be created
# and that the process would be repeated 2 times (repeats)
# The class probabilities in each run will be stored
# And we'll use the twoClassSummary* function to measure the model
# Performance
diab_control<- trainControl("repeatedcv", number = 3, repeats = 2,
classProbs = TRUE, summaryFunction = twoClassSummary)


# Build the model
# We used the train function of caret to build the model
# As part of the training process, we specified a tunelength** of 5
# This parameter lets caret select a set of default model parameters
# trControl = diab_control indicates that the model will be built
# Using the cross-validation method specified in diab_control
# Finally preProc = c("center", "scale") indicate that the data
# Would be centered and scaled at each pass of the model iteration

rf_model<- train(diabetes ~ ., data = diab_train, method = "rf", preProc =
c("center", "scale"), tuneLength = 5, trControl = diab_control, metric =
"ROC")
```

You can get a more detailed explanation of `summaryFunction` from `https://cran.r-project.org/web/packages/caret/vignettes/caret.pdf`.

The `summaryFunction` argument is used to pass in a function that takes the observed and predicted values and estimates some measure of performance. Two such functions are already included in the package: `defaultSummary` and `twoClassSummary`. The latter will compute measures specific to two-class problems, such as the area under the ROC curve, the sensitivity and specificity. Since the ROC curve is based on the predicted class probabilities (which are not computed automatically), another option is required. The `classProbs = TRUE` option is used to include these calculations.

Here is an explanation of `tuneLength` from the help file for the train function of `caret`.

`tuneLength` is an integer denoting the amount of granularity in the tuning parameter grid. By default, this argument is the number of levels for each tuning parameter that should be generated by train. If `trainControl` has the option `search = random`, this is the maximum number of tuning parameter combinations that will be generated by the random search.

 Note that if this argument is given it must be named.

Creating the model

The final step after creating the model is to use the model against the test dataset to get the predictions. This is generally done using the `predict` function in R, with the first argument being the model that was created and the second argument being the dataset against which you'd like to get the predictions for.

Taking our example of the `PimaIndiansDiabetes` dataset, after the model has been built, we can get the predictions on the test dataset as follows:

```
# Install the R Package e1071, if you haven't already
# By running install.packages("e1071")

# Use the predict function and the rf_model that was previously built
# To get the predictions on the test dataset
# Note that we are not including the column diabetes in the test
# dataset by using diab_test[,-ncol(diab_test)]

predictions<- predict(rf_model, diab_test[,-ncol(diab_test)])

# First few records predicted
head(predictions)
[1] negnegpospospospos
Levels: negpos

# The confusion matrix allows us to see the number of true positives
# False positives, True negatives and False negatives

cf<- confusionMatrix(predictions, diab_test$diabetes)
cf

# Confusion Matrix and Statistics
#
#            Reference
```

```
# Prediction negpos
#        neg  89  21
#        pos  11  32
#
# Accuracy : 0.7908
# 95% CI : (0.7178, 0.8523)
# No Information Rate : 0.6536
# P-Value [Acc> NIR] : 0.0001499
#
# Kappa : 0.5167
# Mcnemar's Test P-Value : 0.1116118
#
# Sensitivity : 0.8900
# Specificity : 0.6038
# PosPredValue : 0.8091
# NegPredValue : 0.7442
# Prevalence : 0.6536
# Detection Rate : 0.5817
# Detection Prevalence : 0.7190
# Balanced Accuracy : 0.7469
#
# 'Positive' Class :neg
```

Let's check what the confusion matrix tells us:

```
# This indicates that of the records that were marked negative (neg)
# We predicted 89 of them as negative and 11 as positive (i.e., they
# were negative but we incorrectly classified them as a positive

# We correctly identified 32 positives but incorrectly classified
# 21 positives as negative

#
#           Reference
# Prediction neg  pos
#        neg  89  21
#        pos  11  32

# The overall accuracy was 79%
# This can be improved (significantly) by using more
# Accuracy : 0.7908

# We can plot the model using plot(rf_model) as follows
plot(rf_model)
```

The plot is as follows:

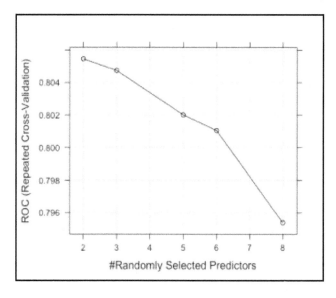

```
# And finally we can also visualize our confusion matrix using the
# inbuilt fourfoldplot function in R
```

fourfoldplot(cf$table)

We get the plot as follows:

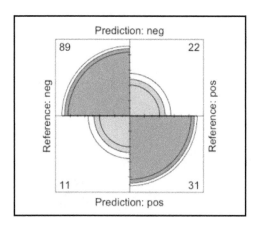

Per the documentation of `fourfoldplot` *[Source:* `https://stat.ethz.ch/R-manual/` `R-devel/library/graphics/html/fourfoldplot.html`*], an association (odds ratio different from 1) between the binary row and column variables is indicated by the tendency of diagonally opposite cells in one direction to differ in size from those in the other direction; color is used to show this direction. Confidence rings for the odds ratio allow a visual test of the null of no association; the rings for adjacent quadrants overlap if and only if the observed counts are consistent with the null hypothesis.*

Leveraging multicore processing in the model

The exercise in the previous section is repeated here using the PimaIndianDiabetes2 dataset instead. This dataset contains several missing values. As a result, we will first impute the missing values and then run the machine learning example.

The exercise has been repeated with some additional nuances, such as using multicore/parallel processing in order to make the cross-validations run faster.

To leverage multicore processing, install the package doMC using the following code:

```
Install.packages("doMC")  # Install package for multicore processing
Install.packages("nnet") # Install package for neural networks in R
```

Now we will run the program as shown in the code here:

```
# Load the library doMC
library(doMC)

# Register all cores
registerDoMC(cores = 8)

# Set seed to create a reproducible example
set.seed(100)

# Load the PimaIndiansDiabetes2 dataset
data("PimaIndiansDiabetes2",package = 'mlbench')
diab<- PimaIndiansDiabetes2

# This dataset, unlike PimaIndiansDiabetes has 652 missing values!
> sum(is.na(diab))
[1] 652

# We will use knnImputation to fill in the missing values
```

```
diab<- knnImputation(diab)

# Create the train-test set split
training_index<- createDataPartition(diab$diabetes, p = .8, list = FALSE,
times = 1)

# Create the training and test dataset
diab_train<- diab[training_index,]
diab_test<- diab[-training_index,]

# We will use 10-Fold Cross Validations
diab_control<- trainControl("repeatedcv", number = 10, repeats = 3, search
= "random", classProbs = TRUE)

# Create the model using methodnnet (a Neural Network package in R)
# Note that we have changed the metric here to "Accuracy" instead of # ROC
nn_model<- train(diabetes ~ ., data = diab_train, method = "nnet",
preProc = c("center", "scale"), trControl = diab_control, tuneLength = 10,
metric = "Accuracy")

predictions<- predict(nn_model, diab_test[,-ncol(diab_test)])
cf<- confusionMatrix(predictions, diab_test$diabetes)
cf

# >cf
# Confusion Matrix and Statistics
#
#          Reference
# Prediction negpos
#          neg  89  19
#          pos  11  34
#
# Accuracy : 0.8039
# 95% CI : (0.7321, 0.8636)
# No Information Rate : 0.6536
# P-Value [Acc> NIR] : 3.3e-05
#
```

Even with 650+ missing values, our model was able to achieve an accuracy of 80%+.

It can certainly be improved, but as a baseline, it shows the kind of performance that can be expected of machine learning models.

In a case of a dichotomous outcome variable, a random guess would have had a 50% chance of being accurate. An accuracy of 80% is significantly higher than the accuracy we could have achieved using just guess-work:

```
plot(nn_model)
```

The resulting plot is as follows:

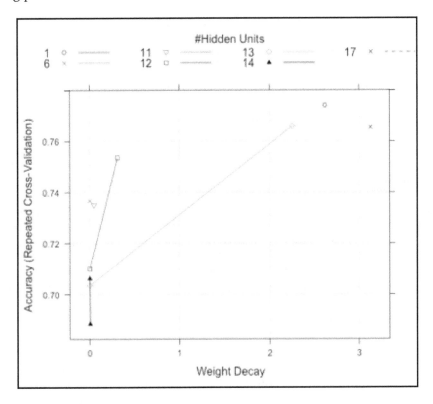

```
fourfoldplot(cf$table)
```

The result is depicted in the following plot:

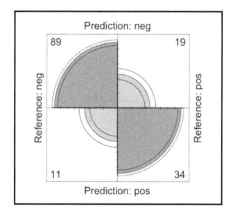

Summary

In this chapter, we learnt about the basic fundamentals of Machine Learning, the different types such as Supervised and Unsupervised and major concepts such as data pre-processing, data imputation, managing imbalanced classes and other topics.

We also learnt about the key distinctions between terms that are being used interchangeably today, in particular the terms AI and Machine Learning. We learned that artificial intelligence deals with a vast array of topics, such as game theory, sociology, constrained optimizations, and machine learning; AI is much broader in scope relative to machine learning.

Machine learning facilitates AI; namely, machine learning algorithms are used to create systems that are *artificially intelligent*, but they differ in scope. A regression problem (finding the line of best fit given a set of points) can be considered a machine learning *algorithm*, but it is much less likely to be seen as an AI algorithm (conceptually, although it technically could be).

In the next chapter, we will look at some of the other concepts in Machine Learning such as Bias, Variance and Regularization. We will also read about a few important algorithms and learn how to apply them using machine learning packages in R.

8
Machine Learning Deep Dive

The prior chapter on machine learning provided a preliminary overview of the subject, including the different classes and core concepts in the subject area. This chapter will delve deeper into the theoretical aspects of machine learning such as the limits of algorithms and how different algorithms work.

Machine learning is a vast and complex subject, and to that end, this chapter focuses on the breadth of different topics, rather than the depth. The concepts are introduced at a high level and the reader may refer to other sources to further their understanding of the topics.

We will start out by discussing a few fundamental theories in machine learning, such as Gradient Descent and VC Dimension. Next, we will look at Bias and Variance, two of the most important factors in any modelling process and the concept of bias-variance trade-off.

We'll then discuss the various machine learning algorithms, their strengths and areas of applications.

We'll conclude with exercises that leverage real-world datasets to perform machine learning operations using R.

We will cover the following topics in this chapter:

- The bias, variance, and regularization properties
- Gradient descent and VC dimension theories
- Machine learning algorithms
- Tutorial: Machine learning with R

The bias, variance, and regularization properties

Bias, variance, and the closely related topic of regularization hold very special and fundamental positions in the field of machine learning.

Bias happens when a machine learning model is too 'simple', leading to results that are consistently off from the actual values.

Variance happens when a model is too 'complex', leading to results that are very accurate on test datasets, but do not perform well on unseen/new datasets.

Once users become familiar with the process of creating machine learning models, it would seem that the process is quite simplistic - get the data, create a training set and a test set, create a model, apply the model on the test dataset, and the exercise is complete. Creating models is easy; creating a *good* model is a much more challenging topic. But how can one test the quality of a model? And, perhaps more importantly, how does one go about building a 'good' model?

The answer lies in a term called regularization. It's arguably a fancy word, but all it means is that during the process of creating a model, one benefits from penalizing an overly impressive performance on a training dataset and relaxing the same on a poorly performing model.

To understand regularization, it would help to know the concepts of overfitting and underfitting. For this, let us look at a simple but familiar example of drawing lines of best fit. For those who have used Microsoft Excel, you may have noticed the option to draw the *line of best fit* - in essence, given a set of points, you can draw a line that represents the data and approximates the function that the points represent.

The following table shows the prices vs square footage of a few properties. In order to determine the relationship between house prices and the size of the house, we can draw a line of best fit, or a trend line, as shown as follows:

Sq. ft.	Price ($)
862	170,982
1235	227,932
932	183,280
1624	237,945

1757	275,921
1630	274,713
1236	201,428
1002	193,128
1118	187,073
1339	202,422
1753	283,989
1239	228,170
1364	230,662
995	169,369
1000	157,305

If we were to draw a *line of best fit* using a linear trend line, the chart would look somewhat like this:

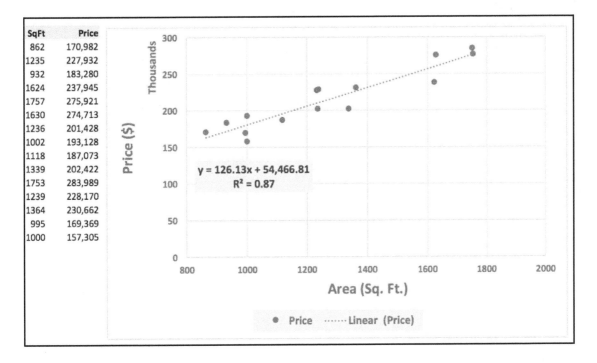

Excel provides an useful additional feature that allows users to draw an extension of the trend line which can provide an estimate, or a *prediction*, of unknown variables. In this case, extending the trendline will show us, based on the function, what the prices for houses in the 1,800-2,000 sq. ft. range are likely to be.

The linear function that describes the data is as follows:

y=126.13x + 54,466.81

The following chart with an extended trend line shows that the price is most likely between $275,000 and $300,000:

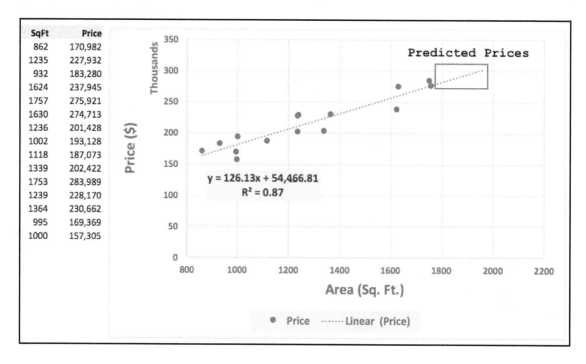

However, one may argue that the line is not the best approximation and that it may be possible to increase the value of R2, which in this case is 0.87. In general, the higher the R^2, the better the model that describes the data. There are various different types of R^2 values, but for the purpose of this section, we'll assume that the higher the R^2, the better the model.

In the next section, we will draw a new trend line that has a much higher R^2, but using a polynomial function. This function has a higher R^2 (0.91 vs 0.87) and visually appears to be closer to the points on average.

The function in this case is a 6th-order polynomial:

$$y = -0.00x^6 + 0.00x^5 - 0.00x^4 + 2.50x^3 - 2,313.40x^2 + 1,125,401.77x - 224,923,813.17$$

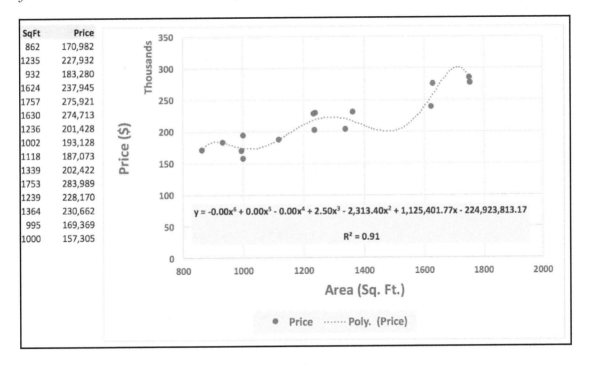

SqFt	Price
862	170,982
1235	227,932
932	183,280
1624	237,945
1757	275,921
1630	274,713
1236	201,428
1002	193,128
1118	187,073
1339	202,422
1753	283,989
1239	228,170
1364	230,662
995	169,369
1000	157,305

$y = -0.00x^6 + 0.00x^5 - 0.00x^4 + 2.50x^3 - 2,313.40x^2 + 1,125,401.77x - 224,923,813.17$

$R^2 = 0.91$

But, even though the line has a higher R^2, if we extend the trend line, intending to find what the prices of houses in the 1,800-2,000 sq. ft. range are likely to be, we get the following result.

Houses in the 1,800-2,000 sq. ft. range go from approx. $280,000 to negative $2 million at the 2,000[th] sq. ft. In other words, people purchasing houses with 1800 sq. ft. are expected to spend $ 280,000 and those purchasing houses with 2,000 sq. ft. should, according to this function, with a 'higher R^2', receive $2 million! This, of course, is not accurate, but what we have just witnessed is what is known as **over-fitting**. The image below illustrates this phenomenon.

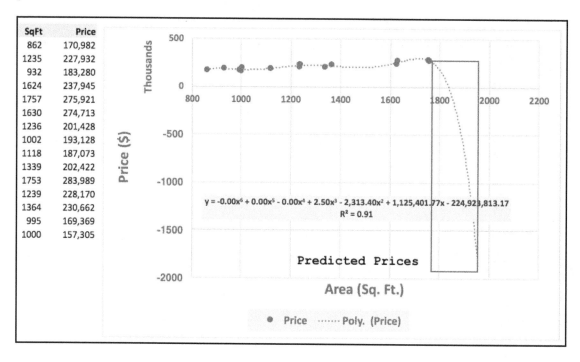

SqFt	Price
862	170,982
1235	227,932
932	183,280
1624	237,945
1757	275,921
1630	274,713
1236	201,428
1002	193,128
1118	187,073
1339	202,422
1753	283,989
1239	228,170
1364	230,662
995	169,369
1000	157,305

$y = -0.00x^6 + 0.00x^5 - 0.00x^4 + 2.50x^3 - 2,313.40x^2 + 1,125,401.77x - 224,923,813.17$

$R^2 = 0.91$

At the other end of the spectrum is **under-fitting**. This happens when the model built does not describe the data. In the following chart, the function $y = 0.25x - 200$ is one such example:

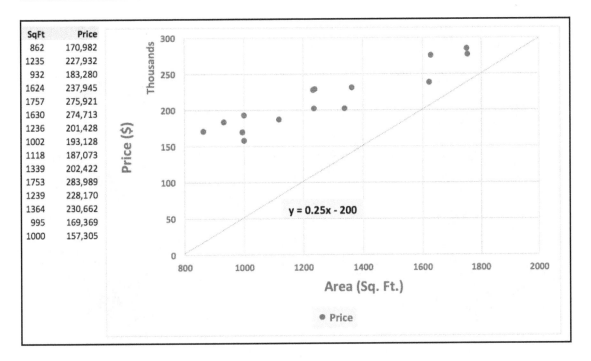

SqFt	Price
862	170,982
1235	227,932
932	183,280
1624	237,945
1757	275,921
1630	274,713
1236	201,428
1002	193,128
1118	187,073
1339	202,422
1753	283,989
1239	228,170
1364	230,662
995	169,369
1000	157,305

In brief, this section can be abbreviated as follows:

- A function that fits the data too well, such that the function can approximate nearly all of the points in the training dataset is considered overfitting.
- A function that does not fit the data at all, or in other words is far from the actual points in the training dataset, is considered underfitting.
- Machine learning is the process of balancing between overfitting and underfitting the data. This is arguably not an easy exercise, which is why even though building a model may be trivial, building a model that is reasonably good is a much more difficult challenge.
- Underfitting is when your function is *not thinking at all* - it has a high bias.
- Overfitting is when your function is *thinking too hard* - it has a high variance.
- Another example for underfitting and overfitting is given in coming example.

Say we are tasked with determining if a bunch of fruit are oranges or apples, and have been given their location in a fruit basket (left-side or right-side), size and weight:

| Basket 1 (Training Dataset) | Basket 2 (Test Dataset) |

An example of overfitting could be that, based on the training dataset, with regard to Basket 1 we could conclude that the only fruits located on the right hand side of the basket are oranges and those on the left are all apples.

An example of underfitting could be that I conclude that the basket has only oranges.

Model 1: In the first case - for overfitting - I have, in essence, memorized the locations.

Model 2: In the second case - for underfitting - I could not remember anything precisely at all.

Now, given a second basket - the test dataset where the positions of the apples and oranges are switched - if I were to use Model 1, I would incorrectly conclude that all the fruits on the right hand side are oranges and those on the left hand side are apples (since I memorized the training data).

If I were to use Model 2, I would, again, incorrectly conclude that all the fruits are oranges.

There are, however, ways to manage the balance between underfitting and overfitting - or in other words, between high bias and high variance.

One of the methods commonly used for bias-variance trade-off is known as regularization. This refers to the process of penalizing the model (for example, the model's coefficients in a regression) in order to produce an output that generalizes well across a range of data points.

The table on the next page illustrates some of the key concepts of bias and variance and illustrates options for remedial steps when a model has high bias or high variance:

To Fix	The Issue	Remedies
High Variance Unable to 'Generalise'	Not enough information	Get more training examples
	Too many features (variables) are being considered	Reduce number of features
	Too less penalisation	Increase Regularisation parameter (lambda)
High Bias We have generalised way too much	Not enough features to build a more thorough model	Add more number of features
	Model is too simple	Add more complex features (eg., polynomial features)
	Too much penalisation	Decrease Regularisation parameter (lambda)

In terms of the modeling process, a high bias is generally indicated by the fact that both the training set error as well as the test set error remain consistently high. For high variance (overfitting), the training set error decreases rapidly, but the test set error remains unchanged.

The gradient descent and VC Dimension theories

Gradient descent and VC Dimension are two fundamental theories in machine learning. In general, **gradient descent** gives a structured approach to finding the optimal co-efficients of a function. The hypothesis space of a function can be large and with gradient descent, the algorithm tries to find a minimum (*a minima*) where the cost function (for example, the squared sum of errors) is the lowest.

VC Dimension provides an upper bound on the maximum number of points that can be classified in a system. It is in essence the measure of the richness of a function and provides an assessment of what the limits of a hypothesis are in a structured way. The number of points that can be exactly classified by a function or hypothesis is known as the VC Dimension of the hypothesis. For example, a linear boundary can accurately classify 2 or 3 points but not 4. Hence, the VC Dimension of this 2-dimensional space would be 3.

VC Dimension, like many other topics in computational learning theory, is both complex and interesting. It is a lesser known (and discussed) topic, but one that has a profound implication as it attempts to answer questions about what the limits of learning can be.

Popular machine learning algorithms

There are various different classes of machine learning algorithms. As such, since algorithms can belong to multiple 'classes' or categories at the same time at a conceptual level, it is hard to specifically state that an algorithm belongs exclusively to a single class. In this section, we will briefly discuss a few of the most commonly used and well-known algorithms.

These include:

- Regression models
- Association rules
- Decision trees
- Random forest
- Boosting algorithms
- Support vector machines
- K-means
- Neural networks

Note that in the examples, we have shown the basic use of the R functions using the entire dataset. In practice, we'd split the data into a training and test set, and once we have built a satisfactory model apply the same on the test dataset to evaluate the model's performance.

Regression models

Regression models range from commonly used linear, logistic, and multiple regression algorithms used in statistics to Ridge and Lasso regression, which penalizes co-efficients to improve model performance.

In our earlier examples, we saw the application of **linear regression** when we created trend-lines. **Multiple linear regression** refers to the fact that the process of creating the model requires multiple independent variables.

For instance:

Total Advertising Cost = x* Print Ads, would be a simple linear regression; whereas

Total Advertising Cost = X + Print Ads + Radio Ads + TV Ads, due to the presence of more than one independent variable (Print, Radio, and TV), would be a multiple linear regression.

Logistic regression is another commonly used statistical regression modelling technique that predicts the outcome of a discrete categorical value, mainly for cases where the outcome variable is dichotomous (for example, 0 or 1, Yes or No, and so on). There can, however, be more than 2 discrete outcomes (for example, State NY, NJ, CT) and this type of logistic regression is known as **multinomial logistic regression**.

Ridge and Lasso Regressions include a regularization term (λ) in addition to the other aspects of Linear Regression. The regularization term, Ridge Regression, has the effect of reducing the β coefficients (thus 'penalizing' the co-efficients). In Lasso, the regularization term tends to reduce some of the co-efficients to 0, thus eliminating the effect of the variable on the final model:

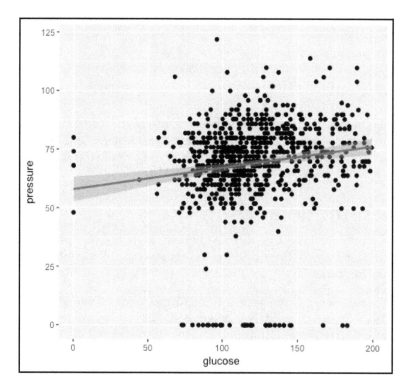

```
# Load mlbench and create a regression model of glucose (outcome/dependent
variable) with pressure, triceps and insulin as the independent variables.

> library("mlbench")
>lm_model<- lm(glucose ~ pressure + triceps + insulin,
data=PimaIndiansDiabetes[1:100,])
> plot(lm_model)
```

Association rules

Association rules mining, or **apriori**, attempts to find relationships between variables in a dataset. Association rules are frequently used for various practical real-world use cases. Given a set of variables, apriori can indicate the patterns inherent in a transactional dataset. One of our tutorials will be based on implementing an R Shiny Application for apriori and hence, more emphasis is being provided for the same in this section.

For instance, let's say a supermarket chain is deciding the order for placing items on the shelves. An apriori algorithm run against a database containing sales transactions would identify the items that, say, are most often bought together. This permits the supermarket to determine which items, when placed strategically in close proximity to one another, can yield the most sales. This is also often referred to as *market basket analysis*.

A simple example that reflects this could be as follows:

```
# The LHS (left-hand side) leads to the RHS (right-hand side) in the
relationships shown below.

# For instance, {Milk, Bread} --> {Butter} indicates that someone
purchasing milk and bread is also likely to purchase butter.

{Milk, Bread} --> {Butter}
{Butter, Egg} --> {Baking Tray}
{Baking Tray, Butter} --> {Sugar}
...
```

In all these cases, the act of purchasing something on the left-hand side led to the purchase of the item mentioned on the right-hand side of the expression.

It is also possible to derive association rules from databases that do not necessarily contain *transactions*, but instead use a sliding window to go through events along a temporal attribute, such as with the WINEPI algorithm.

There are 3 primary measures in apriori. To illustrate them, let us use a sample dataset containing items purchased in 4 separate transactions:

Transaction	Item 1	Item 2	Item 3
1	Milk	Bread	Butter
2	Milk	Egg	Butter
3	Bread	Egg	Cheese
4	Butter	Bread	Egg

Confidence

Confidence refers to how often the right-hand side of the apriori expression is valid when the left-hand side is valid. For instance, given an expression:

```
{Milk} à {Bread}
```

We would like to know how often Bread was purchased *when Milk was also purchased*.

In this case:

- **Transaction 1**: Milk and Bread are both present
- **Transaction 2**: Milk is present, but not Bread
- **Transactions 3 and 4**: Milk is not present

Hence, based on the what we saw, there were 2 transactions where Milk was present and of them, Bread was present in 1 transaction. Hence, the confidence for the rule {Milk} à {Bread} would be ½ = 50%

Taking another expression:

```
{Bread} à {Butter}
```

We would like to know, when Bread was purchased, how often was Butter also purchased?:

- **Transaction 1**: Bread and Butter are both present
- **Transaction 2**: There is no Bread (Butter is present, but our point of reference is Bread and hence this does not count)
- **Transaction 3**: Bread is present but no Butter
- **Transaction 4**: Bread and Butter are both present

Hence, we have Bread in 3 of the transactions, and Bread & Butter in 2 of the 3 transactions. Hence, in this case, the 'confidence' of the rule {Bread} à {Butter} is *2/3 = 66.7.*

Support

Support refers to the number of times the rule is satisfied relative to the total number of transactions in the dataset.

For instance:

{Milk} --> {Bread}, occurs in 1 out of 4 Transactions (in Transaction 1). Hence, the support for this rule is ¼ = 0.25 (or 25%).

{Bread} --> {Butter}, occurs in 2 out of 4 Transactions (in Transaction 1 and 4). Hence, the support for this rule is ½ = 0.50 (or 50%).

Lift

Lift is arguably the most important of the 3 measures; it measures the support of the rule relative to the support of the individual sides of the expression; put differently, it measures how strong the rule is with respect to a random occurrence of the LHS and RHS of the expression. It is formally defined as:

Lift = Support (Rule)/(Support(LHS) * Support (RHS))

A low value for lift (say, less than or equal to 1) indicates that the LHS and RHS occurrence are independent of one another, whereas a higher lift measure indicates that the co-occurrence is significant.

In our prior example,

{Bread} --> {Butter} has a lift of:

Support ({Bread} --> {Butter})
Support {Bread} * Support {Butter}

= 0.50/((3/4) * (3/4)) = 0.50/(0.75 * 0.75) = 0.89.

This indicates that although the Confidence of the rule was high, the rule in and of itself is not significant relative to other rules that may be higher than 1.

An example of a rule with a Lift higher than 1 would be:

{Item 1: Bread} --> {Item 3: Cheese}

This has a Lift of:

Support {Item 1: Bread --> Item 3: Cheese}/(Support {Item 1: Cheese} * Support {Item 3: Cheese})

= (1/4)/((1/4)*(1/4)) = 4.

Decision trees

Decision Trees are a predictive modeling technique that generates rules that derive the likelihood of a certain outcome based on the likelihood of the preceding outcomes. In general, decision trees are typically constructed similar to a **flowchart**, with a series of nodes and leaves that denote a parent-child relationship. Nodes that do not link to other nodes are known as leaves.

Decision Trees belong to a class of algorithms that are often known as **CART (Classification and Regression Trees)**. If the outcome of interest is a categorical variable, it falls under a classification exercise, whereas if the outcome is a number, it is known as a regression tree.

An example will help to make this concept clearer. Take a look at the chart:

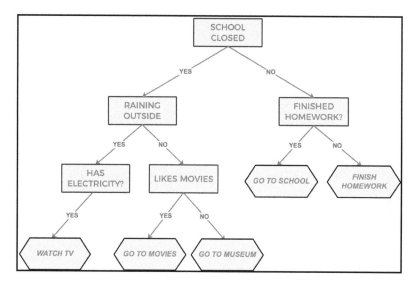

The chart shows a hypothetical scenario: if school is closed/not closed. The rectangular boxes (in blue) represent the nodes. The first rectangle (School Closed) represent the *root* node, whereas the inner rectangles represent the *internal* nodes. The rectangular boxes with angled edges (in green and italic letters) represent the '*leaves*' (or *terminal* nodes).

Decision Trees are simple to understand and one of the few algorithms that are not a 'black box'. Algorithms such as those used to create Neural Networks are often considered black boxes, as it is very hard - if not impossible - to intuitively determine the exact path by which a final outcome was reached due to the complexity of the model.

In R, there are various facilities for creating Decision Trees. A commonly used library for creating them in R is `rpart`. We'll revisit our `PimaIndiansDiabetes` dataset to see how a decision tree can be created using the package.

We would like to create a model to determine how glucose, insulin, (body) mass, and age are related to diabetes. Note that in the dataset, diabetes is a categorical variable with a yes/no response.

For visualizing the decision tree, we will use the `rpart.plot` package. The code for the same is given as follows:

```
install.packages("rpart")
install.packages("rpart.plot")

library(rpart)
library(rpart.plot)

rpart_model<- rpart (diabetes ~ glucose + insulin + mass + age, data =
PimaIndiansDiabetes)


>rpart_model
n= 768

node), split, n, loss, yval, (yprob)
      * denotes terminal node

  1) root 768 268 neg (0.6510417 0.3489583)
    2) glucose< 127.5 485   94neg (0.8061856 0.1938144) *
    3) glucose>=127.5 283 109 pos (0.3851590 0.6148410)
      6) mass< 29.95 76   24neg (0.6842105 0.3157895)
       12) glucose< 145.5 41    6 neg (0.8536585 0.1463415) *
       13) glucose>=145.5 35   17pos (0.4857143 0.5142857)
         26) insulin< 14.5 21    8 neg (0.6190476 0.3809524) *
         27) insulin>=14.5 14    4 pos (0.2857143 0.7142857) *
      7) mass>=29.95 207   57pos (0.2753623 0.7246377)
```

```
14) glucose< 157.5 115   45pos (0.3913043 0.6086957)
  28) age< 30.5 50   23neg (0.5400000 0.4600000)
    56) insulin>=199 14    3 neg (0.7857143 0.2142857) *
    57) insulin< 199 36   16pos (0.4444444 0.5555556)
     114) age>=27.5 10    3 neg (0.7000000 0.3000000) *
     115) age< 27.5 26    9 pos (0.3461538 0.6538462) *
  29) age>=30.5 65   18pos (0.2769231 0.7230769) *
15) glucose>=157.5 92   12pos (0.1304348 0.8695652) *
```

```
>rpart.plot(rpart_model, extra=102, nn=TRUE)
```

```
# The plot shown below illustrates the decision tree that the model,
rpart_model represents.
```

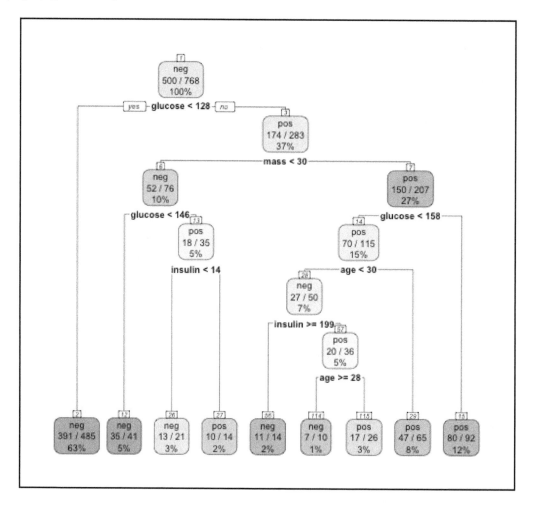

Reading from the top, the graph shows that that there are 500 cases of `diabetes=neg` in the dataset (out of a total of 768 records).

```
> sum(PimaIndiansDiabetes$diabetes=="neg")
[1] 500
```

Of the total number of records in the dataset (768) with value of glucose < 128, there were 485 records marked as negative. Of these, the model correctly predicted 391 cases as negative (Node Number 2, the first one on the left from the bottom).

For the records which had a glucose reading of > 128, there were 283 records marked as positive (Node Number 3, the node immediately below the topmost/root node). The model correctly classified 174 of these cases.

Another, more recent package for intuitive decision trees with comprehensive visual information is **FFTrees (Fast and Frugal Decision Trees)**. The following example has been provided for informational purposes:

```
install.packages("FFTrees")
library(caret)
library(mlbench)
library(FFTrees)
set.seed(123)

data("PimaIndiansDiabetes")
diab<- PimaIndiansDiabetes
diab$diabetes<- 1 * (diab$diabetes=="pos")

train_ind<- createDataPartition(diab$diabetes,p=0.8,list=FALSE,times=1)

training_diab<- diab[train_ind,]
test_diab<- diab[-train_ind,]

diabetes.fft<- FFTrees(diabetes ~.,data = training_diab,data.test =
test_diab)
plot(diabetes.fft)

# The plot below illustrates the decision tree representing diabetes.fft
using the FFTrees package.
```

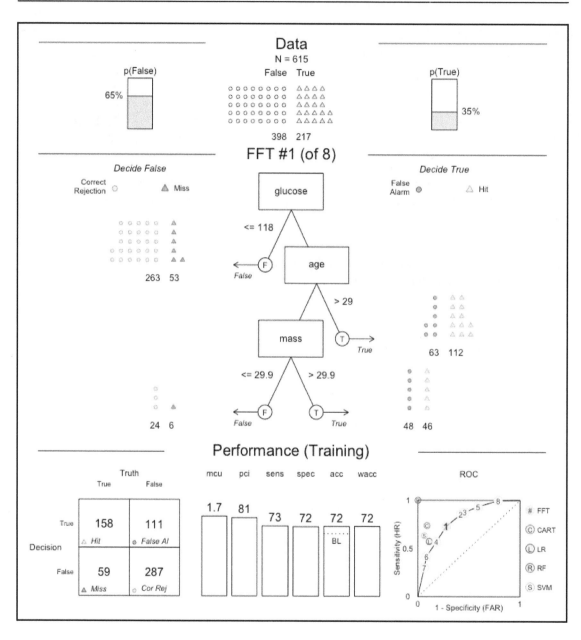

Decision Trees work by splitting the data recursively until a stopping criterion, such as when a certain depth has been reached, or the number of cases, is below a specified value. Each split is done based on the variable that will lead to a 'purer subset'.

In principle, we can grow an endless number of trees from a given set of variables, which makes it a particularly hard and intractable problem. Numerous algorithms exist which provide an efficient method for splitting and creating decision trees. One such method is Hunt's Algorithm.

Further details about the algorithm can be found at:
`https://www-users.cs.umn.edu/~kumar/dmbook/ch4.pdf`.

The Random forest extension

Random forest is an extension of the decision tree model that we just discussed. In practice, Decision Trees are simple to understand, simple to interpret, fast to create using available algorithms, and overall, intuitive. However, Decision Trees are sensitive to small changes in the data, permit splits only along an axis (linear splits) and can lead to overfitting. To mitigate some of the drawbacks of decision trees, whilst still getting the benefit of their elegance, algorithms such as Random Forest create multiple decision trees and sample random features to leverage and build an aggregate model.

Random forest works on the principle of **bootstrap aggregating** or **bagging**. Bootstrap is a statistical term indicating random sampling with replacement. Bootstrapping a given set of records means taking a random number of records and possibly including the same record multiple times in a sample. Thereafter, the user would measure their metric of interest on the sample and then repeat the process. In this manner, the distribution of the values of the metric calculated from random samples multiple times is expected to represent the distribution of the population, and so the entire dataset.

An example of Bagging a set of 3 numbers, such as (1,2,3,4), would be:

(1,2,3), (1,1,3), (1,3,3), (2,2,1), and others.

Bootstrap Aggregating, or *bagging*, implies leveraging a voting method using *multiple bootstrap samples* at a time, building a model on each individual sample (set of n records) and then finally aggregating the results.

Random forests also implement another level of operation beyond simple bagging. It also randomly selects the variables to be included in the model building process at each split. For instance, if we were to create a random forest model using the `PimaIndiansDiabetes` dataset with the variables pregnant, glucose, pressure, triceps, insulin, mass, pedigree, age, and diabetes, in each bootstrap sample (draw of n records), we would select a random subset of features with which to build the model--for instance, glucose, pressure, and insulin; insulin, age, and pedigree; triceps, mass, and insulin; and others.

In R, the package commonly used for RandomForest is called by its namesake, RandomForest. We can use it via the package as is or via caret. Both methods are shown as follows:

1. Using Random Forest using the RandomForest package:

```
> rf_model1 <- randomForest(diabetes ~ ., data=PimaIndiansDiabetes) >
rf_model1 Call: randomForest(formula = diabetes ~ ., data =
PimaIndiansDiabetes)
Type of random forest: classification Number of trees: 500 No. of variables
tried at each split: 2 OOB estimate of error rate: 23.44% Confusion matrix:
negposclass.error neg430 70 0.1400000 pos 110 158 0.4104478
```

2. Using Random Forest via caret using the `method="rf"` function:

```
> library(caret)
> library(doMC)

# THE NEXT STEP IS VERY CRITICAL - YOU DO 'NOT' NEED TO USE MULTICORE
# NOTE THAT THIS WILL USE ALL THE CORES ON THE MACHINE THAT YOU ARE
# USING TO RUN THE EXERCISE

# REMOVE THE # MARK FROM THE FRONT OF registerDoMC BEFORE RUNNING
# THE COMMAND

># registerDoMC(cores = 8) # CHANGE NUMBER OF CORES TO MATCH THE NUMBER OF
CORES ON YOUR MACHINE

>rf_model<- train(diabetes ~ ., data=PimaIndiansDiabetes, method="rf")
>rf_model
Random Forest

768 samples
  8 predictor
  2 classes: 'neg', 'pos'

No pre-processing
Resampling: Bootstrapped (25 reps)
Summary of sample sizes: 768, 768, 768, 768, 768, 768, ...
Resampling results across tuning parameters:

mtry  Accuracy   Kappa
  2    0.7555341  0.4451835
  5    0.7556464  0.4523084
  8    0.7500721  0.4404318

Accuracy was used to select the optimal model using  the largest value.
```

```
The final value used for the model was mtry = 5.

>getTrainPerf(rf_model)

TrainAccuracyTrainKappa method
1      0.7583831  0.4524728rf
```

It is also possible to see the splits and other related information in each tree of the original Random Forest model (which did not use caret). This can be done using the `getTree` function as follows:

```
>getTree(rf_model1,1,labelVar = TRUE)
      left daughter right daughter split var split point status prediction
1                2              3      mass      27.8500      1      <NA>
2                4              5       age      28.5000      1      <NA>
3                6              7   glucose     155.0000      1      <NA>
4                8              9       age      27.5000      1      <NA>
5               10             11      mass       9.6500      1      <NA>
6               12             13  pregnant       7.5000      1      <NA>
7               14             15   insulin      80.0000      1      <NA>
8                0              0     <NA>       0.0000     -1       neg
9               16             17  pressure      68.0000      1      <NA>
10               0              0     <NA>       0.0000     -1       pos
11              18             19   insulin     131.0000      1      <NA>
12              20             21   insulin      87.5000      1      <NA>

    [...]
```

Boosting algorithms

Boosting is a technique that uses weights and a set of *weak learners*, such as decision trees, in order to improve model performance. Boosting assigns weights to data based on model misclassification and future learner's (created during the boosting machine learning process) focus on the misclassified examples. Examples that were correctly classified will be reassigned new weights which will generally be lower than those that were not correctly classified. The weight can be based on a cost function, such as a majority vote, using subsets of the data.

In simple and non-technical terms, boosting uses *a series of weak learners, and each learner 'learns' from the mistakes of the prior learners.*

Boosting is generally more popular compared to bagging as it assigns weights relative to model performance rather than assigning equal weights to all data points as in bagging. This is conceptually similar to the difference between a weighted average versus an average function with no weighting criteria.

There are several packages in R for boosting algorithms and some of the commonly used ones are as follows:

- Adaboost
- **GBM (Stochastic Gradient Boosting)**
- XGBoost

Of these, XGBoost is a widely popular machine learning package that has been used very successfully in competitive machine learning platforms such as Kaggle. XGBoost has a very elegant and computationally efficient way to creating ensemble models. Because it is both accurate and extremely fast, users have often used XGBoost for compute-intensive ML challenges. You can learn more about Kaggle at http://www.kaggle.com.

```
# Creating an XGBoost model in R

library(caret)
library(xgboost)

set.seed(123)
train_ind<-
sample(nrow(PimaIndiansDiabetes),as.integer(nrow(PimaIndiansDiabetes)*.80))

training_diab<- PimaIndiansDiabetes[train_ind,]
test_diab<- PimaIndiansDiabetes[-train_ind,]

diab_train<- sparse.model.matrix(~.-1, data=training_diab[,-
ncol(training_diab)])
diab_train_dmatrix<- xgb.DMatrix(data = diab_train,
label=training_diab$diabetes=="pos")

diab_test<- sparse.model.matrix(~.-1, data=test_diab[,-ncol(test_diab)])
diab_test_dmatrix<- xgb.DMatrix(data = diab_test,
label=test_diab$diabetes=="pos")



param_diab<- list(objective = "binary:logistic",
eval_metric = "error",
            booster = "gbtree",
max_depth = 5,
```

```
            eta = 0.1)

xgb_model<- xgb.train(data = diab_train_dmatrix,
param_diab, nrounds = 1000,
watchlist = list(train = diab_train_dmatrix, test = diab_test_dmatrix),
print_every_n = 10)


predicted <- predict(xgb_model, diab_test_dmatrix)
predicted <- predicted > 0.5

actual <- test_diab$diabetes == "pos"
confusionMatrix(actual,predicted)


# RESULT

Confusion Matrix and Statistics

          Reference
Prediction FALSE TRUE
     FALSE    80   17
     TRUE     21   36

Accuracy : 0.7532
                95% CI : (0.6774, 0.8191)
    No Information Rate : 0.6558
    P-Value [Acc> NIR] : 0.005956

Kappa : 0.463
Mcnemar's Test P-Value : 0.626496

Sensitivity : 0.7921
Specificity : 0.6792
PosPredValue : 0.8247
NegPredValue : 0.6316
Prevalence : 0.6558
        Detection Rate : 0.5195
   Detection Prevalence : 0.6299
      Balanced Accuracy : 0.7357

       'Positive' Class : FALSE
```

Support vector machines

Support vector machines, commonly known as **SVMs**, are another class of machine learning algorithm that are used to classify data into one or another category using a concept called **hyperplane**, which is used to demarcate a linear boundary between points.

For instance, given a set of black and white points on an x-y axis, we can find multiple lines that will separate them. The line, in this case, represents the function that delineates the category that each point belongs to. In the following image, lines H1 and H2 both separate the points accurately. In this case, how can we determine which one of H1 and H2 would be the optimal line?:

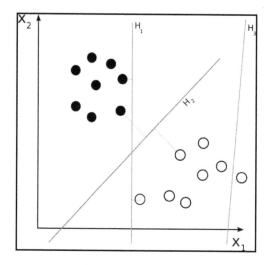

Intuitively, we can say the line that is closest to the points - for instance, the vertical line H1 - might *not* be the optimal line to separate the points. Since the line is too close to the points, and so too specific to the points on the given dataset, a new point may be misclassified if it is even slightly off to the right or the left side of the line. In other words, the line is too sensitive to small changes in the data (which could be due to stochastic/deterministic noise, such as imperfections in the data).

On the other hand, the line H2 manages to separate the data whilst maintaining the maximum possible distance from the points closest to the line. Slight imperfections in the data are unlikely to affect the classification of the points to the extent line H1 may have done. This, in essence, describes the principle of the maximum margin of separation as shown in the image below.

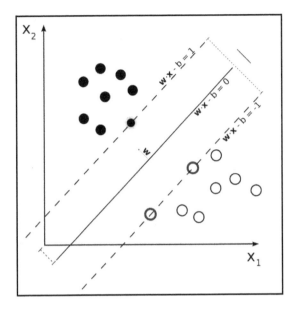

The points close to the line, also known as the hyperplane, are known as the 'support vectors' (hence the name). In the image, the points that lie on the dashed line are therefore the support vectors.

In the real world, however, not all points may be 'linearly separable'. SVMs leverage a concept known as the 'kernel trick'. In essence, points that might not be linearly separable can be projected or mapped onto a higher dimensional surface. For example, given a set of points on a 2D x-y space that are not linearly separable, it may be possible to separate them if we were to project the points on a 3-dimensional space as shown in the following image. The points colored in red were not separable by a 2D line, but when mapped to a 3-dimensional surface, they can be separated by a hyperplane as shown in the following image:

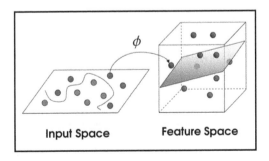

There are several packages in R that let users leverage SVM, such as `kernlab`, `e1071`, `klaR`, and others. Here, we illustrate the use of SVM from the `e1071` package, as shown as follow:

```
library(mlbench)
library(caret)
library(e1071)
set.seed(123)


data("PimaIndiansDiabetes")
diab<- PimaIndiansDiabetes

train_ind<- createDataPartition(diab$diabetes,p=0.8,list=FALSE,times=1)

training_diab<- diab[train_ind,]
test_diab<- diab[-train_ind,]

svm_model<- svm(diabetes ~ ., data=training_diab)
plot(svm_model,training_diab, glucose ~ mass)

# The plot below illustrates the areas that are classified 'positive' and
'negative'
```

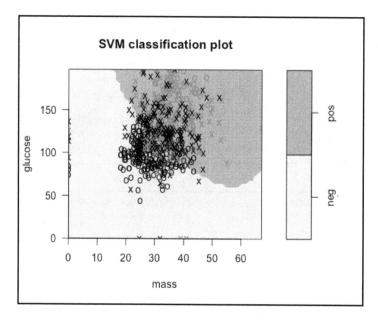

```
# Creating and evaluating the Confusion Matrix for the SVM model

svm_predicted<- predict(svm_model,test_diab[,-ncol(test_diab)])
```

```
confusionMatrix(svm_predicted,test_diab$diabetes)

Confusion Matrix and Statistics

          Reference
Prediction negpos
neg  93  26
pos7  27

Accuracy : 0.7843
                95% CI : (0.7106, 0.8466)
    No Information Rate : 0.6536
    P-Value [Acc> NIR] : 0.0003018

Kappa : 0.4799
Mcnemar's Test P-Value : 0.0017280

Sensitivity : 0.9300
Specificity : 0.5094
PosPredValue : 0.7815
NegPredValue : 0.7941
Prevalence : 0.6536
        Detection Rate : 0.6078
    Detection Prevalence : 0.7778
      Balanced Accuracy : 0.7197

      'Positive' Class :neg
```

The K-Means machine learning technique

K-Means is one of the most popular unsupervised machine learning techniques that is used to create clusters, and so categorizes data.

An intuitive example could be posed as follows:

Say a university was offering a new course on American History and Asian History. The university maintains a 15:1 student-teacher ratio, so there is 1 teacher per 15 students. It has conducted a survey which contains a 10-point numeric score that was assigned by each student to their preference of studying American History or Asian History.

We can use the in-built K-Means algorithm in R to create 2 clusters and presumably, by the number of points in each cluster, it may be possible to get an estimate of the number of students who may sign up for each course. The code for the same is given as follows:

```
library(data.table)
library(ggplot2)
library()

historyData<- fread("~/Desktop/history.csv")
ggplot(historyData,aes(american_history,asian_history)) + geom_point() +
geom_jitter()

historyCluster<- kmeans(historyData,2) # Create 2 clusters
historyData[,cluster:=as.factor(historyCluster$cluster)]
ggplot(historyData, aes(american_history,asian_history,color=cluster)) +
geom_point() + geom_jitter()

# The image below shows the output of the ggplot command. Note that the
effect of geom_jitter can be seen in the image below (the points are nudged
so that overlapping points can be easily visible)
```

The following image could provide an intuitive estimate of the number of students who may sign up for each course (and thereby determine how many teachers may be required):

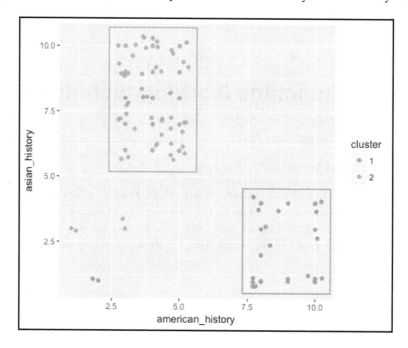

There are several variations of the K-Means algorithm, but the standard and the most commonly used one is Lloyd's Algorithm. The algorithm steps are as follows:

Given a set of n points (say in an x-y axis), in order to find k clusters:

1. Select k points at random from the dataset to represent the mid-points for k clusters (say, the *initial centroids*).
2. The distance from each of the other points to the selected k points (representing k clusters) is measured and assigned to the cluster that has the lowest distance from the point.
3. The cluster centers are recalculated as the mean of the points in the cluster.
4. The distance between the centroids and all the other points are again calculated as in Step 2 and new centroids are calculated as in Step 3. In this manner, Steps 2 and 3 are repeated until no new data is re-assigned.

Various *distance and similarity measures* exist for clustering, such as **Euclidean Distance** (straight-line distance), **Cosine Similarity** (Cosine of angles between vectors), **Hamming Distance** (generally used for categorical variables), **Mahalanobis Distance** (named after P.C. Mahalanobis; this measures the distance between a point and the mean of a distribution), and others.

Although the optimal number of clusters cannot always be unambiguously identified, there are various methods that attempt to find an estimate. In general, clusters can be measured by how close points within a cluster are to one another (within cluster variance, such as the sum of squares--WSS) and how far apart the clusters are (so higher distances between clusters would make the clusters more readily distinguishable). One such method that is used to determine the optimal number is known as the **elbow method**. The following chart illustrates the concept:

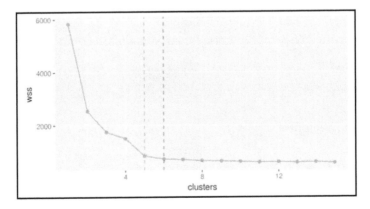

The chart shows a plot of the WSS (within the cluster sum of squares that we're seeking to minimize) versus the number of clusters. As is evident, increasing the number of clusters from 1 to 2 decreases the WSS value substantially. The value for WSS decreases rapidly up until the 4th or 5th cluster, when adding more clusters does not lead to a significant improvement in WSS. By visual assessment, the machine learning practitioner can conclude that the ideal number of clusters that can be created is between 3-5, based on the image.

 Note that a low WSS score is not enough to determine the optimal number of clusters. It has to be done by inspecting the improvement in the metric. The WSS will eventually reduce to 0 when each point becomes an independent cluster.

The neural networks related algorithms

Neural Network related algorithms have existed for many decades. The first computational model was described by Warren McCulloch and Walter Pitts in 1943 in the Bulletin of Mathematical Biophysics.

 You can learn more about these concepts at `https://pdfs.semanticscholar.org/5272/8a99829792c3272043842455f3a110e841b1.pdf` and `https://en.wikipedia.org/wiki/Artificial_neural_network`.

Various man-made objects in the physical world, such as aeroplanes, have drawn inspiration from nature. A neural network is in essence a representation of the phenomenon of data exchange between the axons and dendrons (also known as dendrites) of neurons in the *human nervous system*. Just as data passes between one neuron to multiple other neurons to make complex decisions, an artificial neural network in similar ways creates a network of neurons that receive input from other neurons.

At a high level, an artificial neural network consists of 4 main components:

- Input Layer
- Hidden Layer(s)
- Output Layer
- Nodes and Weights

This is depicted in the following image:

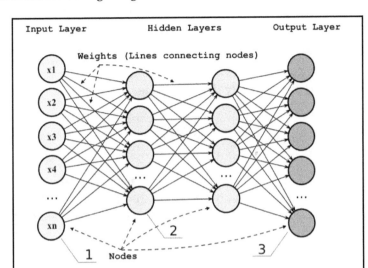

Each node in the diagram produces an output based on the input from the preceding layer. The output is produced using an **activation function**. There are various types of activation functions and the output produced depends on the type of function used. Examples include binary step (0 or 1), tanh (between -1 and +1), sigmoid, and others.

The following diagram illustrates the concept:

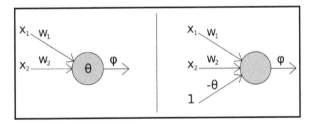

The values x1 and x2 are the inputs, w1 and w2 represent the weights, and the node represents the point at which the inputs and their weights are evaluated and a specific output is produced by the activation function. The output f can thus be represented by:

$$f\left(\sum_i (w_i * x_i) + b\right)$$

Here, f represents the activation function, and b represents the bias term. The bias term is independent of the weights and the input values and allows the user to shift the output to achieve a better model performance.

Neural networks with multiple hidden layers (generally 2 or more) are computationally intensive, and in recent days, neural networks with multiple hidden layers, also known as deep neural networks or more generally deep learning, have become immensely popular.

A lot of the developments in the industry, driven by machine learning and artificial intelligence, have been the direct result of the implementation of such multi-layer neural networks.

In R, the package nnet provides a readily usable interface to neural networks. Although in practice, neural networks generally require sophisticated hardware, GPU cards, and so on for illustration purposes, we have leveraged the nnet package to run the earlier classification exercise on the PimaIndiansDiabetes dataset. In the example, we will leverage caret in order to execute the nnet model:

```
library(mlbench)
library(caret)
set.seed(123)


data("PimaIndiansDiabetes")
diab<- PimaIndiansDiabetes

train_ind<- createDataPartition(diab$diabetes,p=0.8,list=FALSE,times=1)

training_diab<- diab[train_ind,]
test_diab<- diab[-train_ind,]

nnet_grid<- expand.grid(.decay = c(0.5,0.1), .size = c(3,5,7))

nnet_model<- train(diabetes ~ ., data = training_diab, method = "nnet",
metric = "Accuracy", maxit = 500, tuneGrid = nnet_grid)

# Generating predictions using the neural network model
nnet_predicted <- predict(nnet_model, test_diab)

> plot (nnet_model)
```

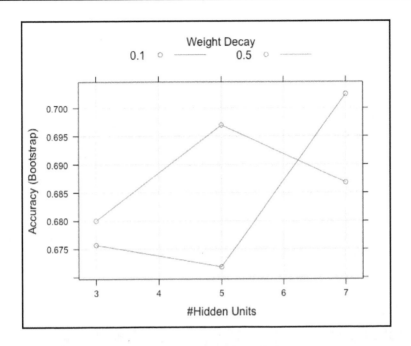

```
# Confusion Matrix for the Neural Network model

confusionMatrix(nnet_predicted,test_diab$diabetes)

Confusion Matrix and Statistics

          Reference
Prediction negpos
neg  86   22
pos  14   31

Accuracy : 0.7647
               95% CI : (0.6894, 0.8294)
    No Information Rate : 0.6536
    P-Value [Acc> NIR] : 0.001988

Kappa : 0.4613
Mcnemar's Test P-Value : 0.243345

Sensitivity : 0.8600
Specificity : 0.5849
PosPredValue : 0.7963
NegPredValue : 0.6889
Prevalence : 0.6536
        Detection Rate : 0.5621
```

```
Detection Prevalence : 0.7059
    Balanced Accuracy : 0.7225

      'Positive' Class :neg
```

Tutorial - associative rules mining with CMS data

This tutorial will implement an interface for accessing rules created using the Apriori Package in R.

We'll be downloading data from the CMS OpenPayments website. The site hosts data on payments made to physicians and hospitals by companies:

The site provides various ways of downloading data. Users can select the dataset of interest and download it manually. In our case, we will download the data using one of the Web-based APIs that is available to all users.

Downloading the data

The dataset can be downloaded either at the Unix terminal (in the virtual machine) or by accessing the site directly from the browser. If you are downloading the dataset in the Virtual Machine, run the following command in the terminal window:

```
time wget -O cms2016_2.csv
'https://openpaymentsdata.cms.gov/resource/vq63-hu5i.csv?$query=select
Physician_First_Name as firstName,Physician_Last_Name as
lastName,Recipient_City as city,Recipient_State as
state,Submitting_Applicable_Manufacturer_or_Applicable_GPO_Name as
company,Total_Amount_of_Payment_USDollars as
payment,Nature_of_Payment_or_Transfer_of_Value as
paymentNature,Product_Category_or_Therapeutic_Area_1 as
category,Name_of_Drug_or_Biological_or_Device_or_Medical_Supply_1 as
product where covered_recipient_type like "Covered Recipient Physician" and
Recipient_State like "NY" limit 1200000'
```

Alternatively, if you are downloading the data from a browser, enter the following URL in the browser window and hit *Enter*:

```
https://openpaymentsdata.cms.gov/resource/vq63-hu5i.csv?$query=s
elect Physician_First_Name as firstName,Physician_Last_Name as
lastName,Recipient_City as city,Recipient_State as
state,Submitting_Applicable_Manufacturer_or_Applicable_GPO_Name
as company,Total_Amount_of_Payment_USDollars as
payment,Nature_of_Payment_or_Transfer_of_Value as
paymentNature,Product_Category_or_Therapeutic_Area_1 as
category,Name_of_Drug_or_Biological_or_Device_or_Medical_Supply_
1 as product where covered_recipient_type like "Covered
Recipient Physician" and Recipient_State like "NY"
```

As shown in the following image:

Writing the R code for Apriori

The Apriori algorithm, as explained earlier, allows users to find relationships or patterns inherent in a dataset. For this, we will use the arules package in R/RStudio. The code will read the dataset downloaded (called `cms2016_2.csv` in the example) and run the apriori algorithm in order to find associative rules.

Create a new R file in RStudio and enter the following code. Make sure that you change the location of the csv file that you downloaded to the appropriate directory where the file has been stored:

```
library(data.table)
library(arules)

cms<- fread("~/cms2016_2.csv") # CHANGE THIS TO YOUR LOCATION OF THE DATA

cols <-
c("category","city","company","firstName","lastName","paymentNature","produ
ct")

cms[ ,(cols) := lapply(.SD, toupper), .SDcols = cols]

cms[,payment:=as.numeric(payment)]

quantile_values<- quantile(cms$payment,seq(0,1,.25))
interval_values<-
```

```
findInterval(cms$payment,quantile_values,rightmost.closed=TRUE)

cms[,quantileVal:=factor(interval_values,
labels=c("0-25","25-50","50-75","75-100"))]

rules_cols<-
c("category","city","company","paymentNature","product","quantileVal")

cms[ ,(rules_cols) := lapply(.SD, factor), .SDcols = rules_cols]

cms_factor<-
cms[,.(category,city,company,paymentNature,product,quantileVal)]

rhsVal<- paste0("quantileVal","=",c("0-25","25-50","50-75","75-100"))

cms_rules<-
apriori(cms_factor,parameter=list(supp=0.001,conf=0.25,target="rules",minle
n=3))

cms_rules_dt<- data.table(as(cms_rules,"data.frame"))
cms_rules_dt[, c("LHS", "RHS") := tstrsplit(rules, "=>", fixed=TRUE)]
num_cols<- c("support","confidence","lift")
cms_rules_dt[,(num_cols) := lapply(.SD, function(x){round(x,2)}), .SDcols =
num_cols]

saveRDS(cms_rules_dt,"cms_rules_dt.rds")
saveRDS(cms_factor,"cms_factor_dt.rds")
```

Shiny (R Code)

In RStudio, select **File** | **New File** | **Shiny Web App:**

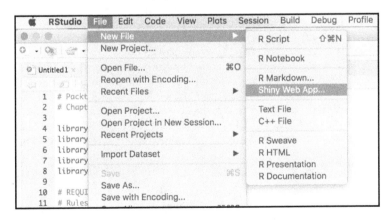

Enter the following code in app.R:

```r
# Packt: Big Data Analytics
# Chapter 8 Tutorial

library(shiny)
library(shinydashboard)
library(data.table)
library(DT)
library(shinyjs)


cms_factor_dt<- readRDS("~/r/rulespackt/cms_factor_dt.rds")
cms_rules_dt<- readRDS("~/r/rulespackt/cms_rules_dt.rds")

# Define UI for application that draws a histogram
ui<- dashboardPage (skin="green",
dashboardHeader(title = "Apriori Algorithm"),
dashboardSidebar(
useShinyjs(),
sidebarMenu(
uiOutput("company"),
uiOutput("searchlhs"),
uiOutput("searchrhs"),
uiOutput("support2"),
uiOutput("confidence"),
uiOutput("lift"),
downloadButton('downloadMatchingRules', "Download Rules")


    )
),dashboardBody(
tags$head(
tags$link(rel = "stylesheet", type = "text/css", href = "packt2.css"),
tags$link(rel = "stylesheet", type = "text/css", href =
"//fonts.googleapis.com/css?family=Fanwood+Text"),
tags$link(rel = "stylesheet", type = "text/css", href =
"//fonts.googleapis.com/css?family=Varela"),
tags$link(rel = "stylesheet", type = "text/css", href = "fonts.css"),

tags$style(type="text/css", "select { max-width: 200px; }"),
tags$style(type="text/css", "textarea { max-width: 185px; }"),
tags$style(type="text/css", ".jslider { max-width: 200px; }"),
tags$style(type='text/css', ".well { max-width: 250px; padding: 10px; font-
size: 8px}"),
tags$style(type='text/css', ".span4 { max-width: 250px; }")

        ),
```

```
fluidRow(
dataTableOutput("result")
)
        ),
        title = "Aprior Algorithm"
)


# Define server logic required to draw a histogram
server <- function(input, output, session) {

  PLACEHOLDERLIST2 <- list(
    placeholder = 'Select All',
onInitialize = I('function() { this.setValue(""); }')
  )

output$company<- renderUI({
datasetList<- c("Select
All",as.character(unique(sort(cms_factor_dt$company))))
selectizeInput("company", "Select Company" ,
datasetList, multiple = FALSE,options = PLACEHOLDERLIST2,selected="Select
All")
  })

output$searchlhs<- renderUI({
textInput("searchlhs", "Search LHS", placeholder = "Search")
  })

output$searchrhs<- renderUI({
textInput("searchrhs", "Search RHS", placeholder = "Search")
  })

  output$support2 <- renderUI({
sliderInput("support2", label =
'Support',min=0,max=0.04,value=0.01,step=0.005)
  })

output$confidence<- renderUI({
sliderInput("confidence", label = 'Confidence',min=0,max=1,value=0.5)
  })

output$lift<- renderUI({
sliderInput("lift", label = 'Lift',min=0,max=10,value=0.8)
  })

dataInput<- reactive({
    print(input$support2)
    print(input$company)
    print(identical(input$company,""))
```

```r
    temp <- cms_rules_dt[support > input$support2 & confidence
>input$confidence& lift >input$lift]

    if(!identical(input$searchlhs,"")){
searchTerm<- paste0("*",input$searchlhs,"*")
      temp <- temp[LHS %like% searchTerm]
    }

    if(!identical(input$searchrhs,"")){
searchTerm<- paste0("*",input$searchrhs,"*")
      temp <- temp[RHS %like% searchTerm]
    }

if(!identical(input$company,"Select All")){
      # print("HERE")
      temp <- temp[grepl(input$company,rules)]
    }
    temp[,.(LHS,RHS,support,confidence,lift)]
  })

output$downloadMatchingRules<- downloadHandler(
    filename = "Rules.csv",
    content = function(file) {
      write.csv(dataInput(), file, row.names=FALSE)
    }
  )

output$result<- renderDataTable({
    z = dataInput()
    if (nrow(z) == 0) {
      z <- data.table("LHS" = '', "RHS"='', "Support"='', "Confidence"='',
"Lift" = '')
    }
setnames(z, c("LHS", "RHS", "Support", "Confidence", "Lift"))
datatable(z,options = list(scrollX = TRUE))
  })

}  shinyApp(ui = ui, server = server)
```

The following image shows the code being copied and saved in a file called `app.R`.

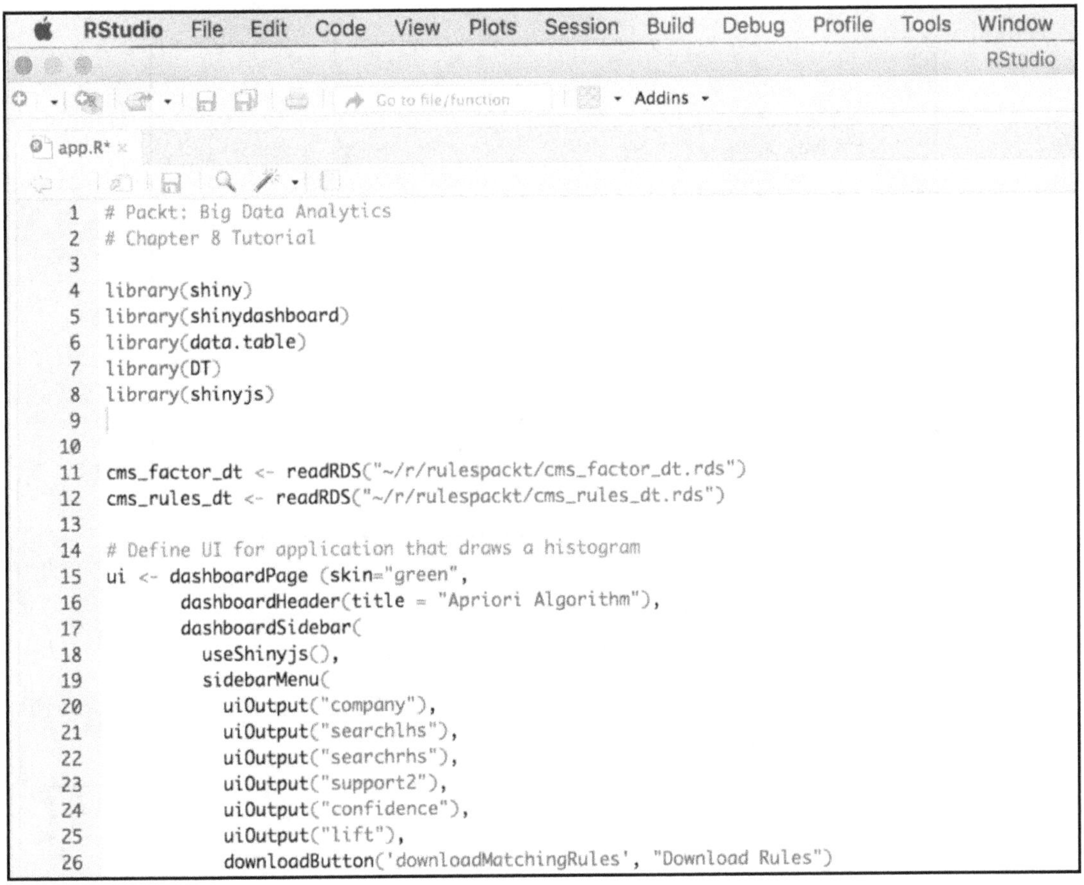

Using custom CSS and fonts for the application

For our application, we will use a custom CSS File. We will also use custom fonts in order to give the application a nice look-and-feel.

You can download the custom CSS File from the software repository for this book.

The CSS, Fonts, and other related files should be stored in a folder called `www` in the directory where you created the R Shiny Application:

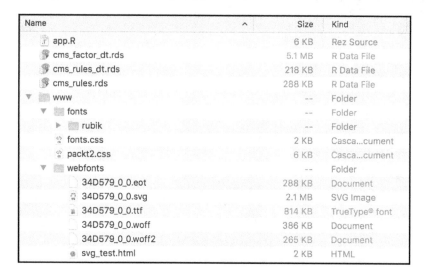

Running the application

If all goes well, you should be now able to run the application by clicking on the **Run App** option on the top of the page, as shown in the following images:

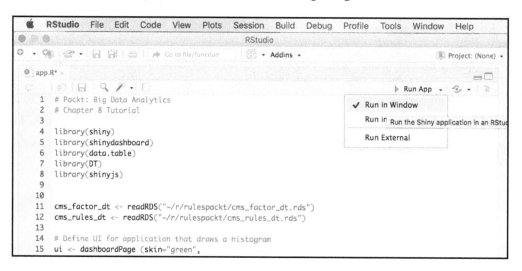

Upon clicking the "Run" button, the user will see a popup window similar to the one shown below. Note that popups should be enabled in the browser for this to function.

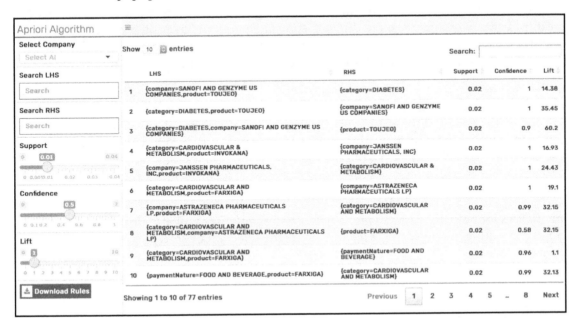

The app has multiple controls, such as:

- **Search LHS/RHS**: Enter any test that you want to filter for, in the Left-Hand Side or the Right-Hand Side of the rule.
- **Support**: Indicates the prevalence of the rule in the dataset.
- **Confidence**: Of the rules, how many were exact matches.
- **Lift**: Variable defining the importance of a rule. Numbers above 1 are considered significant.

You can use this app for any other rules file as long as they are processed in a way similar to the one outlined before in the R Script section.

Summary

Machine learning practitioners are often of the opinion that creating models is easy, but creating a good one is much more difficult. Indeed, not only is creating a *good* model important, but perhaps more importantly, knowing how to identify a *good* model is what distinguishes successful versus less successful Machine Learning endeavors.

In this chapter, we read up on some of the deeper theoretical concepts in Machine Learning. Bias, Variance, Regularization, and other common concepts were explained with examples as and where needed. With accompanying R code, we also learnt about some of the common machine learning algorithms such as Random Forest, Support Vector Machines, and others. We concluded with a tutorial on how to create an exhaustive web-based application for Association Rules Mining against CMS OpenPayments data.

In the next chapter, we will read about some of the technologies that are being used in enterprises for both big data as well as machine learning. We will also discuss the merits of cloud computing and how they are influencing the selection of enterprise software and hardware stacks.

9
Enterprise Data Science

We have thus far discussed various topics regarding both data mining and machine learning. Most of the examples shown were designed so that anyone with a standard computer would be able to run them and complete the exercises. In real-world situations, datasets would be much larger than those encountered in general home use.

Traditionally, we have relied on well-known database technologies such as SQL Server, Oracle, and others for organizational data warehouse and data management. The advent of NoSQL and Hadoop-based solutions made a significant change to this model of operation. Although companies were at first reluctant, the popular appeal of these tools became too large to ignore, and today, most, if not all, large organizations leverage one or more non-traditional contemporary solution for their enterprise data requirements.

Furthermore, the advent of cloud computing has transformed most businesses, and in-house data centers are being rapidly replaced by cloud-based infrastructures. The primary market leaders in the cloud space are Amazon (Amazon Web Services), Microsoft (Azure), and, to a lesser extent, Google (Google Compute Engine).

Data warehousing, data science, and machine learning needs are being delivered primarily on such platforms.

In this section, we will look at the various technical platforms that are prevalent in the corporate/enterprise market, their strengths, use cases, and potential pitfalls. In addition, we will also complete a tutorial using AWS to launch new instances on-demand using a trial account.

We will cover the following topics in this chapter:

- Enterprise data science overview
- Enterprise data mining
- Enterprise AI and machine learning
- Enterprise infrastructure
- Other considerations, such as data strategy, governance, and tool selection
- Amazon Web Services tutorial

Enterprise data science overview

Data science is a relatively new topic in terms of enterprise IT and analytics. Traditionally, researchers and analysts belonged broadly to one of two categories:

- Highly technical researchers who used complex computing languages and/or hardware for their professional tasks
- Analysts who could use tools such as Excel and BI platforms in order to perform both simple and complex data analysis

Organizations started looking into **Big Data** and, more generally, data science platforms in the late 2000s. It had gained immense momentum by 2013, when solutions such as Hadoop and NoSQL platforms were released. The following table shows the developments in data science:

Year	Developments
1970s to late 1990s	Widespread use of relational database management systems. Entity relationship model, structured query language (SQL), and other developments eventually led to a rapid expansion of databases in the late 90s.
Early 2000s	The anti-climatic, yet expensive, non-event of Y2K, coupled with the collapse of the dot-com `bubble` led to a period of stagnation. In terms of databases, or more generally, data mining platforms, this meant that companies were less focused on new innovations than they were on keeping the business running.

2005-2010	The industry slowly recovered, but it was not until 2005 that newer developments began to emerge. Some notable events included: • 2006: GoogleBigTable paper published • 2006: Amazon Web Services cloud platform launched • 2007: Amazon Dynamo paper published • 2008: Facebook makes Cassandra open source • 2009: MongoDB released • 2009: Redis released
2010-2012	2010: NoSQL conferences and related events start gaining popularity and *NoSQL* becomes a commonly accepted technical term. At the same time, Hadoop becomes widely popular, and nearly all major companies begin the process of implementing Hadoop-related technologies. 2011: Market leaders start adopting Big Data and forming Big Data strategies. Numerous articles and research papers claiming the huge potential of Big Data makes it very popular. McKinsey publishes a paper on Big Data and calls it the next frontier of *innovation, competition, and productivity*. The October 2012 edition of, *Harvard Business Review* includes a very positive outlook on data scientists, which becomes immediately popular.
2013-2015	The growth of Big Data technologies leads to the development of a concept called data science, which moves the focus from just the data to the value of the data. Coupled with developments in machine learning and the rise of the popularity of R, Python, and other data science-oriented platforms, the industry shifts attention to getting insights from data as opposed to merely managing data. Machine learning is the new buzzphrase.
2016-	The evolution of smart devices, wearables, AI-enabled cell phones, autonomous driving cars, and other such innovative solutions adds a new component of artificial intelligence to the existing trend of Big Data and machine learning. Manufacturers start broadly advertising the intelligent capabilities, as opposed to merely the machine learning capabilities, of technical solutions.

The responsibility for implementing a Big Data platform or, more generally, a Big Data Initiative, is generally delegated to the IT or Analytics Department of a company, if such a department exists.

In a general survey of Big Data and data science delegations in organizations, we observed that, in most cases, the Chief Information Officer or the Chief Data/Digital Officer was responsible for the **Enterprise Big Data Strategy**, as shown in the following figure:

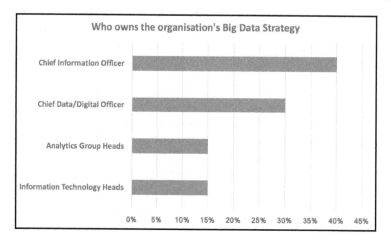

Although analytics and IT teams played a significant role, not surprisingly, the final responsibility was delegated to the C-level management of the company.

Investment in Big Data within the enterprise was also varied, with most organizations in the $100k to $1M range. An analysis of mid/large-scale organizations produced an expected result. What was evident, though, was that nearly *all respondents had made at least some investment in Big Data*:

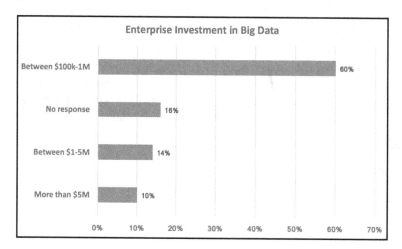

Most organizations also reported having a corporate mandate for **Advanced Analytics**. This helped in securing the required budget to implement and advance the state of analytics within the organization.

Furthermore, the predicted forecast of the revenue potential of data science greatly helped in making the case to senior management that a suitable investment in Big Data was essential to the future growth of a company.

With a current Big Data and Business Analytics revenue that has grown exponentially to more than $150 billion, the pressure on corporations to implement such capabilities, at least at a preliminary level, has been immense.

Another aspect of organizational awareness and acceptance of Big Data as a corporate mandate is the cultural perception of the utility of such tools. In a survey conducted with C-level management at large companies, most respondents stated that analytics was being used by managers in their departments, but there wasn't a uniform level of engagement across all departments, as shown in the following figure:

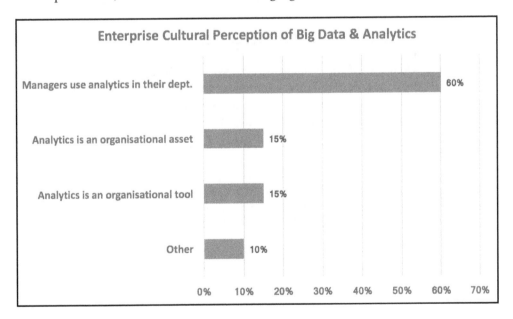

Furthermore, it appeared that the partnership strategies for Big Data across the organization were also not structured to the extent needed for commercial success. Respondents to the survey indicated that the partnership, as in, the cross-functional collaboration of analytics initiatives, was loosely defined:

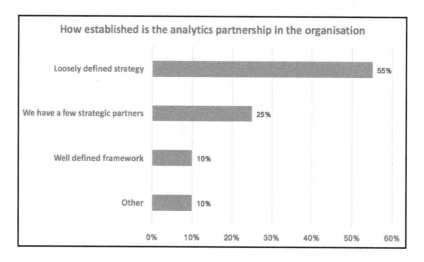

While the responses to some of the questions were skewed, with one category being the overwhelming majority, the feedback on organizational challenges with Big Data and analytics in general had a broad uniform consensus. The following chart shows the feedback on analytics challenges from each participant in the survey:

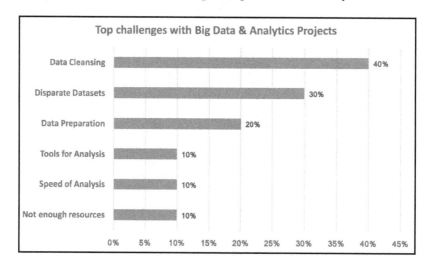

All of this leads to an interesting but paradoxical analytics dilemma in the enterprise. Although the merit of Big Data and analytics is widely understood and accepted, there is a sense of ambiguity regarding the appropriate approach, as shown in the following diagram:

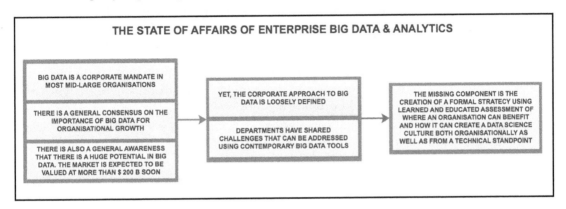

A roadmap to enterprise analytics success

In our experience, analytics, which is a fairly recent term compared to well-established terms such as data warehouse and others, requires a careful approach in order to ensure both immediate success and the consequent longevity of the initiative.

Projects that prematurely attempt to complete an initial analytics project with large-scale, high-budget engagement run the risk of jeopardizing the entire initiative if the project does not turn out as expected.

Moreover, in such projects, the outcome measures are not clearly defined. In other words, measuring the value of the outcome is ambiguous. Sometimes, it cannot be quantified either. This arises because the success of an analytics initiative has benefits beyond simply the immediate monetary or technical competencies. A successful analytics project often helps to foster executive confidence in the department's ability to conduct said projects, which in turn may lead to bigger endeavors.

The **general challenges** associated with Big Data analytics are as follows:

- Nearly every company is investing in Big Data, machine learning, and AI
- Often, the company has a corporate mandate
- Finding the right use cases can be challenging

- Even after you *find* them, the outcome may be uncertain (will this resonate, how long will it take, and so on)
- Even after you *achieve* them, whether or not the optimal targets have been identified can be elusive (for example, when using HDFS for storing only data)

Now, let's look at some **general guidelines** for data science and analytics initiatives:

- **Conduct meetings and one-on-one reviews with business partners** in the organization to review their workflows and get feedback on where analytics and/or data mining would provide the most value
- **Identify specific aspects of business operations** that are important and related to the firm's *revenue stream*; the use case would have a measurable impact once completed
- The use cases do not have to be *complex*; they can be simple tasks, such as ML or Data Mining
- Intuitive, easily understood, you can explain it to friends and family
- Ideally the use case takes effort to accomplish today using conventional means. The solution should not only benefit a **range of users**, but also have **executive visibility**
- Identify **Low Difficulty - High Value (Short)** vs **High Difficulty - High Value (Long)** use cases
- Educate business sponsors, share ideas, show **enthusiasm** (like a long job interview)
- Score **early wins** for **Low Difficulty - High Value**, create **Minimum Viable Solutions**, and get management to buy in before further enhancing the use solutions developed. (takes time)

Early wins act as a **catalyst** to a) foster executive confidence, and b) also makes it easier to justify budgets, which then makes it easier to move onto High Difficulty - High Value tasks.

The last two points are important as it is essential to identify Low Difficulty - High Value projects. This could be a task that appears *basic* to an experienced practitioner but is very valuable to the end user.

One of the executives of an analytics group in a large enterprise organization once remarked that the most successful project of the year was the *change of timing of an email report*. Instead of sending the report in the morning, the timing was changed to late afternoon. It appeared that engagement with the report became more active after the timing was changed. Morning schedules tend to be very busy and afternoon reports, on the other hand, provide recipients with the time to review the report at a more relaxed pace.

A few examples of *low difficulty* but *potentially high value* projects could be:

- Automating manual tasks conducted on a frequent basis by a business group; for instance, reports that are created in Excel may be easily automated using a combination of open source tools and databases.
- Converting manual stock analytics to automated versions using programming scripts. This could involve tasks such as creating regular tables, pivot tables, and charts that are created in Excel but can be converted into automated processes.
- Creating web interfaces using R Shiny for business applications and implementing predictive analytics functionalities.
- Moving certain parts of the IT infrastructure to a cloud platform. This may seem counter-intuitive, especially if the organization is not used to working in cloud environments. However, the ease and simplicity of managing cloud deployments can mean an overall reduction in the total cost of ownership and operational overhead.

The ultimate choice of the use case would depend on various factors, and the previous ones have been mentioned to set an approximate idea of the type of projects that may be attempted, and the workflows that may yield positive results. In the next section, we will look at some of the specific software and hardware solutions used in the industry for data science.

Data science solutions in the enterprise

As discussed before, in general, we can broadly categorize data science into two primary sections:

- Enterprise data warehouse and data mining
- Enterprise data science: machine learning, artificial intelligence

In this section, we will look at each of these individually and discuss both the software and hardware solutions used in the industry for delivering these capabilities.

Enterprise data warehouse and data mining

Today, there are scores of databases available in the industry that are marketed as NoSQL systems capable of running complex analytical queries. Most of them have one or more features of typical NoSQL systems, such as columnar, in-memory, key-value, document-oriented, graph-based, and so on. The next section highlights some of the key enterprise NoSQL systems in use today.

Traditional data warehouse systems

Traditional data warehouses might be a misnomer, since most of the *traditional* systems have also incorporated core concepts of NoSQL. However, in this case, the term is intended to indicate databases that existed well before the advent of NoSQL systems, and that have also added features that make them aligned with the requirements of Enterprise data science.

Oracle Exadata, Exalytics, and TimesTen

Oracle Exadata, Exalytics, and Exalogic belong to Oracle's Exa family of products. **Exadata** is Oracle's high performance *Engineered Database Platform* that is designed for resource intensive queries. In general, it is expected to significantly improve query performance over non-Exadata systems, and supports advanced software features such as in-memory computing, independent row and column-based filtering, and other hardware features such as support for the latest storage devices, including NVMe, in-memory fault tolerance, and others.

Exalytics is a complementary solution that is intended primarily for **BI** workloads. The Exa family of products are considered *engineered systems* as opposed to *appliances*. Whereas the latter may indicate preset and pre-loaded software-hardware stacks, an engineered system is expected to support a higher level of flexibility regarding the choice of installed components which are installed selectively depending on client needs. One of the key components of Exalytics commonly found in enterprise installations is **OBIEE (Oracle Business Intelligence Enterprise Edition)**. This is a complete BI suite and benefits from an underlying in-memory database called **Times Ten**, which is also a part of the Exalytics ecosystem.

Business use case: Oracle Exadata is used for OLTP transactional workloads where speed and performance is critical.

Exalytics, on the other hand, is used for analytical workloads. The integrated OBIEE interface together with TimesTen provides a strongly coupled analytics environment. Oracle Exadata is also available as a cloud-based service.

HP Vertica

Vertica from HP is a column-oriented, massively parallel processing database system with key software features such as support for in-database machine learning, and native integration to open source systems such as Apache Kafka and Apache Spark, and is generally deployed on a multi-node hardware architecture. Vertica is supported on popular cloud environments such as **Amazon Web Services** (**AWS**), Google, and Azure. Vertica supports a standard interactive SQL interface, thus making it readily compatible with most contemporary BI tools.

HP Vertica, interestingly, is one of the few enterprise databases that is also available as a Community Edition. This means that users who are interested in trying out Vertica (within the scope of its licensing), or who are simply learning more about the platform can leverage the Community Edition, which can be downloaded from HP Vertica's website at no charge.

Business use case: Similar to the other databases indicated in this section, Vertica incorporates several notable features such as in-database processing, parallel processing capabilities, and others. Vertica supports a wide range of analytical workloads and comes with associated commercial licensing fees (as do all the other commercial database products). The availability of a Community Edition, along with HP's willingness, in most cases, to engage in proof of concept for large deployments provides ample opportunities for business to try and test the platform with company-specific use cases prior to making a decision.

Teradata

Teradata is widely recognized as a leader in enterprise database technology. Its database, which also goes by the same name, shares several of the same features as other competitor products. Some key features of Teradata include native integration with many open source solutions, such as R, RStudio, Jupyter, and SAS; time series support; built-in analytic functions for machine learning and AI; support for a wide range of data types, such as CSV, JSON, and text, and spatial/temporal data.

The analytics platform, also known as Aster Analytics, is available as a Community Edition from `https://aster-community.teradata.com/community/download`.

While, traditionally, Teradata was available as an appliance solution, as in both the database as well as the hardware were available as a single integrated unit, today, it is also possible to use Teradata in the cloud using Teradata Everywhere. The software can be deployed in a hybrid architecture (both on-premises as well as in the cloud), as well as in public cloud environments such as AWS and Microsoft Azure. Bundled services, subscription-based services, and as-a-service options are available. Teradata Intellicloud is a subscription-based cloud offering from Teradata that includes several products from the Teradata ecosystem in a managed environment.

Business use case: Teradata has been a popular enterprise database for several decades and has strong credibility with large organizations. In recent years, Teradata's proactive integration with open source systems such as R, Jupyter, and other products made it more appealing and arguably helped increase its visibility. Teradata appliances can be relatively expensive and, as with other commercial options, require proper POCs to assess suitability for use cases specific to the organization.

IBM data warehouse systems (formerly Netezza appliances)

IBM Netezza used to be sold as a separate data warehouse appliance, in some ways similar to how Teradata was also marketed. Recently, Netezza has been moved under the broader categorization of IBM Data Warehouse systems which is more aligned with the contemporary Big Data requirements for managing very large volumes of data. IBM Pure Systems, PureSystems for Analytics, and IBM Integrated Analytics System are some of the newer solutions that provide essentially the same functionalities of Netezza in an integrated ecosystem.

The Integrated Analytics environment includes embedded Apache Spark for machine learning, Jupyter Notebooks for data science workloads, a common SQL engine that connects to other NoSQL and Hadoop implementations, and support for deployments on high performance architecture with the option of managed, cloud-based environments

Business use case: Netezza has been favored by firms that have traditionally had strong dependency on IBM-related technologies, such as DB2, AIX, and other products from IBM. The new integrated product environment provides an opportunity to continue using whilst adding data science capabilities to existing IBM investments in the organization.

PostgreSQL

PostgreSQL is an interesting choice in this section because, technically, there is no separate NoSQL version of PostgreSQL, but rather PostgreSQL has added various features in recent releases that have added NoSQL capabilities to the existing Postgres implementation.

Proponents of PostgreSQL rightly point out that it is a much older, and, by extension tested technology, having been first released in the mid-1990s. **Postgres** now supports hierarchical document data storage, JSON, a key-value store (called **HStore**), and sharding, and includes interfaces for various programming languages as well as diverse data sources. In other words, PostgreSQL has been extended to support NoSQL-like functionalities while maintaining its existing capabilities as a traditional RDBMS.

PostgreSQL is available as a fully-functional, open source product.

Business use cases: While most of the technologies in this section are available under commercial licensing (to get access to all their capabilities), PostgreSQL, being open source, is a very cost-effective way to try out a mature database without making large initial investments. It can also serve as a testing platform for trying out NoSQL features, such as handling JSON data prior to making a final decision. In either case, PostgreSQL is a formidable platform and can support enterprise needs. There are also commercial derivatives of PostgreSQL—databases that build on top of PostgreSQL such as Greenplum, which is also available as an open source product.

Greenplum

Greenplum Database® is built on top of PostgreSQL, and adds a number of significant analytic capabilities. These include an innovative cost-based query optimizer, integration with Apache MADlib, and choices for ®">row or columnar storage. It has native interfaces for popular programming languages such as R, Python, and Java, and supports massively-parallel architectures. Greenplum is available for download at no charge from `http://greenplum.org/download/`.

Business use cases: A commercial distribution of Greenplum with full support is available from **Pivotal**. Greenplum has been very successful, not least because of its proven performance for large enterprise workloads. The availability of commercial support has been beneficial to organizations who require dedicated support and service-level agreements (**SLA**) that guarantee critical business operations.

SAP Hana

SAP Hana is a columnar, in-memory database from SAP with support for NoSQL features. Hana supports multicore parallel operations, multi-tenancy, and is fully **ACID** compliant and can handle a diverse range of analytical workloads including predictive modelling, streaming analytics, time series analysis, and spatial, text, and graph-based analysis. You can also manage JSON based unstructured data within an SAP Hana system.

Hana also works natively with other SAP products such as SAP Fiori, which includes a wide range of SAP UX applications used in HR, finance, accounting, and other departments.

Business use cases: SAP has been a mainstay for enterprise organizations for several decades and is used for a wide range of applications, most notably perhaps for manufacturing and financial/accounting requirements. SAP Hana adds a formidable high-performance database to existing SAP installations. In general, due to the high cost involved with enterprise-grade deployments, SAP is used mainly for business-critical needs. The benefits of Hana for large organizations that are dependent on SAP may outweigh the costs. Furthermore, while Hana can deliver a wide range of NoSQL capabilities, companies may find that they will end up with two or more different solutions based on budget, performance needs, and other factors.

Enterprise and open source NoSQL Databases

The prior section outlined some of the well-known traditional database/RDBMS solutions that have added enterprise-grade NoSQL capabilities. This upcoming sections looks at some of the more niche business use cases specific to database solutions.

Kdb+

The **kdb+** from Kx Systems is one of the fastest, most efficient and lightweight databases that has been used in high-frequency trading and other similar environments for almost two decades. Its popularity outside of finance has been much less pronounced, but nevertheless, it is arguably one of the most efficiently designed and optimized systems in the world of databases.

Kdb+ supports in-memory columnar storage from the outset and is technically an extension of the **q** programming language. A table in kdb+ is in essence a data structure in the q language. However, unlike similar concepts in other programming languages, a kdb+ table is enterprise-grade and can easily handle terabytes and petabytes of data.

Due to its inherent programming language, code that is written in q can be run against data stored in kdb+, so a custom *function* can be run in-database with very minimal effort.

Additionally, the size of the kdb+ binary is about 500 to 600KB, small enough to fit in the L3 cache of most modern CPUs.

Kdb+ also includes built-in MapReduce capabilities so that queries are automatically executed in parallel across muticore CPUs.

Business use case: Kdb+ is one of the most formidable databases to have existed in an enterprise setting. It was traditionally available only for perpetual core-based licensing, but in recent days, the company has added support for subscription-based and on-demand licensing. Its low footprint and simplicity of use makes it well suited for enterprise needs. However, this comes with a caveat. The q language is very terse and can appear cryptic to new users. The language, arguably, has a slightly steeper learning curve than others and requires practice and first-hand experience. That said, there are ample online resources to learn and utilize the features of the database. Native interfaces for R, Python, C, Java, and other programming languages, along with libraries used for machine learning, make it particularly well suited for data science workloads involving large datasets.

While kdb+ is not available as an open source product, it is generally available for personal use at no charge from: `https://kx.com/download/`.

MongoDB

MongoDB is a market leader in the space of document-oriented databases for the storage of data in JSON format. It supports on-demand querying, indexing, and aggregations, and has a rich interface for Python, Java, and JavaScript, among other languages. Other features, such as horizontal scaling and sharding, high availability, an integrated data exploration tool called Compass, and others, add to the existing capabilities of the database.

Business use cases: Companies considering databases for storing unstructured or semi-structured data may find the features of MongoDB well suited for querying such datasets. The database does not require a fixed schema to be defined at the onset, making it flexible and extensible to support new attributes that are added to existing data. MongoDB is available as a free open source download from
`https://www.mongodb.com/download-center` and can also be implemented as a managed and hosted cloud solution via MongoDB Atlas. An enterprise version that supports features such as in-memory and encrypted storage is also available on a subscription basis.

Cassandra

Cassandra is one of the most successful and widely used enterprise NoSQL systems. It incorporates both columnar and key-value concepts and stores data in row-based partitions. Each partition is in turn a primary key. Rows can have multiple columns and the number of columns may differ from one row to another.

Cassandra databases can be queries done via CQL, which uses a SQL-like syntax and makes the process of data querying, saving, and other common tasks much easier. Cassandra also uses a decentralized architecture; it does not have any single point of failure and supports multi-node architecture.

In addition to the standard horizontal scalability of Cassandra DBMS, the platform also supports Elastic scalability and is able to transparently allocate and de-allocate nodes depending upon needs. On the whole, Cassandra is one of the most formidable options for enterprise NoSQL systems and is used in production environment across multiple large firms globally.

Business use case: Cassandra is a fully open source solution and implements multiple key features of NoSQL systems. It is used in production workloads globally and has matured into a stable, enterprise-grade, open source platform. In other words, Cassandra is well suited for managing large organizational needs and does not incur any additional licensing costs. A commercial, licensed, and paid version of Cassandra is also available from Datastax: `https://www.datastax.com/products/datastax-enterprise`. It is known as **DSE** (**Datastax Enterprise**). DSE incorporates various enterprise features such as security and search, and can also be accessed via the Datastax Managed Cloud environment using popular cloud providers such as AWS.

Neo4j

Neo4j is a graph-based database that is used to model relationships between different entities. The database uses familiar concepts in graph theory to create tree-based representations (with nodes and relationships) of interconnected subjects. It is used most commonly in conjunction with recommendation engines. Conceptually, a Neo4j graph database could represent individuals as nodes who are connected to one another by, say, their degree of separation. This would hypothetically allow an end user to trace the degrees of separation between any arbitrary node or one individual to another.

Various graph-based representations such as weighted, directed, unidirectional, and labelled are available in the Neo4j platform.

Business use case: Companies that require deep customer-level or user-level analysis such as social networks or recommendation systems (such as Netflix), stand to gain an immense benefit from deploying graph-based databases such as Neo4j. Today, the platform supports AI and machine learning, iOT, real-time recommendations, and many other useful characteristics used in enterprise.

Although Neo4j is available as open source software from `https://neo4j.com/download/?ref=hro`, there is also a commercial licensed version known as Neo4j Enterprise Edition.

Cloud databases

Cloud databases, as the name suggests refers to data warehouse or database systems available from cloud vendors such as Amazon, Google, and Microsoft.

Amazon Redshift, Redshift Spectrum, and Athena databases

One of the most commonly used cloud-based data warehouse platforms is **Amazon Redshift**. It is the most prominent platform for data management in the cloud-based ecosystem. It is based on PostgreSQL and is intended mainly for analytical workloads. Redshift is highly scalable and requires significantly less effort relative to on-premises databases with similar characteristics. It can be deployed directly from the AWS console (after signing up for an AWS account). Nodes can be added or removed seamlessly via the AWS Console to increase and/or decrease capacities respectively.

A more recent release of Redshift known as **Redshift Spectrum** permits the querying of data that has been stored in Amazon S3, the standard storage layer in AWS. This means that users can directly query data stored on disk without having to load it into a Redshift-specific instance. Overall, Redshift is relatively fast, inexpensive, and more importantly easy to use and deploy. Redshift Spectrum uses a pay-per-query model—users pay only for the queries that are executed at a nominal charge for each terabyte of data scanned.

Amazon Athena is in many respects similar to Amazon Redshift Spectrum, in that it is also used to query data that is stored on S3. However, while the features of Amazon Redshift Spectrum cannot be used without first purchasing Amazon Redshift, users can leverage Amazon Athena on-demand and do not need to reserve any additional hardware. On the other hand, because Amazon Redshift Spectrum is closely integrated with the Redshift ecosystem, users can distribute their workload on either of the two solutions. Data that needs faster processing can remain on Amazon Redshift, whereas less frequently used/less critical data can be stored on S3 and queried using Redshift Spectrum:

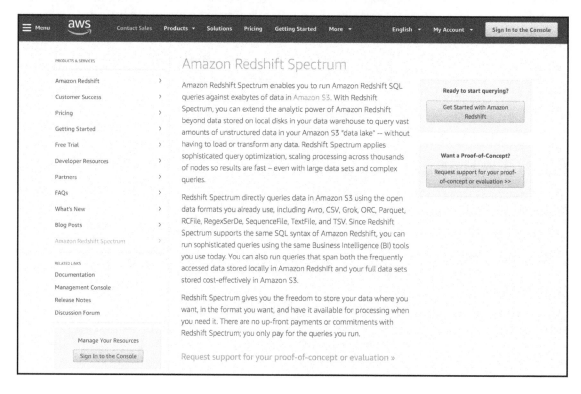

You can learn more about Amazon Redshift Spectrum at `https://aws.amazon.com/redshift/spectrum/`.

Google BigQuery and other cloud services

Google BigQuery is similar to Amazon Redshift, in that it is also a large-scale data warehouse system that is fully cloud-based. However, while Redshift requires separate provisioning (of an AWS cluster and Redshift resources), Google BigQuery is the *plug-and-play* equivalent of the same. To use BigQuery, the user simply needs to create an account at `https://bigquery.cloud.google.com` and begin running queries after loading their datasets.

The charging method of BigQuery is also quite different in comparison to Redshift. Users can query a cumulative of 1 terabyte of data at no charge per month. BigQuery uses a pay-per-use model whereby queries have allocated costs. In essence, BigQuery abstracts the complexity of setting up a database and allows the end user to dedicate time to writing queries and/or performing analytics without the overhead of setting up an infrastructure. Scaling queries, allocating resources, and tasks that may have otherwise required manual intervention (by a DBA for example), hence become redundant.

Google also has a set of other NoSQL products on its cloud platform, including Google Cloud Datastore, a NoSQL document-based database; Google BigTable; Google Spanner; and several others. The following figure shows the Google BigQuery database:

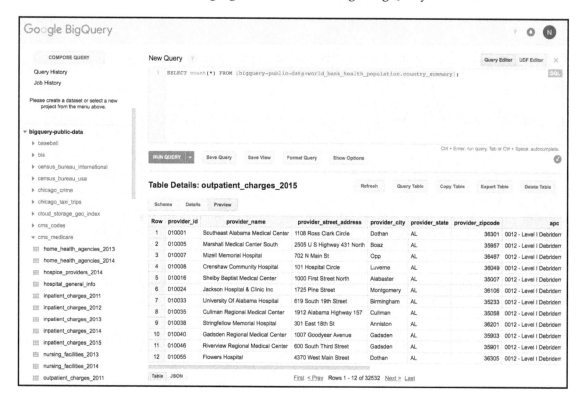

Azure CosmosDB

The **Azure CosmosDB** is one of Microsoft's NoSQL cloud-based databases. Other NoSQL systems in Azure include Table Storage, Azure Redis Cache, and others. CosmosDB is considered a *multi-model* database; it can support key-value pairs, document-based queries, graph-based models, and also relational database queries.

Traditional Microsoft databases, such as, SQL Server are also available and are supported as fully managed and hosted solutions on the Azure platform. You can learn more about the Azure platform at `https://azure.microsoft.com/en-in/services/cosmos-db/`. The following figure shows the Microsoft Azure platform's **Solutions** window:

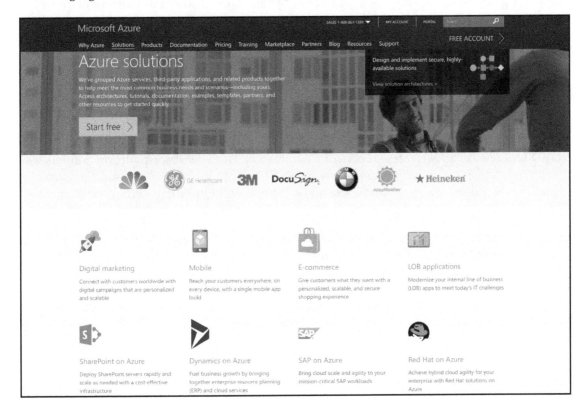

GPU databases

GPU databases are a more recent development that came with the growth of Graphics Processing Unit cards for data science related tasks, such as machine learning. GPUs work best when the query can be parallelized. This is due to the fact that GPUs contain thousands of cores. By delegating each core to work on a small subset of the data, a GPU can often calculate at an impressively fast rate that far exceeds the CPU-based query performance.

Brytlyt

Brytlyt is a recent entrant in the space of GPU databases. It is complemented by a visualization product called **Spotlyt**. Early testing has shown that Brytlyt surpasses several challenging benchmarks. However, how well it generalizes in other use cases remains to be seen.

Brytlyt is available in the Amazon AWS Marketplace (`https://aws.amazon.com/marketplace/pp/B074JZNSWZ?qid=1513342415797sr=0-1ref_=srh_res_product_title`) for those wish to try it.

MapD

MapD was one of the early developers of a commercial GPU database platform. Similarly to Brytlyt, it has also shown impressive early results. Nevertheless, as GPU-based databases are still in their early stages, popular use and adoption will ultimately determine whether they will become commonplace in enterprise.

One of the primary challenges of GPU-based databases is the need to configure a GPU-based system properly. This can require specialized skills, as using GPU cards for computation is quite different than using GPU cards for common tasks such as rendering images. Due to this, users wishing to try out GPU-based databases prior to adopting a formal version would find it easier to leverage a pre-configured image in AWS (AMI Image), which would require minimal system configuration.

Other common databases

There are various other types of databases, such as ones that are used for analyzing streaming data (Amazon Kinesis), and those that process data using specialized Accelerator Cards using FPGAs from Baidu.

Enterprise data science – machine learning and AI

Data science solutions have matured rapidly over the past 4 - 5 years, similar to the movement in other areas of data science such as NoSQL, Hadoop, and other data mining solutions. Although many of the prior database systems also incorporate key features of *data science*, such as machine learning and others, this section highlights some of the solutions at a high level that are primarily used for machine learning and/or AI, as opposed to data management.

Indeed, the distinction between *Big Data* products and *data science* products has become blurred, since products that were originally intended for Big Data handling have incorporated key features of data science, and vice versa.

The R programming language

R, as we have seen in prior chapters, is an environment originally designed for statistical programming. It emerged out of a project at the University of New Zealand, where *Ross Ihanka* and *Robert Gentleman* developed R as a variation of the S programming language developed by John Chambers in Bell Labs. Although R was initially intended for *statistical programming*, over the last 7 to 8 years it has evolved into a mature, multifaceted language with enhanced support for a diverse range of related disciplines such as machine learning, high performance computing, visualization, econometrics, TimeSeries analysis, and much more. Some of these areas are also described with accompanying information at `https://cran.r-project.org/web/views/`.

A commercial version of R with enterprise support was available from Revolution Analytics. In 2015, it was rebranded as **Microsoft R Open** (open-source version) and **Microsoft R Server** (commercial version).

Although marketed under the Microsoft brand, note that Microsoft R is also available for Linux and Mac OS.

Popular machine learning packages in R include `e1071`, `randomForest`, `gbm`, `kernlab`, `arules`, and many more. These are listed at `https://cran.r-project.org/web/views/MachineLearning.html`. Another popular package, called caret, acts as a wrapper around various algorithm packages and provides a useful unified interface to run algorithms without having to conform to the nuances of the packages individually.

R also supports multicore programming via packages such as `multicore`, `doMC`, and others. These are listed at
`https://cran.r-project.org/web/views/HighPerformanceComputing.html`.

Python

The `scikit-learn` package in Python is arguably the most comprehensive machine learning package among all platforms that incorporates an extensive list of machine learning algorithms. It is also considered to be faster compared to R, and is the tool of choice for various enterprise organizations. The following screenshot shows the web page from which we can download the `scikit-learn` package:

A commercially supported enterprise version of Python that comes pre-configured with useful machine learning and data mining packages is `Anaconda`, available from Continuum Analytics. A cloud version of Anaconda called **Anaconda Cloud** allows new users to start leveraging the features of Anaconda Python without the overhead of downloading and installing it separately.

OpenCV, Caffe, and others

Image recognition is one of the more successful areas of machine learning. While most machine learning tasks require a relatively long period of time before their true benefits can be measured and quantified, image recognition is a familiar subject area that can be readily understood. In essence, it involves identifying objects and correctly categorizing them. It has several applications, ranging from identifying license plate numbers to face recognition, and is available in mobile devices and robotics.

OpenCV provides a standard interface for various image recognition tasks, and can also leverage hardware acceleration features to optimize performance.

Other well-known machine learning software for image processing include Caffe, cuDNN, TensorFlow, and others. Note that these packages are not limited to simply image recognition, but can be also used for other deep learning use cases.

Spark

The MLlib library in Spark provides a formal implementation of various machine learning algorithms that can be used in a Spark platform. The availability of pySpark makes the process of using the functionality easier for those with Python programming knowledge. If the organization had an existing Spark platform, it would be worth exploring the machine learning capabilities in MLlib.

The following screenshot gives you a brief overview of MLlib:

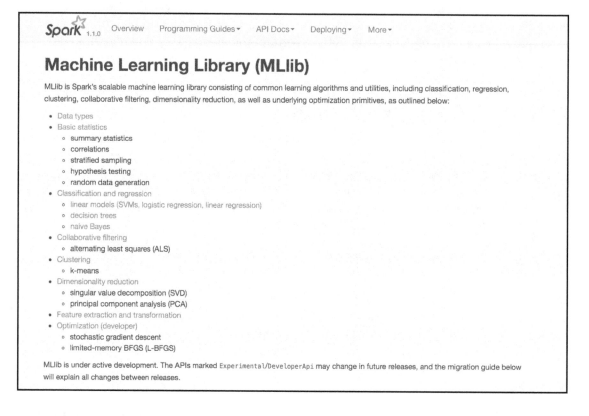

Deep learning

Neural Networks with multiple hidden layers (generally more than two) and/or nodes are generally categorized as **deep learning**. Several contemporary advances in machine learning, such as autonomously driving cars, are a direct result of the use of deep learning for practical day-to-day tasks.

There are various deep learning frameworks/packages, and some notable ones include:

- TensorFlow
- cuDNN
- Theano
- Torch
- PaddlePaddle, from Baidu

H2O and Driverless AI

A popular platform for Kaggle competitions, **H2O** provides a massively scalable, real-time machine learning interface with native integration for R, Python, Spark, and much more. It is available for download, at no charge, from `https://www.h2o.ai/h2o/`.

Driverless AI is a recent addition to the H2O line of products. It aims to make machine learning easier for practitioners by implementing an automated interface that attempts to create models and optimize accuracy by building and evaluating multiple models in an automated manner. The following screenshot shows the homepage of the H2O platform:

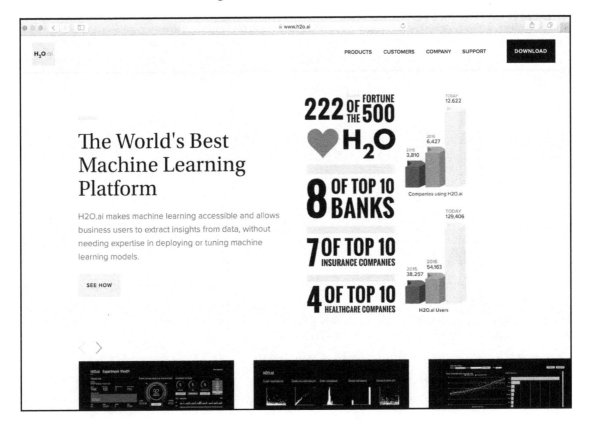

Datarobot

Conceptually, Datarobot is similar to H2O's Driverless AI in that it also attempts to build machine learning models in an automated manner by creating and evaluating multiple models against a given dataset.

However, unlike H2O, although it can be very powerful, Datarobot requires a licensing fee and can be expensive for smaller firms.

Command-line tools

There are multiple machine learning tools that are executed at the Unix command-line. There are existing interfaces for some of these tools in R, Python, and other languages that permit users to leverage their capabilities without having to use them from the Unix terminal. Some of the popular command-line utilities include:

- LIBSVM
- LIBLINEAR
- Vowpal Wabbit
- MLPACK
- libFM

Apache MADlib

One of the lesser-known but feature-rich platforms is **Apache MADlib**, which aims to perform analytics and run algorithms *in-database*, as in, it can execute functions locally without requiring an external programming interface. It supports parallel processing and can work seamlessly with multiple data sources such as Greenplum, PostgreSQL, and others.

As an example, an apriori model can be created by simply running an SQL command, as shown here, from `http://madlib.apache.org/docs/latest/group__grp__assoc__rules.html`:

```
SELECT * FROM madlib.assoc_rules(.25,            -- Support
                                 .5,             -- Confidence
                                 'trans_id',     -- id col
                                 'product',      -- Product col
                                 'test_data',    -- Input data
        NULL,           -- Output schema
```

```
                                    TRUE              -- Verbose output
);
```

Further information about Apache MADlib (screenshot of site shown below) is available at http://madlib.apache.org.

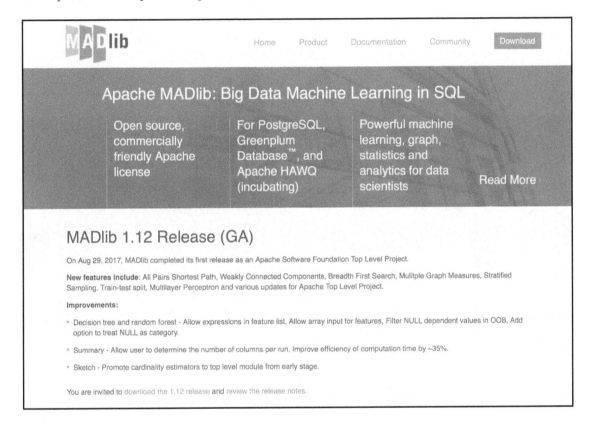

Machine learning as a service

Cloud-based machine learning platforms that integrate with other cloud resources have also proliferated. Some of the well-known platforms include AzureML, BigML, IBM Watson, and others.

The screenshot below is from IBM Watson, one of the most well-known platforms for machine learning and artificial intelligence. The platform gained prominence after it won the Jeopardy championship in 2011 [Source: `https://www.techrepublic.com/article/ibm-watson-the-inside-story-of-how-the-jeopardy-winning-supercomputer-was-born-and-what-it-wants-to-do-next/`]. At the time, the Machine Learning trend was in a nascent state and Watson was one of the first AI technologies that took the world by surprise. It proved that AI can be powerful and capable asset. Users can today leverage some of the same computing capabilities of IBM Watson by signing up for an account on the site `https://www.ibm.com/watson/`.

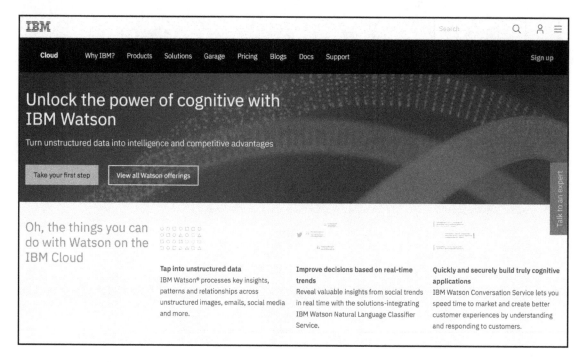

Enterprise infrastructure solutions

The proper choice of infrastructure also plays a key role in determining the efficiency of the organization's data science platform. Too little, and the algorithms will take too long to execute; too much and you may have a lot of resources remaining unutilized. As such, the latter is preferable to having too little, which thwarts progress and the ability of any machine learning researcher to efficiently perform his or her tasks.

Cloud computing

Over the past 5 - 7 years, organizations have gradually shifted their resources to cloud-based platforms such as Amazon Web Services, Microsoft Azure, and Google Compute Engine. Today, all of these contain extremely sophisticated and extensive architecture to support machine learning, data mining, and in general *data science* at an enterprise level to meet the needs of organizations of all sizes.

In addition, the concept of *images*, such as AMI images in Amazon's AWS, allows users to initiate a pre-built snapshot of an OS with pre-installed components. As a result, users can almost entirely avoid the setup overhead prior to trying out new platforms.

Hadoop and map-reduce operations in general are also supported extensively in AWS. The **EMR**, or **Elastic Map Reduce** in AWS, and HDInsight in Azure, are two well-known and very popular Big Data frameworks.

The tutorial at the end of this chapter will demonstrate how to set up an AWS account and start using a sample AMI Image.

Virtualization

Virtualization—the process of creating isolated, self-contained environments within a larger host, has allowed organizations to consolidate servers and dramatically reduce data center footprints. If, say, an organization leverages six servers for their websites, and of those, two get utilized frequently whereas the others have relatively lower loads most of the time, it may be possible to consolidate all the servers into one or two servers at most. In this regard, technologies from Dell EMC, such as VxBLOCK, are well-known enterprise virtualization hardware used in physical data centers. This also allows companies to create their own private cloud infrastructure. However, it can be fairly expensive and requires the proper assessment of the cost-to-benefit ratio.

An open source software used for creating public and private clouds is Openstack. It is an enterprise-grade ecosystem with multiple products that works seamlessly within the Openstack platform. Further details about Openstack are available at `https://www.openstack.org`:

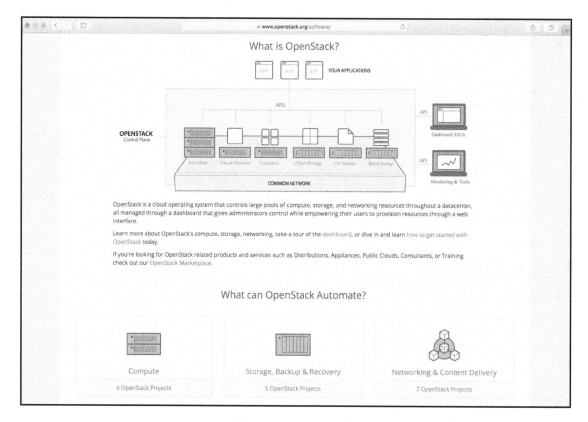

Users may be familiar with Oracle Virtualbox, which, in essence, is also a type of virtualization software that permits users to create isolated environments. This allows users to run Linux within Windows, and vice versa.

Specialized software or hardware, known as hypervisors, are used to manage and administer virtual machines.

Containers – Docker, Kubernetes, and Mesos

Containers, like virtualization, create isolated guest systems, but, while Virtual Machines create a completely separate environment, containers share the same kernel as the host system and hence are considered to be closer to the hardware. Both virtualization and containers incur performance penalties due to multiple layers of abstraction—the translation of functionalities between a host and guest OS. However, containers in general have a higher level of performance because they rely on and directly use features of the guest OS instead of creating a separate OS ecosystem.

Popular containers include Docker, CoreOS, and many others. Today, containers are used for the large-scale management of mainly web-related services. Containers can be started up and shut down on demand much more readily than VMs, and popular cloud providers have added dedicated support for containers, making it easy to start up thousands of containers to service web requests with simply a few lines of code. Orchestration software such as Kubernetes provide enterprise-grade capabilities for managing containers. Furthermore, platforms, such as Mesos, not only provide support for managing containers, but also add the capability of managing other legacy hardware for application-aware scheduling and other services:

On-premises hardware

Finally, on-premises hardware, such as the traditional data center, still has a place in modern-day computing. With a physical data center, users do not have to pay recurring fees for cloud-based services. For small to mid-sized organizations that do not have large administrative overhead, or for organizations that do not require high-performance/specialized computing capabilities, on-premises systems are fully capable of delivering cost-efficient, permanent solutions.

Companies such as ScaleMP provide specialized hardware that is used for high-performance computing. Consumers of such hardware usually have specific requirements that cannot be provided by cloud-based vendors:

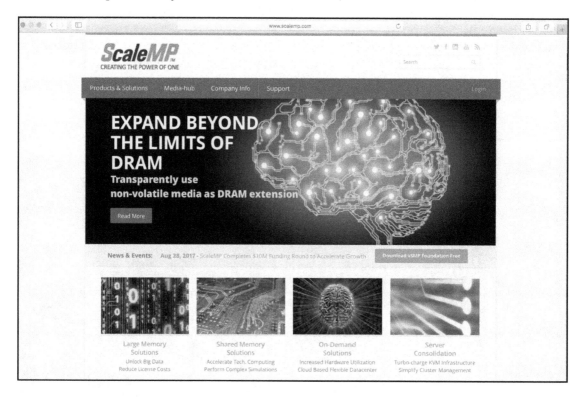

A summary of some of the differences between on-premises and cloud-based systems is shown below:

On-premises	Cloud
You own the hardware	You lease the hardware
Requires full maintenance	Maintenance is managed by a cloud-hosting provider
Requires IT resources for managing computing hardware resources	Much less overhead in terms of managing computing hardware resources, as they can be added on-demand in the cloud
Cost efficient for small to mid-sized environments with low or no data center operation cost	Cost efficient for large organizations that are looking to simplify data center operation costs
No recurring cost for using hardware other than resources required to manage them	Recurring cost to use the hardware; uses a subscription model for pricing
Mainly static architecture; new requirements for Hadoop will require a complete range of new purchases	Extremely flexible; companies can provision thousands of servers in multiple operating systems on-demand
Are readily accepted by organizational, legal, and associated departments	Faces obstacles, in particular from legal departments, due to the delegation of management to a third-party/cloud-hosting provider

Enterprise Big Data

The overall strategy of Big Data implementation in large organizations depends on the particular needs of the organization. Today, there are hundreds of options to choose from between Big Data, data science, machine learning and, of late, AI providers.

As such, there are two main considerations while implementing Big Data in large organizations:

- **Technical**: The selection of the proper software and hardware stack
- **Operational**: Management of the organizational data, creating a formal data governance strategy, and creating an adequate data management framework

Apart from these, hiring the right talent and possibly creating well-defined roles for the company's Big Data/data science implementations are additional but equally essential tasks.

Some key questions in the creation of such a strategy include:

- Is the software/hardware licensing based on size or cores? If it is based on the size of data and my data size increases, what will be my 3 year/5 year cost?
- Does the solution have enterprise support?
- Do we need to hire external resources?
- What business questions will the new capabilities answer?
- Have we done short and long-term cost-benefit analysis?
- What are the present unmet needs of the organization that the new solutions can answer?
- Is the solution scalable enough to meet my potential future needs?

In terms of technical needs, although there are many solutions in the marketplace, it is extremely essential in practice to conduct testing or proof of concept using real-world/actual data that the solution will be used for. It is not uncommon to find solutions that claim grand capabilities but do not deliver expectations. **In other words, it is crucial to gather thorough empirical results and not purchase solely on the basis of a marketing pitch.**

Lastly, as Big Data/data science is constantly evolving, the long-term scalability and adaptability of the solution needs to be properly evaluated. The cloud-based option should be considered in light of the fact that it provides an efficient medium to access and use new and emerging solutions in an easy and affordable manner.

Tutorial – using RStudio in the cloud

The following tutorial will demonstrate how to create an account on **AWS** (Amazon Web Services), load an AMI Image for RStudio, and thereafter use RStudio, all at *no charge*. Readers who are experienced in using cloud platforms may find the instructions quite basic. For other users, the tutorial should provide helpful initial guidance on using AWS.

Please read the **Warning** message below prior to proceeding.

Warning: Note that AWS requires a credit card for signup. Users must be careful and select only the options for the FREE TIER. The AWS agreement permits Amazon to bill users for incurred charges. Due to this reason, users should use the platform judiciously to avoid potentially expensive unexpected charges from servers or services that are left running.

 As of this time, Azure and Google Cloud offer user signups with provisions to avoid inadvertent charges. However, AWS has the highest market share among all cloud vendors, and users are likely to encounter AWS in most workplace situations. Hence, this tutorial focuses on AWS rather than the alternatives.

Instructions on how to close your account have also been provided at the end of the tutorial, should you wish to discontinue your use of AWS (and thus also prevent any charges):

1. Go to `https://aws.amazon.com/`and click on the **Create an AWS Account** button at the top-right:

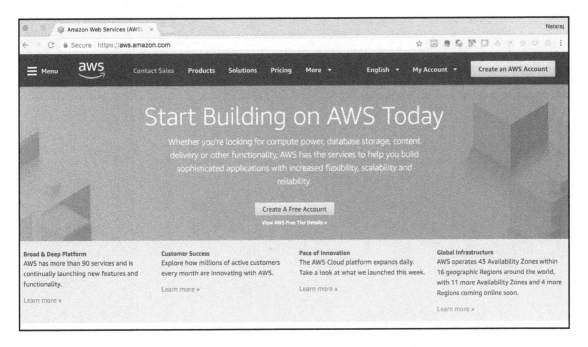

2. An AWS account generally includes 12 months of initial free tier access. Enter your information and click on **Continue**:

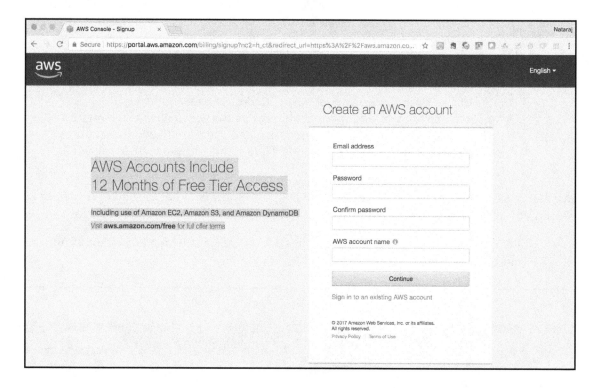

3. Select your **Account type** (such as **Personal**) and enter your contact information:

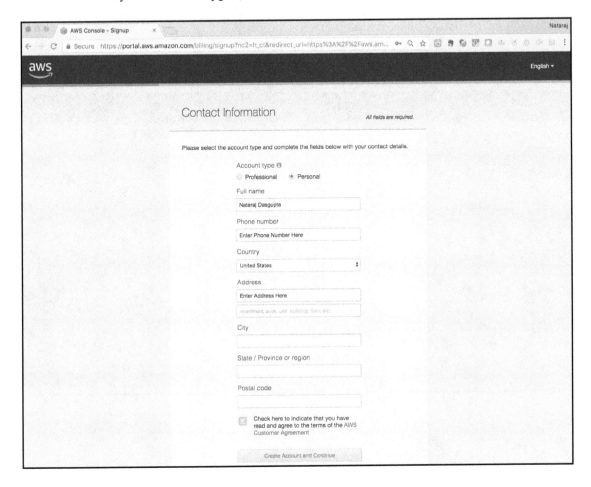

4. Enter the payment information. AWS requires a credit card for signup. Note that users must utilize AWS resources very carefully and judiciously in order to ensure that there are no inadvertent charges:

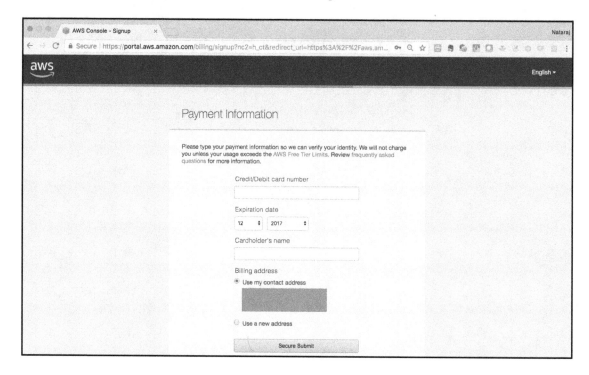

5. You'll receive a confirmation once the payment information has been verified:

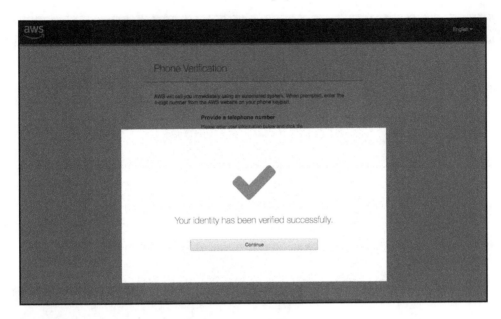

6. Select the **Basic Plan** (Free):

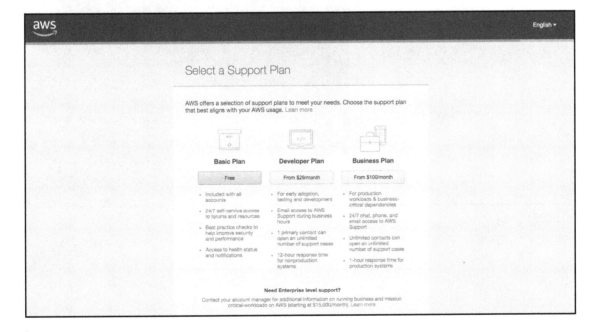

The confirmation page after selecting the **Basic Plan** is as follows:

7. Log in to AWS with your credentials:

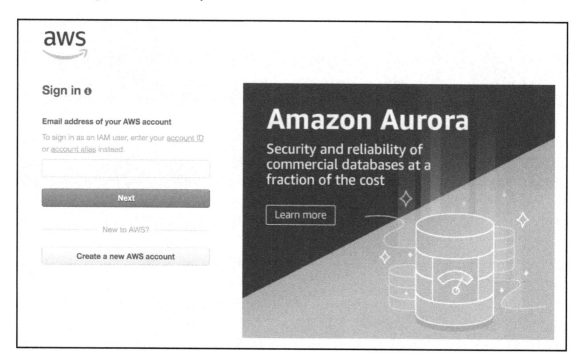

8. The first page shows some of the services in AWS. The top-right shows the **region** of your instance. AWS supports multiple regions, and users can select from a range of geographically-dispersed locations:

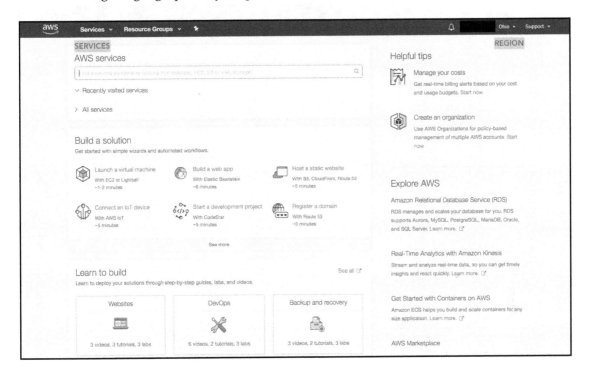

9. Clicking on the top-left drop-down menu for **Services** will bring up the different services available. Some of the important ones are highlighted here:

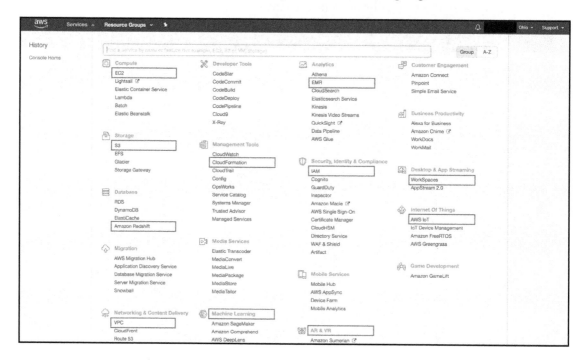

10. Click on **EC2**:

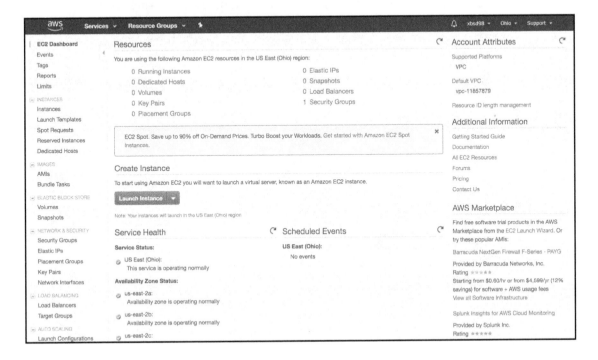

11. AWS provides the option to launch multiple different OSs. While we can start a new instance afresh with a selected OS, we will be instead using an AMI image. AMIs are preconfigured images with installed software. Note that using an AMI image is **not** required, but one is being used here for the tutorial:

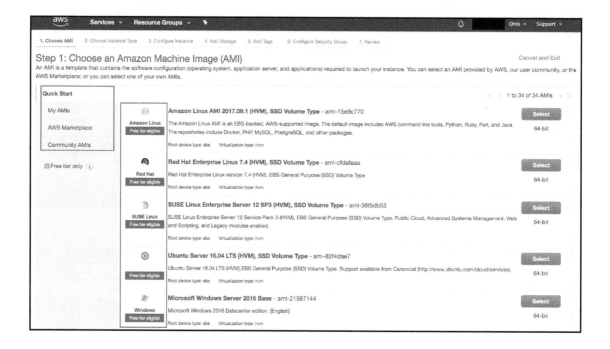

12. Click on **Community AMIs** on the left menu bar and search for **RStudio**. Select the first option and click on the Select button:

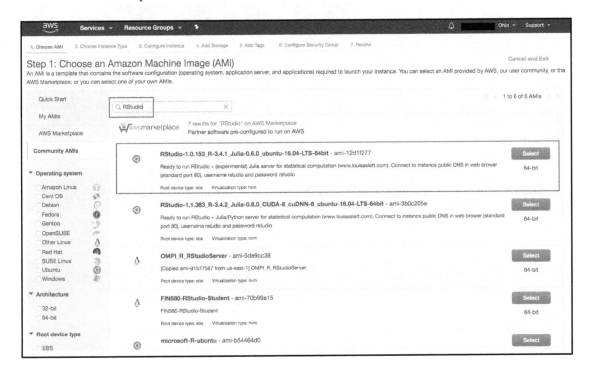

13. Select the free tier option (**t2.micro**) and click **Next: Configure Instance Details**:

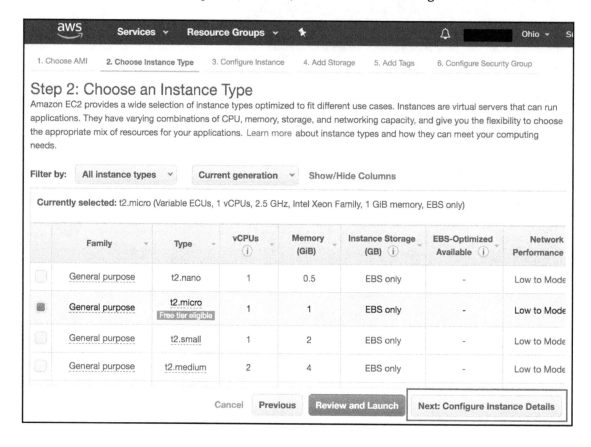

14. Select the default options on the next page and click **Next:Add Storage**:

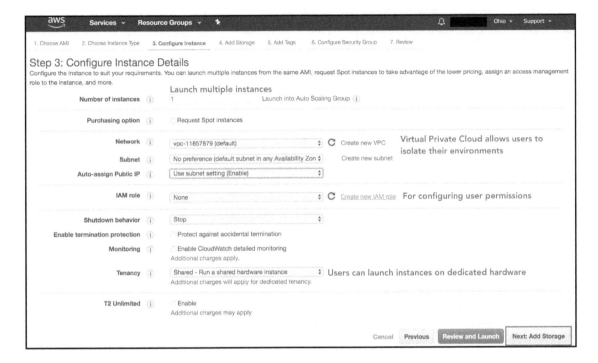

15. Select the default storage options and click on **Add Tags**:

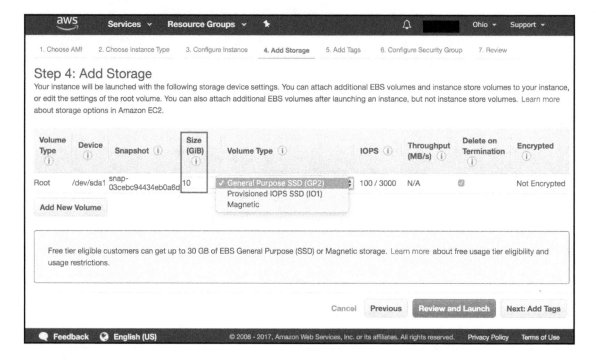

16. Click **Next:Configure Security Group**:

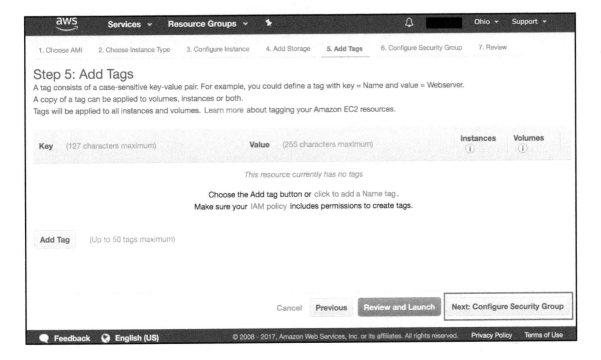

17. Security groups specify the network access rules for the server. For our tutorial, we will select **All TCP** and click **Review and Launch**:

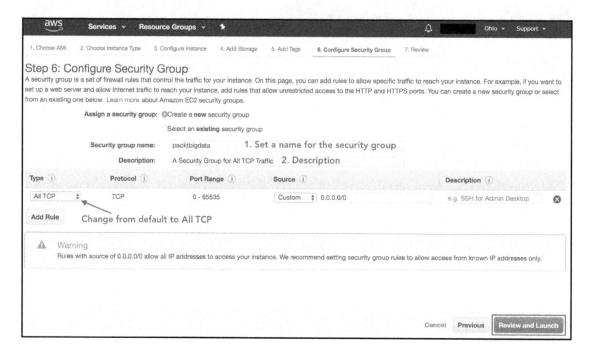

18. Click **Launch**:

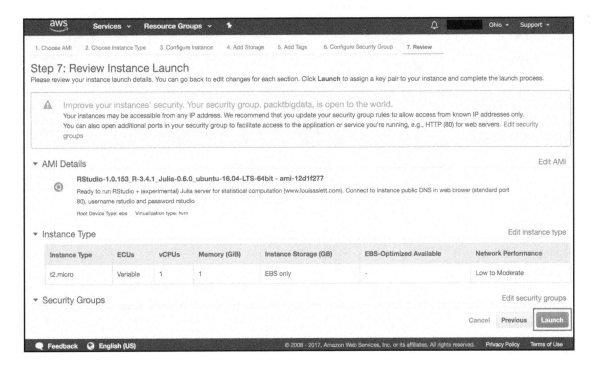

19. Select **Create a new key pair**, and click **Download Key Pair**. Once the key finishes downloading, click on the **Launch Instances** button:

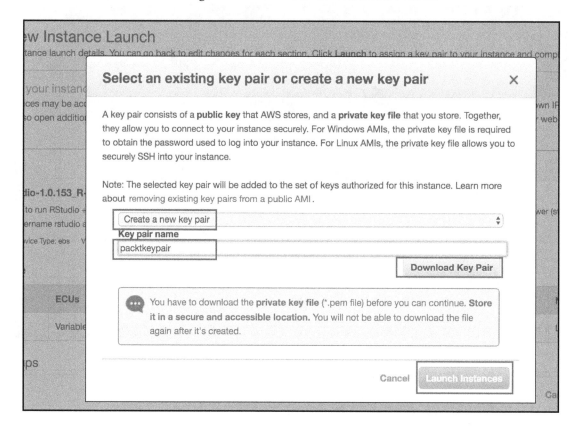

20. Click on the instance ID:

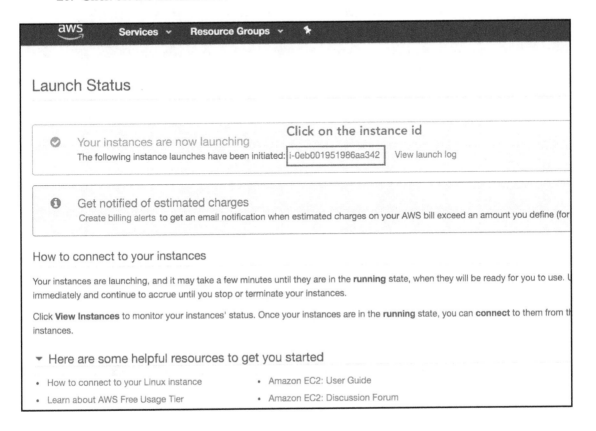

21. Once the status of the instance ID is displayed as **running**, copy the name of the server, which can be viewed in the bottom panel:

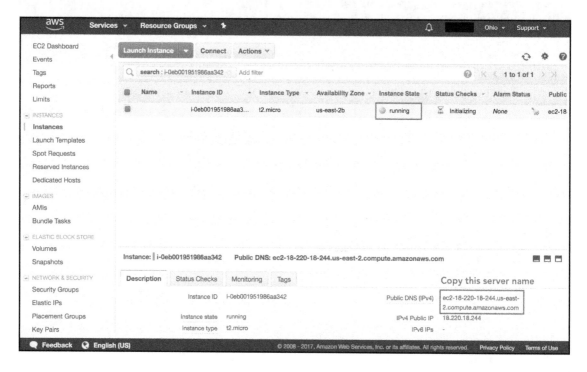

22. Open a new browser, enter the name of the server as the URL, and hit Enter. This will bring up RStudio. Log in with the ID **rstudio** and password **rstudio**:

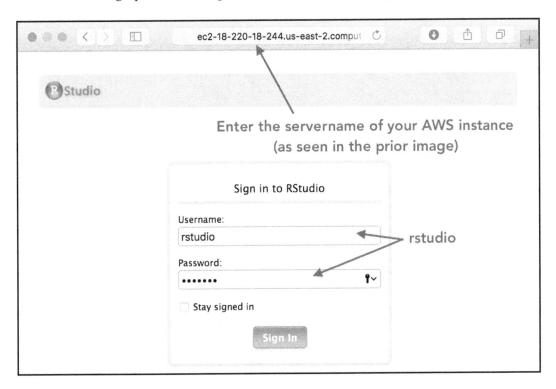

23. This will bring up the RStudio console. This is a complete R environment and you can execute R code just as you would in a local installation of R and RStudio:

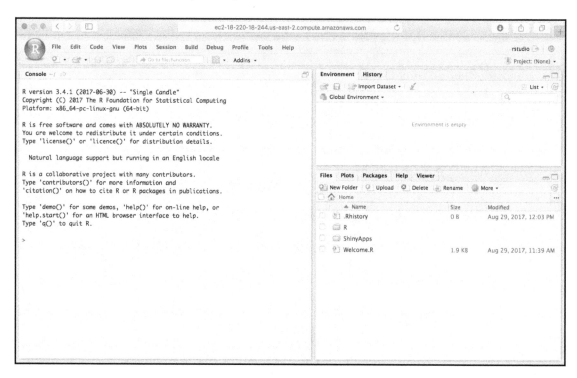

24. Once you have finished using R Studio, make sure that you `terminate` the instance. Termination stops the billing process. Even though we are using the free tier account, it is good practice to stop or terminate the instance once you have finished your work:

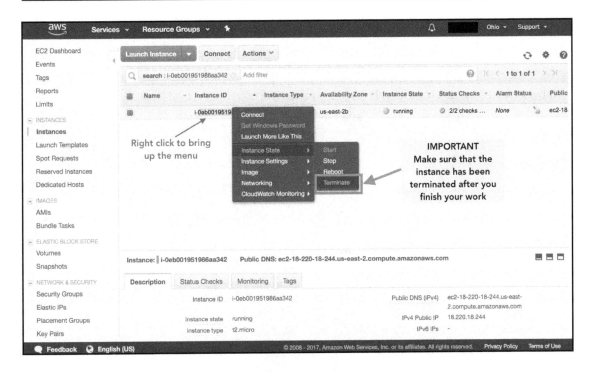

25. Click **Sign Out** to log out of the AWS console:

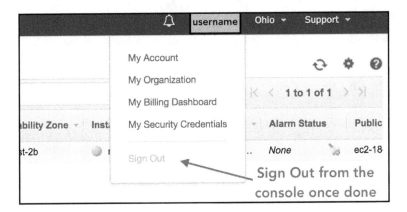

Azure also offers free account signups at `https://azure.microsoft.com/en-us/free/`, as shown in the following screenshot:

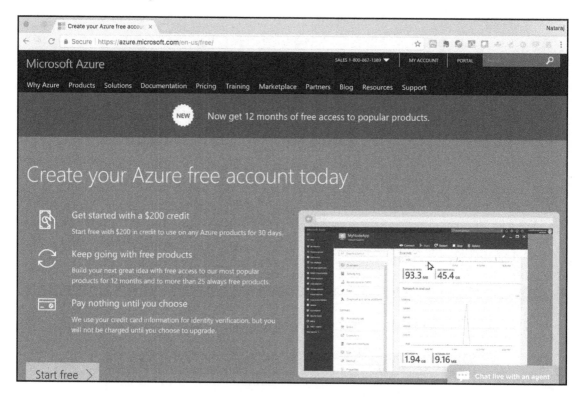

Google's free cloud signup form is available at `https://cloud.google.com/free/`, as shown in the following screenshot:

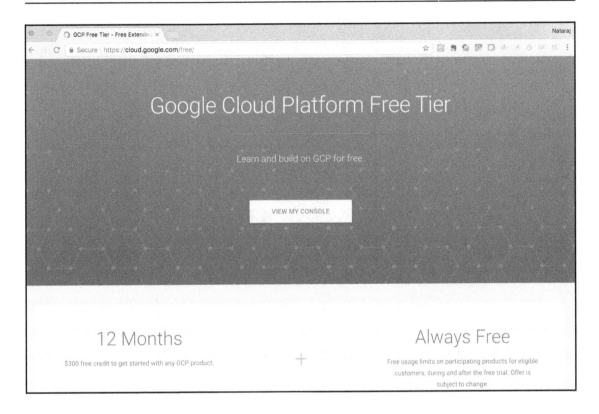

Summary

In this chapter, we discussed the requirements for deploying enterprise-scale data science infrastructures, both at a software as well as a hardware level. We shared key common questions around such initiatives at a management level. This was followed by an extensive section on key enterprise solutions that are being used for data mining and machine learning in large organizations.

The tutorial involved launching an RStudio Server on Amazon Web Services (a cloud-based system). AWS has become the leading provider of cloud services in the world today, and the exercise showed how simple it can be to launch entire machines in a few seconds. Appropriate pros and cons about the judicious and careful use of AWS to prevent very expensive charges were mentioned.

The next and final chapter will include some closing thoughts, the next steps, and links to useful resources you can use to learn more about the topics that have been discussed in this book.

10
Closing Thoughts on Big Data

We have covered a broad range of topics thus far. We have looked at technologies used for big data, for data science, and for machine learning. We have learned about how companies are implementing their big data corporate strategies. We have also developed a handful of real-world applications along the way.

This chapter discusses the practical considerations of big data or data science initiatives at corporations. The field is continually evolving, with the introduction of newer technologies, newer open source tools, and new concepts in data mining. Due to this, organizations of all sizes share common challenges.

Data science success stories are everywhere in the media. In fact, most, if not all, of the investment happening in technology today has some connection to aspects of data science. Indeed, it has become an indispensable and integral aspect of IT development.

In this chapter, we will discuss a few of the common themes of implementing data science, the shared challenges, and what you can do to make your initiative successful. Further, we'll look at major successes in data science as well as examples where data science failed to live up to its promise. We'll also provide a set of links to resources where you can go to learn more about the relevant topics.

The following subjects will be covered in this chapter:

- Corporate big data and data science strategy
- Ethical considerations
- Silicon Valley and data science
- The human factor
- Links for further reading

Corporate big data and data science strategy

You have read about it in the papers, you have seen it on the evening news, you have heard about it from your friends – big data and data science are everywhere and they are here to stay.

The success stories from Silicon Valley have made the effect even more pronounced. Who would have thought that a ride-sharing and ride-hailing phone application, Uber, could become one of the most popular companies in the world with an estimated valuation of close to $70 billion. Sites and apps such as Airbnb turned apartment-sharing into a booming business, becoming the second most valued company at $30 billion.

These and other similar events transformed the topics of big data and data science from being purely theoretical and technical subjects into common terminology that people have come to associate with unbounded investment success.

Since nearly all major technology vendors have started adding features categorized as *big data*, nearly all companies that invest in technology today are using some facets of big data, knowingly or otherwise.

The process of implementing however, is very loosely defined. As such, there is no definitive framework, other than perhaps Hadoop, which has been the de facto framework that most companies have adopted. Senior level management are often aware of the big picture, namely, the value that big data can bring to their organizations. However, the path to realizing the vision is challenging and as such there is no definitive solution that can guarantee success.

Broadly speaking, there are three stages of implementation:

- **Dormant**: When the company has not yet established a firm mandate, but there are discussions about big data
- **Passive**: The discussions start taking a more formal shape, usually leading to the delegation of a team/teams to assess the impact and value to the organization
- **Active**: The company starts assessing technologies and engages in active implementation

The ownership of the big data and/or data science strategy can be somewhat confusing. This is due to the fact that the field encompasses elements of both analytics as well as technology. The former, analytics, is usually owned by the business-facing divisions of the organization, whereas technology is owned by IT departments. However, in data science, both elements are required. Individuals who are data *specialists*, that is, those who understand the domain very well and have experience with the data used in the domain, can be great business subject matter experts. They may also be able to comprehensively identify the ideal use cases and how the data can be best utilized. However, without having strong technical acumen, it would be difficult to identify the right tools to realize the vision.

In similar terms, an IT manager may be very knowledgeable about big data-related technologies, but would require the feedback of business stakeholders to effectively determine which of the various solutions will meet the specific immediate and long-term needs of the organization.

In other words, multiple cross-disciplinary streams need to collaborate in order to implement a truly effective organizational big data ecosystem.

The process of realizing the strategy is generally either *top-down* or *bottom-up*. However, rather than adopting a rigid directional approach, a collaborative, iterative, and agile process is often the best solution. There will be decisions, and changes to decisions based on new requirements and discoveries during the course of assessing big data needs, and prior evaluations may need to be modified in order to meet modified objectives.

The bottom-up approach involves structuring decisions starting at the IT level. The top-down approach, which is arguably more common, involves making decisions starting at the management level. Neither is generally optimal. The ideal approach is one where there is a continuous feedback loop that adjusts requirements based on a process of discovery:

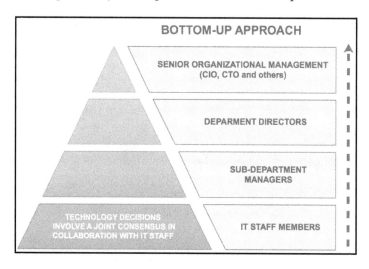

In contrast, the top-down approach is as follows:

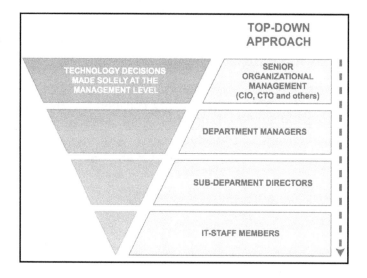

Neither the bottom-up nor the top-down approach is optimal for a successful big data initiative. A better option is a collaborative process that takes into account the shifting needs and diverse requirements of different departments that stand to benefit from the implementation of a big data platform:

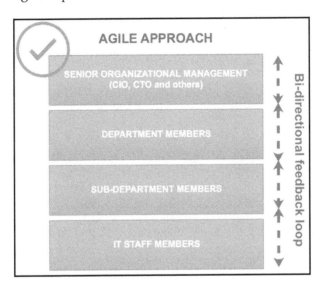

Ethical considerations

Big data often involves the gathering of large volumes of data that may contain users' personal information. Companies such as Facebook and Google have flourished on analyzing individual information to target ads and perform other types of marketing. This evidently poses an ethical dilemma. To what extent should personal data be collected? And how much is *too much?* There are, of course, no correct answers to these questions. The rise of hacking in which information from hundreds of millions of user accounts has been compromised is so commonplace today that we have almost become complacent about the consequences.

In October 2017, Yahoo! disclosed that 3 billion accounts, in fact every single account on Yahoo!, had suffered a data breach. **Equifax**, one of the largest credit reporting companies in the US suffered a data breach that exposed the personal details of more than 140 million consumers. There were scores of other similar incidents, and in all of them, the common denominator was that all the companies collected some level of users' personal information, whether directly or via third parties.

In essence, whenever user-related information is involved, it begets the implementation of suitable IT security in order to ensure that the data does not get compromised. The repercussions are not limited to only the loss of data, but collateral damage due to impact on reputation and goodwill, apart from the primary fact that real people are involved whose data has been compromised.

Thus, the security of big data, whenever it involves sensitive information and/or any personal information, becomes critically important. Cloud providers, such as AWS and Azure, have gained traction partly due to the fact that they have very stringent standards of security as well as certifications that allow organizations to offload the responsibility to a trusted and formidable entity.

The EU **GDPR** (**General Data Privacy Regulation**), effective May 2018, is an excellent step toward securing the personal data of its citizens. In a nutshell, the GDPR regulates the use of any personal data. In this context, the term any is extremely broad, including even the very name of an individual. Violators of the rule will be fined up to 20 million euro, or 4 percent of the global turnover of the defaulting organization.

While this will evidently reduce the availability of *Big Data* datasets, especially those that relate to individual data, it may also stir a debate and perhaps innovations on how data can be put to best use within the constraints, that is, getting value from data without using personal information.

On the other hand, countries such as the US have been relaxing laws around the collection of personal data. In early 2017, the US removed privacy protections around collection of personal information by internet service providers and in fact made it legal for ISPs such as AT&T to not only collect but also sell users' browsing and app data.

Silicon Valley and data science

Several of the key innovations we see today in big data have emerged from Silicon Valley. The region has been a tech hub for decades and has launched some of the most successful companies such as Apple, Google, Facebook, and eBay. The presence of universities, such as the University of California at Berkeley, has made access to talent relatively easy.

That said, the cost of living in the region has sky-rocketed, especially in the wake of the growth of the big data and data science industry. Today, the average rent for a one-bedroom apartment is well above $3,500 per month, making it more expensive than even New York City.

Silicon Valley, however, is synonymous with success and many new entrepreneurs are drawn to the region. Startups have sprung up, many of them commanding tens of millions of dollars in VC investment. However, entrepreneurs should heed statistical warnings given the high failure percentage of startup businesses. It is one thing to have a great idea, with a potential high commercial value. Turning the idea into a commercial success requires a different kind of skill and business acumen.

For those interested, the website Crunchbase offers a very comprehensive view into activities in the startup arena. The following image shows the average figures on investments that have happened on any given 7-day period, which may be in the tens of billions of dollars:

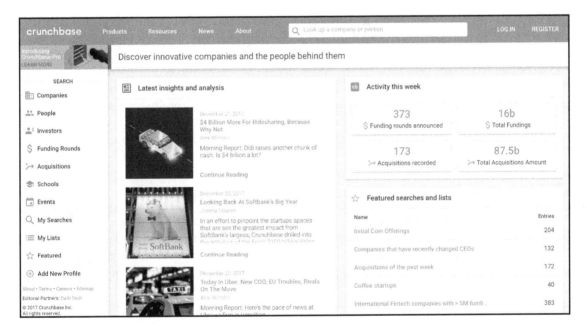

The human factor

The significant advantages of big data and data science notwithstanding, their successes and breakthrough growth, it is still important to bear in mind that the element of human thinking is essential in all endeavors.

Big data technologies will allow us to analyze data more efficiently. But we still need to use proper judgment to decide on our ideal use cases. This is not trivial. Large companies find initiatives just as challenging (although at a higher scale) as seasoned big data professionals.

Similarly, data science and machine learning can empower us to make predictions and gain foresight with the help of sophisticated algorithms and code. However, it is still incumbent upon the user to evaluate the results and make decisions not solely based on the predicted output. Users should apply common sense and experience in making such assessments. If the GPS instructs the driver to go on a certain road on a snowy winter night and the driver knows that the road won't have been cleared by the snowplow, it wouldn't be prudent to follow the GPS instructions blindly.

A recent example that illustrated this concept is the disconnect between man and machine during the 2016 election. Extensive models that estimated, using very sophisticated algorithms, the high probability of Clinton winning the elections were all proven wrong. Eminent data scientists and leading statistical organizations estimated that there was an 80-90 percent chance of a Clinton presidency. What we all missed was the human element of making decisions. We relied too intently on model sophistication instead of trying to understand how people really felt and whether their assertions on, say, an informal survey would be aligned with their final choice of candidate and true feelings about them.

Characteristics of successful projects

Data science projects, by their very nature, take a long time to realize a return on investment. In particular, it is hard to accurately measure the success of projects that involve making long-term predictions. As noted in an earlier chapter, for departments to advance the cause of data science, it is essential for them to show early successes. In general, projects that a) are short term; b) have a measurable outcome; and c) can benefit and will be used a wide range of users are some of the key factors that help to establish credibility and ensure success of data science related projects.

An example of such a project is Arterys, a cloud-based company that developed a deep learning algorithm in late 2016 that could assess the flow of blood to the heart in a fraction of the time compared to conventional scanners. It met all the key criteria of success. The benefits were obvious almost immediately, the algorithm provided a directly measurable outcome since you could compare the results with those from scanners and it was useful to a broad range of users, namely, patients. Further, the topic was very intuitive.

Anyone who has ever had a blood test can intuitively relate to measuring bloodflow. The benefits of such a product are also quite obvious. Being able to get results in a fraction of the time could help save lives. In November 2016, the FDA approved the algorithm. It was a monumental achievement.

Summary

Overall, while the path to big data and data science success may seem arduous, hopefully the preceding chapters have provided a comprehensive overview of various topics in big data. We discussed data mining and machine learning, learned about the various tools and technologies in the respective disciplines, and developed applications on real-world data and provided parting thoughts on the nuances of organizational big data and data science initiatives.

The next few pages list some links to resources that the reader may find useful for learning more about the respective subject areas.

External Data Science Resources

The book has covered a very wide range of materials, from Hadoop to NoSQL and machine learning to enterprise data science. The information has been exhaustive, but due to space limitations, we have not gone deep into any one particular area.

In the next few sections, we have provided links to external material for further reading that you may find useful should you want to learn more about the respective topics.

 Several of the solutions here are either open source or community versions of enterprise software. The latter can be especially useful if you are considering enterprise solutions for big data and/or data science.

Big data resources

Apache Hadoop:
`https://hadoop.apache.org`

Apache Spark:
`https://spark.apache.org`

Databricks Spark: Community access to Spark clusters:
`https://community.cloud.databricks.com/`

NoSQL products

Redis: In-Memory Key-Value NoSQL Database:
https://redis.io

Cassandra: One of the most powerful production NoSQL systems:
http://cassandra.apache.org

MongoDB: Document-based NoSQL database:
https://www.mongodb.com

Vertica: Community Edition:
https://www.vertica.com/try/

Teradata: Aster Community Edition:
https://aster-community.teradata.com/community/download

Languages and tools

Open Source R:
https://www.r-project.org

Microsoft Open R (with additional features for enterprise):
https://mran.microsoft.com/open

RStudio: Development Interface for R:
https://www.rstudio.com

Open Source Python:
https://www.python.org

Anaconda Python: Python preinstalled with data science and other important packages:
https://anaconda.org

Creating dashboards

R Shiny: Dashboards in R:
https://www.rstudio.com/products/shiny/

Dash: Dashboards in Python:
https://plot.ly/products/dash/

Notebooks

Jupyter: Notebook interface for R, Python and various other languages:
`http://jupyter.org`

Beaker Notebook: Similar to Jupyter but not as widely used:
`http://beakernotebook.com`

Visualization libraries

Bokeh: An excellent plotting library for Python:
`https://bokeh.pydata.org/en/latest/`

Plotly: Dashboard and Reporting: Enterprise and Open-Source:
`https://plot.ly`

RCharts: A widely used plotting package in R:
`https://ramnathv.github.io/rCharts/`

HTMLWidgets: Interactive dashboards in R using JavaScript:
`http://www.htmlwidgets.org`

ggplot2: The ultimate R graphics library:
`http://ggplot2.tidyverse.org`

Courses on R

edX Courses on R:
`https://www.edx.org/course?search_query=R+programming`

A concise R tutorial:
`http://www.cyclismo.org/tutorial/R/`

Coursera: Big Data and R courses:
`https://www.coursera.org/specializations/big-data`
`https://www.coursera.org/courses?languages=enquery=r+programming`

Courses on machine learning

Harvard CS109: THE MOST Comprehensive Machine Learning Course using Python (per author):
`http://cs109.github.io/2015/pages/videos.html`

Caltech Learning from Data: THE MOST Comprehensive MOOC on Machine Learning Theory:
`https://work.caltech.edu/telecourse.html`

Coursera: Various courses on Machine Learning:
`https://www.coursera.org/learn/machine-learning`

Stanford: Statistical Learning by Trevor Hastie and Rob Tibshirani:
`https://lagunita.stanford.edu/courses/HumanitiesSciences/StatLearning/Winter2016/about`

Machine Learning by Andrew Ng: One of THE MOST widely known MOOC on Machine Learning:
`https://www.coursera.org/learn/machine-learning`

Machine learning and deep learning links

Scikit-Learn: The most comprehensive Machine Learning package in Python:
`http://scikit-learn.org/stable/`

Tensorflow: A well-known solution for Deep Learning from Google:
`https://www.tensorflow.org`

MLPACK: Machine Learning using C++ and Unix Command Line:
`http://www.mlpack.org`

Word2Vec: One of the well-known packages for Natural Language Processing:
`https://deeplearning4j.org/word2vec`

Vowpal Wabbit: Excellent Machine Learning software used in many Kaggle competitions:
`https://github.com/JohnLangford/vowpal_wabbit/wiki/Tutorial`

LIBSVM & LIBLINEAR: Highly regarded command line machine learning tools:
`https://www.csie.ntu.edu.tw/~cjlin/libsvm/`
`https://www.csie.ntu.edu.tw/~cjlin/liblinear/`

LIBFM: Matrix Factorization:
http://www.libfm.org

PaddlePaddle: Deep Learning from Baidu:
https://github.com/PaddlePaddle/Paddle

CuDNN: Deep Learning/Neural Network solution from NVIDIA:
https://developer.nvidia.com/cudnn

Caffe: Deep Learning framework from Berkeley:
http://caffe.berkeleyvision.org

Theano: GPU Enabled Machine Learning in Python:
http://deeplearning.net/software/theano/

Torch: High performance Machine Learning in Lua:
http://torch.ch

Keras: Open-Source Neural Network Applications:
https://keras.io

Web-based machine learning services

AzureML: Machine Learning in Microsoft Azure Cloud:
https://azure.microsoft.com/en-us/services/machine-learning/

H2O: High Performance Machine Learning Platform: Works with R, Python and much more:
https://www.h2o.ai

BigML: Visually appealing Web-based machine learning platform:
https://bigml.com

Movies

The Imitation Game: Movie on Alan Turing:
http://www.imdb.com/title/tt2084970/

A Beautiful Mind: Movie on John Nash:
http://www.imdb.com/title/tt0268978/

2001: A Space Odyssey:
`http://www.imdb.com/title/tt0062622/`

Moneyball: Movie on sabermetrics:
`http://www.imdb.com/title/tt1210166/`

Ex Machina: Movie on Artificial Intelligence:
`http://www.imdb.com/title/tt0470752/`

Terminator 2: A movie that has achieved cult status:
`http://www.imdb.com/title/tt0103064/`

Machine learning books from Packt

Getting Started with Tensorflow by Giancarlo Zaccone:
`https://www.packtpub.com/big-data-and-business-intelligence/getting-started-tensorflow`

Machine Learning and Deep Learning by Sebastian Raschka:
`https://www.amazon.com/Python-Machine-Learning-scikit-learn-TensorFlow/dp/1787125939`

Machine Learning with R by Brett Lantz:
`https://www.amazon.com/Machine-Learning-techniques-predictive-modeling/dp/1784393908`

Books for leisure reading

A classic on logic and mathematics:
`https://www.amazon.com/Gödel-Escher-Bach-Eternal-Golden/dp/0465026567`

A simple explanation of Gödel's Incompleteness Theorem:
`https://www.amazon.com/Gödels-Proof-Ernest-Nagel/dp/0814758371/`

Roger Penrose on Artificial Intelligence and much more:
`https://www.amazon.com/Emperors-New-Mind-Concerning-Computers/dp/0198784929/`

Other Books You May Enjoy

If you enjoyed this book, you may be interested in these other books by Packt:

Big Data Analytics with SAS
David Pope

ISBN: 978-1-78829-090-6

- Configure a free version of SAS in order do hands-on exercises dealing with data management, analysis, and reporting.
- Understand the basic concepts of the SAS language which consists of the data step (for data preparation) and procedures (or PROCs) for analysis.
- Make use of the web browser based SAS Studio and iPython Jupyter Notebook interfaces for coding in the SAS, DS2, and FedSQL programming languages.
- Understand how the DS2 programming language plays an important role in Big Data preparation and analysis using SAS
- Integrate and work efficiently with Big Data platforms like Hadoop, SAP HANA, and cloud foundry based systems.

Predictive Analytics with TensorFlow
Md. Rezaul Karim

ISBN: 978-1-78839-892-3

- Get a solid and theoretical understanding of linear algebra, statistics, and probability for predictive modeling
- Develop predictive models using classification, regression, and clustering algorithms
- Develop predictive models for NLP
- Learn how to use reinforcement learning for predictive analytics
- Factorization Machines for advanced recommendation systems
- Get a hands-on understanding of deep learning architectures for advanced predictive analytics
- Learn how to use deep Neural Networks for predictive analytics
- See how to use recurrent Neural Networks for predictive analytics
- Convolutional Neural Networks for emotion recognition, image classification, and sentiment analysis

Leave a review - let other readers know what you think

Please share your thoughts on this book with others by leaving a review on the site that you bought it from. If you purchased the book from Amazon, please leave us an honest review on this book's Amazon page. This is vital so that other potential readers can see and use your unbiased opinion to make purchasing decisions, we can understand what our customers think about our products, and our authors can see your feedback on the title that they have worked with Packt to create. It will only take a few minutes of your time, but is valuable to other potential customers, our authors, and Packt. Thank you!

Index

CPSIA information can be obtained
at www.ICGtesting.com
Printed in the USA
LVHW040003041218
599174LV00007B/36/P

9 781783 554393